WOODWORKING FOR EVERYBODY

JOHN G. SHEA FOURTH EDITION

WOODWORKING
FOR EVERYBODY

 VAN NOSTRAND REINHOLD COMPANY
NEW YORK   CINCINNATI   TORONTO   LONDON   MELBOURNE

ACKNOWLEDGMENTS

For their courteous cooperation in furnishing illustrations, information, and
material, separately identified in this book, the author wishes to thank the
following companies and associations:
Acushnet Process Co., New Bedford, Massachusetts
Adjustable Clamp Co., Chicago, Illinois
American Forest Products Industries, Inc., Washington, D. C.
American Hardboard Association, Washington, D. C.
American Plywood Association, Tacoma, Washington
Arco Tools Inc., New York, N. Y.
Black and Decker Manufacturing Co., Towson, Maryland
The Borden Company, New York, N. Y.
Bostitch Co., East Greenwich, Rhode Island
BVI Corporation, New York, N. Y.
Channellock Tools, Meadville, Pennsylvania
Disston Division, H. K. Porter Co., Pittsburgh, Pennsylvania
Dremel Manufacturing Company, Racine, Wisconsin
E. I. du Pont de Nemours & Co., Wilmington, Delaware
Firestone Tire & Rubber Co., Fall River, Massachusetts
General Foam Corporation, New York, N. Y.
Gerber Wrought Iron Products, Inc., St. Louis, Missouri
Hardwood Plywood Association, Arlington, Virginia
Homecraft Veneers, Latrobe, Pennsylvania
Irwin Bit Co., Wilmington, Ohio
Knape & Vogt Manufacturing Co., Grand Rapids, Michigan
Millers Falls Co., Greenfield, Massachusetts
Minwax Co., Delawanna, New Jersey
Morgan Adhesives Co., Stow, Ohio
G. W. Murphy Industries, Geneva, Illinois
National Lumber Manufacturers Association, Washington, D. C.
Nicholson File Co., Providence, Rhode Island
Pittsburgh Plate Glass Co., Pittsburgh, Pennsylvania
Red Devil Tools, Union, New Jersey
Reynolds Metals Co., Richmond, Virginia
Rockwell Manufacturing Co., Pittsburgh, Pennsylvania
Skil Corporation, Chicago, Illinois
Stanley Tools, New Britain, Connecticut
The 3-M Co., St. Paul, Minnesota
U. S. Forest Service, Washington, D. C.
U. S. M. Corporation, Reading, Pennsylvania
U. S. Plywood-Champion Papers, Inc., New York, N. Y.
Watco-Dennis Corporation, Santa Monica, California
X-Acto, Inc., Long Island City, N. Y.

Van Nostrand Reinhold Company Regional Offices:
  New York, Cincinnati, Chicago, Millbrae, Dallas
Van Nostrand Reinhold Company International Offices:
  London, Toronto, Melbourne

Copyright © 1970 by Litton Educational Publishing, Inc.
Library of Congress Catalog Card No. 75-90315
ISBN 0-442-07540-5

16   15   14   13   12   11   10   9   8   7   6

PREFACE

When prefacing a new edition of a book which has been in print for over one-quarter of a century, the author's first impulse is to express a resounding *thank you* to the thousands of people who have made his work so enduringly popular. But with this expression of gratitude comes reflection on the changes which both the book and the world have undergone in the years since the original edition was published. For the world, this quarter-century spans the advent of the atomic bomb, many major wars, and the fantastic accomplishment of men walking on the moon.

And the book, born in the turmoil of World War II, has also changed. At first it was designed essentially as a school textbook—and used in industrial arts and vocational education classes. In this role it was adopted by many state board of education. The author was gratified by the part it played—and still plays—as a practical educational medium.

Then, during the immediate postwar period, this work was more generally used by homemakers. Many of its new readers had only recently returned from the rigors of military combat and were eager to settle down and apply their creative abilities to the peaceful pursuits of building and furnishing new dwellings. Thus, as the book advanced into its 2nd Edition, additional material was offered to help new homemakers with their domestic woodworking activities. This gave birth to a tandem "trade edition" which soon attained circulation equal to that of the original textbook edition.

Meanwhile, with the dawn of the nuclear age, all things started to change—even the techniques, tools, and materials of woodworking. So much so, in fact, that anybody examining the 4th Edition of *Woodworking for Everybody* and comparing it to the 1st and 2nd Editions will find very little of the text and photographs remain the same. Actually, about the only original elements are the animated chapter headings and caricatured tools, which seem to have endeared themselves to readers as "friendly Gremlins" ever since the book was first published. But aside from these creepy characters and the "Safety First" sketches and standard line illustrations, little else of the original edition remains.

The present emphasis, it will be noted, is on the many new tools and materials which have appeared in recent years to facilitate do-it-yourself enterprise. Recent inventions and modifications of power tools alone demonstrate the competitive acumen of tool manufacturers to engineer something safer, lighter, and more efficient. (Indeed, each new edition of this book had to be "retooled" to keep abreast of constant changes.)

Such advantages as *shockproof insulation, unbreakable casings,* and *vari-speed control* of motors have made power tools—particularly the portable models—safer, more durable, and easier to use. Stationary woodworking machines, too—especially the combination machines—are now designed in detail for increased convenience of operation and greater functional efficiency. Even the cutting blades of hand and power tools may now be treated with the miracle *"Teflon S"* to reduce friction and ease operation.

In order to highlight a few of the new materials and accessories now available, the first chapter of this edition has been devoted to brief exploration of these helpful auxiliaries. There are many others to be found at your building supply dealer.

There have also been minor revolutions in methods and materials of wood finishing. Some of the new finishes, described in Chapter 7, go on easier, look better, and last much longer.

Woodworking projects—whether they be furniture or utility items—have also changed with each new edition of this book. Thus, with the exception of a few ageless designs (mostly colonial antiques), former projects have been replaced in this edition with new designs, fashioned to meet today's needs.

So, in presenting the 4th Edition of *Woodworking for Everybody*, it should be observed that despite an almost complete revision and updating of contents, the purpose of this book remains essentially the same. As with the first edition, this is intended to serve as a practical guide and book of instructions on woodworking practice. It is hoped that this up-to-date edition will serve today's readers as effectively as the earlier editions served in their time.

John G. Shea
Greenwich, Connecticut
March 1, 1970

CONTENTS

1

Materials & Accessories

Lumber

The National Bureau of Standards has established grading and classification rules for lumber selection. Careful inspection determines all grading, and these rules ensure uniform quality throughout the industry.

The best quality of lumber, suitable for natural finishing, is stamped "Select." This is graded into two classes: "A" and "B." The "B" grade allows for small blemishes or defects. The second classification is "Finish" material, which is good in appearance and suitable for paint finishing. This is graded "C" and "D" according to the number and size of its defects. Lumber useful for general utility construction purposes is designated "Common." Numbers 1 and 2 "Common" are usually applicable without waste. But numbers 3 and 4 are for rough construction and contain many flaws.

How to Order Lumber

To the average inexperienced person, the ordering of lumber sometimes seems to be quite an involved and complicated matter. Of course, the lumber dealer will cooperate in seeing that the correct material is supplied. However, it is well to be able to call off the complete order.

Lumber can be purchased in various grades, thicknesses, widths, and lengths. Obviously for cabinet work only the better grades are suitable. So the average home or school woodworker will be interested in purchasing only the finer grades of lumber.

Lumber dealers carry stocks of the woods in greatest demand in their area. But all lumber manufacturers and dealers use a standard size and grade system which simplifies ordering. However, for the sake of economy and better service, the customer should have some understanding of this system.

At the sawmill three principal designations are given to rough lumber. These are: (1) *dimension stuff*, which is cut 2 inches thick and from 4 inches to 12 inches in width; (2) *timbers*, which are cut 4 inches to 8 inches thick and from 6 inches to 10 inches wide; and (3) *common boards*, which are 1 inch thick and from 4 inches to 18 inches wide.

When these general designations of rough lumber are *dressed* by planing machines, the rough surfaces are removed from sides and edges to a depth of approximately ⅛ inch. This finishing process is sometimes called *surfacing*, and lumber thus treated will be designated *S 1 S*, meaning surfaced on one side, or *S 4 S*, which means it has been surfaced or dressed on all sides or edges.

Thus, to avoid confusion, it should be understood that when you order a *two by four*, which is commonly S 4 S, you *don't* get a piece of lumber 2 inches thick and 4 inches wide. But you do get a piece that started out at these dimensions before the planing machine, in the surfacing process, reduced its *surfaced* dimensions to approximately 1⅝″ × 3⅝″.

Oftentimes the inexperienced customer is confused when he orders lumber ¾ inch thick, only to hear his dealer read back his order as 1 inch thick. The dealer may then explain that, as with the two by four, lumber is bought at its *unfinished* thickness and then dressed down to the more or less standard scale of finished thicknesses which the customer requires.

Lumber is generally sold by the *board foot*. This is the standard measure of 1 inch thick by 12 inches wide by 12 inches long. Two by four's, molding, trim, siding, and other small pieces of standard thickness and width may be sold by the *running foot*. But the *board-foot* price of a specified quality and type of lumber determines its cost. Composition panels, plywood, siding, and other materials of this nature are sold by the *square foot*.

Lumber Manufacture

The boards you buy have undergone a long process of manufacture before they reached your workshop. After the trees have been felled and transported by river, rail, or truck to the lumber mill, they are sliced into slabs or heavy timbers which are then squared and reduced to roughly sawed planks.

Planks are then carefully graded and stacked for outdoor seasoning, which, for finer grades, is followed by kiln-drying and planing into smooth boards.

Accompanying photographs highlight the preliminary steps of producing the finished lumber which goes into your projects.

A huge band saw "head rig" slices long slabs from the log. *National Lumber Mfg. Assn.*

After squaring in, "head rig" sections—or "cants"—emerge as planks from a series of gang saws. *National Lumber Mfg. Assn.*

Lumber is sorted for thickness, species, quality. *American Forest Products Industries, Inc.*

In many mills the next step is to move boards outdoors, where they are stacked and air-dried. *U.S. Forest Service.*

Dry kilns are used for scientifically controlled seasoning. These hold over 3,000,000 board feet. *National Lumber Mfg. Assn.*

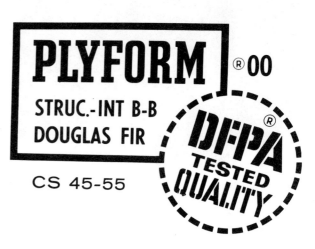

Plywood

Douglas Fir is the most common of the softwood plywoods and is available in panels measuring 4' by 8'. However, greater lengths may also be had — particularly of the exterior-type for use in boat building and exterior construction. Widths range from 24" to 60", with 48" being most common.

Usually, softwood plywoods are made of an odd number of plies, approximately of equal thickness. Panels are available as thin as ⅛" (for special purpose) but run in regular stock thicknesses ranging from ¼" (3-ply) to 1⅛" (7-ply).

As already noted, two types of softwood plywood — exterior and interior — are available. Each type is clearly labeled on the surface and edge stamping of the panel. Exterior plywood is waterproof while interior plywood is only moisture-resistant and thus unsuitable for any type of construction which must be exposed to dampness. Within each type there are several grades.

Standards of Quality

The United States Department of Commerce has established commercial standards for the manufacture of plywood. These standards are augmented by the exacting specifications and high-level, quality identification maintained by the plywood industry itself. Such matters as the type of glue bond, species, testing procedures, grading and labeling, must conform to government standards and to quality codes established within the industry.

Grades of softwood plywood are identified by letters stamped on the edge and surface of the panel. The letter "A" signifies the best quality of veneer while "B," "C," and "D" indicate decline of quality to lower grades. As an example an "A-A" grade of plywood is surfaced on *both* sides with the best quality of veneer. Only minor defects and limited patches are permitted in this quality. But since the "A" designation pertains to *surface* quality only, the inner plys may be fabricated of a patched, but structurally sound, "C" grade.

Of course, the ultimate end-use of the plywood must determine selection of the proper grade. Grade "A-A" will be selected where both appearance and endurance are required. Exterior "A-A" — and special marine versions thereof — may be used for boat hulls and other construction exposed to moisture. Grade "C-D" plywood, which foots the scale, has its place in construction of sub-floors, roof or wall sheathing, where it is covered by other materials.

Manufacture of Plywood

In its manufacturing process, plywood represents a form of wood conservation, for little waste is tolerated in extracting the finished product from the original log. While two methods are employed to remove sheets of veneer from the log, namely by rotary lathe and veneer slicer, by far the most common — particularly in manufacture of softwood plywoods — is the rotary lathe or "peeling" method.

Logs used for plywood are literally unwound or peeled against a keen cutting edge into continuous sheets of wood. These sheets, or veneers, are peeled from the rotating log in much the same way that wrapping paper is unwound from a roll. Illustrations on the facing page highlight the plywood manufacturing process.

1 Rotary-cut plywood veneer is peeled from log as it revolves in lathe against sharp cutting knife. *U.S. Forest Service.*

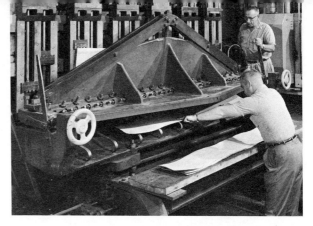

2 Veneer slicer is used to obtain select cuts of surface veneer for many species of hardwood plywood. *U.S. Forest Service.*

3 Turning against a sharp knife in the peeling lathe, wood veneer unwinds (like wrapping paper) to form continuous sheets from which plywood is manufactured. *American Plywood Association.*

4 After cutting to standard sizes, veneer is dried, mended, and prepared for edge jointing prior to passing through glue spreader for panel assembly. *American Plywood Association.*

5 Giant presses bond the assembly of cross-laminated veneers and adhesives into rigid plywood panels of uniform thickness. This operation is controlled under heat and pressure. *American Plywood Association.*

6 After passing through sanding machines and edge trimming to exact size, plywood panels are thoroughly inspected and stamped for type and grade. *American Plywood Association.*

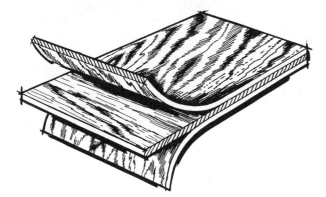

Veneer-core hardwood plywood.

Lumber-core hardwood plywood.

Hardwood Plywood

For the making of fine furniture, wall paneling and an extensive variety of other uses, hardwood plywood is regarded as an ideal building material. Like its softwood counterpart, it comes in both exterior and interior types. But, as illustrated on the facing page, it is veneered with a variety of beautifully grained and highly decorative hardwoods, including rare species of both domestic and foreign origin.

Hardwood plywood differs structurally from the softwood variety. Most hardwood panels use a solid "core," or extra-thick middle ply.

This may vary in both thickness and substance, depending on specific applications of the panel.

Most common is the *veneer core* panel, which is manufactured like softwood plywood but composed of a thicker core and thinner surface veneers. It is used for wall paneling, sheathing, furniture, and for special applications where the panel must be curved or bent.

For the making of table tops, doors, cabinets, and fixtures, *lumber core* plywood is commonly used. This contains a thick, solid wood core fabricated by edge-gluing narrow strips of solid lumber. A variation of this is the *particle-board core* plywood made of a composition, wood-particle core bonded together with a resin binder. This composition offers a maximum of dimensional stability.

Types and Grades of Hardwood Plywood

Hardwood plywoods are made of three, five, seven and nine plies, ranging in thickness from 1/8″ to 1″. Like the softwoods, their manufacture conforms to government standards. Within the industry, standards are scrupulously upheld, with markings devised for labeling and identifying each type and grade.

Four types of hardwood plywood panels are available: Type I is manufactured with waterproof adhesive for use in construction of objects exposed to moisture. Type II, made with water-resistant adhesive, is for interior application. Type III is only moisture-resistant which means it can be damaged by water but resists indoor dampness and humidity. The fourth type, Technical Type I, has the same waterproof qualities as Type I, but varies in thickness and arrangement of plies.

The grading of hardwood plywood falls into five specific categories. Leading the list is Premium Grade #1 with select, matched veneer on surface, avoiding contrasts of color. Good Grade #1 also avoids sharp contrasts in color and grain. Sound Grade #2 allows some surface deficiencies such as imperfect matching of color and grain, but does not permit open defects. Utility Grade #3 allows tight knots, mismatching of veneers, streaks and slight splits. Backing Grade #4 permits larger defects which do not affect strength or serviceability of panels.

Specialty Grade SP hardwood plywood is custom made, of select matching veneers for special requirements.

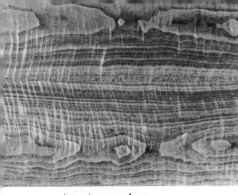

American walnut
Sliced figured
(2-piece matched)

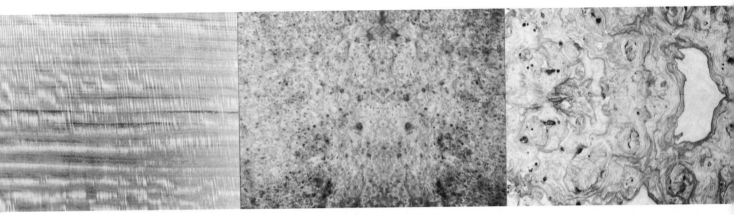

Domestic oak
Quartered

Red gum
Figured
(2-piece matched)

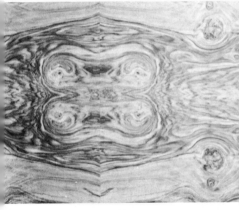

African mahogany
Mottled and fiddleback

Carpathian elm
Burl
(2-piece matched)

Olive
Burl
(2-piece matched)

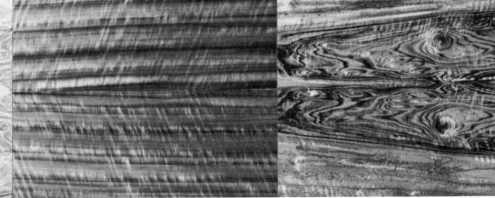

French walnut
Stumpwood
(4-piece matched)

Orientalwood
(2-piece matched)

Paldao
(2-piece matched)

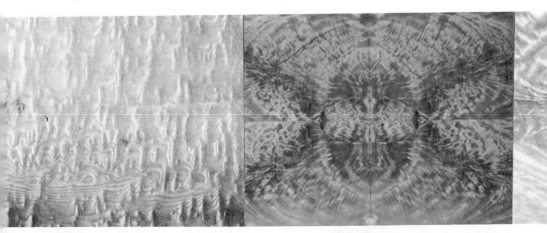

Japanese ash (Tamo)

Avodire
Crotch

Avodire
Crotch

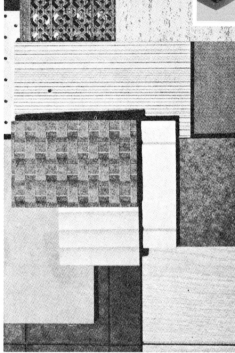

In addition, because hardboard is called upon to serve such a wide variety of applications, manufacturers have developed processes to produce special qualities of hardness. Thus, through addition of chemicals and heat treatment an especially hard product has been developed called *tempered hardboard*.

Hardboard is well adapted for surface veneering with natural woods as well as plastics and various composition materials. It is manufactured with one or both surfaces smooth, referred to as S 1 S or S 2 S. It is also prepared in a broad range of specialty surfaces such as perforated (peg board and filigree), striated, grooved, tiled, and embossed. As well, it can be obtained in pre-finished, prime-coated, and wood-grained patterns.

Hardboard is available through lumber yards and building materials dealers. In size, panel dimensions range up to 5 feet in width and 16 feet in length. Thicknesses are from one-twelfth of an inch to three-fourths of an inch.

Hardboard

The name "hardboard" identifies a wide range of panel products composed of wood fibers. Unlike lumber and plywood, which utilizes wood in the natural grain structure of the growing tree, the manufacture of hardboard reduces the cellulose and lignin of wood to its individual, basic fibers. It is then reconstituted into panels which use lignin (the natural cohesive substances found in all woods which hold the fibers together) to form a new composition.

Because of its durability, structural stability, and adaptability to a vast variety of surface treatments, hardboard has become an extremely practical building material. It can be worked like wood, but for many applications offers advantages over lumber and plywood. Moreover, it can be made of many different kinds of wood including defective tree growth which would otherwise be wasted. It also makes extensive use of wood residues from sawmills and plywood plants.

Planer chips, which in bygone days were a waste product of the lumber mill, are now utilized to manufacture hardboard and particle board. *American Hardboard Association.*

8

Surfacing Materials

In order to enhance the surface characteristics of wood and thus make your projects more serviceable and attractive, a vast variety of surfacing materials are available. These can be easily bonded to any smooth surfaces. Such surfacers come as rigid sheets of hard composition like *Formica*. But they are also available in a wide range of wood-grained veneers and pliable plastics.

As illustrated here, surface coverings include ceramics, tiles, leathers, and an infinite variety of new vinyls in simulated wood grains as well as a full spectrum of colors and patterns.

While the practice of upgrading common woods by veneering them with richer woods dates back many centuries, the techniques involved in applying veneers have never been so simple as they are today. This is because of the nature of the new veneers as well as the excellent new contact cements which provide instant adhesion.

Most easily applied are the self-adhesive surface coverings of vinyl. These are available in facsimile simulations of rich wood grains as well as colors, patterns and textures. Containing their own sealed-in bond, such self-adhesives as "*MACtac*" can be instantly and enduringly bonded to practically any smooth surface.

This is just a small sampling of the many materials available for surfacing. *American Plywood Association.*

Veneers of rare woods may be matched for decorative effects to enrich the surface characteristics of your projects. *Homecraft Veneers.*

Vinyl, self-adhesive surfacers are applied simply by removing the paper backing, which exposes the adhesive for instant bonding. *Morgan Adhesives Co.*

"Flexwood," an especially processed wood veneer made by U.S. Plywood-Champion Papers, Inc., comes in 4' by 8' sheets of exquisite grained pattern and rare woods. It is easily applied with contact cement. *U.S. Plywood-Champion Papers, Inc.*

Accessories

Attachable Legs

As illustrated on this page, attachable legs can be obtained in a variety of types and sizes. They are made of both metal and wood. Of the wooden variety, they come finished or unfinished and are made of many woods, including teak and walnut, to match your projects. Metal legs are usually painted black but can be repainted to any desired color. Some are finished in brass and chromium.

To attach these legs you simply drive a few screws through the top plates. Some, like the Gerber legs, shown below, come with detachable plates threaded for assembly of the legs either in perpendicular or slanted positions. The legs are then screwed to the plates with a threaded spindle. They have adjustable nylon leveling disks threaded to the bottom tips. These are ad-

Pedestal Bases

justed to eliminate wobbling on uneven floors.

If you want to make a table, chair, or stool, in a hurry, there's nothing will hasten the job more effectively than the pedestal bases pictured on these pages. These bases are made of metal and can be bolted together in a jiffy.

As illustrated below, the top plate is pre-drilled to be screwed to an attaching surface. Thus, to make the tables shown here, it is only necessary to fashion a top of plywood to desired dimensions and attach it to the pedestal base with six screws. Stools and chairs are almost as easily assembled.

Pedestal bases may be purchased in two sizes: 15″ tall for low tables, stools, and chairs and 28″ tall for full size tables. They are finished either in brass, chromium, or enamel and can be refinished to match any desired color scheme.

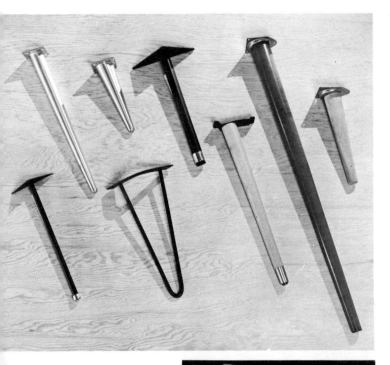

Gerber Wrought Iron Products, Inc.

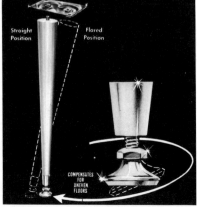

Adjustable brackets and standards provide "open stock" expansion possibilities. You can start with a modest arrangement of two or three shelves and later expand to cover entire walls. *Knape & Vogt Mfg. Co.*

Adjustable Shelving Brackets and Standards

Instant shelving introduces myriads of useful and highly decorative shelving ideas which are made possible with the metal standards and brackets available at your hardware or department store. They come in colors as well as chromium and brass finishes. Application of these accessories is limited only by the imagination of the homemaker. Both standards and brackets are available in varying lengths to accommodate books, magazines, and other items of assorted shapes and sizes.

You can start with simple shelf groupings as illustrated here, or you can line entire walls with shelves spaced to suit your needs.

The woodworker can make his own shelves of lumber or plywood. These can be stained, painted, or veneered. It should be noted, however, that you can also buy prefabricated shelves cut and finished to desired widths and lengths. These come prefinished in natural wood tones and colors.

The only mechanical aptitude involved in installation of such shelves is that of attaching the standards perfectly perpendicular with screws driven securely into wall studding. This is located at 16″ intervals and can usually be located by tapping the wall. Installation on certain types of walls requires predrilling and insertion of "molly" fasteners, which anchor the standards firmly.

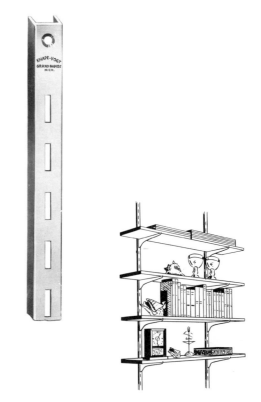

Metal wall standards are slotted to receive brackets which adjust shelves to any desired spacing. Brackets and standards come in several lengths. *Knape & Vogt Mfg. Co.*

Flush Panel Doors

Flush panel doors — the inexpensive kind you can buy unfinished at lumber yards or from your building supply dealer — may be used to make many attractive and useful articles of furniture. When used with attachable legs they make "instant tables" at small cost — and the appearance and practical qualities of such tables does not betray their simplicity.

Flush doors are most commonly made in lengths of 80″ and in widths, graduating by 2″, from 18″ to 36″. Their surface panels are laminated of thin plywood; Philippine mahogany, birch, and maple are the most common woods. Some are hardboard-surfaced for painting.

Most flush doors are "stuffed" with wood staves that are bonded diagonally beneath the panel surfaces. Since these staves are spaced to form a hollow core, fastenings cannot be secured within the hollow areas. Thus when legs are attached, flat cleats must first be glued on to span the undersurface with a couple of screws at each end to catch the solid edges.

Core edges are made of softwood with wider strips — up to 4″ wide — at the ends. Although the structure is light, the doors are fabricated to maintain flat, non-warping stability — as they would have to be to perform their essential functions. However, the light surface panels will not withstand pounding or heavy impact — and they should be reinforced with an additional laminate of plywood surfacing if heavy use is anticipated.

The finishing of furniture made with doors is most easily accomplished with paint. For natural finishes which bring out characteristics of wood graining, stains can be applied followed by clear coatings. But for richer effects the door should be surfaced either with natural wood veneers or with one of the surfacing materials previously described.

Since the 80″ lengths of most flush doors may exceed room requirements it is often necessary to saw them down to more manageable lengths. This can be easily done by following the step-by-step procedures pictured on page 56.

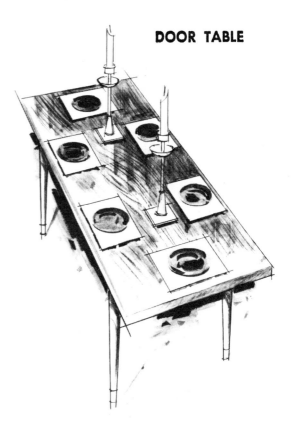

DOOR TABLE

2

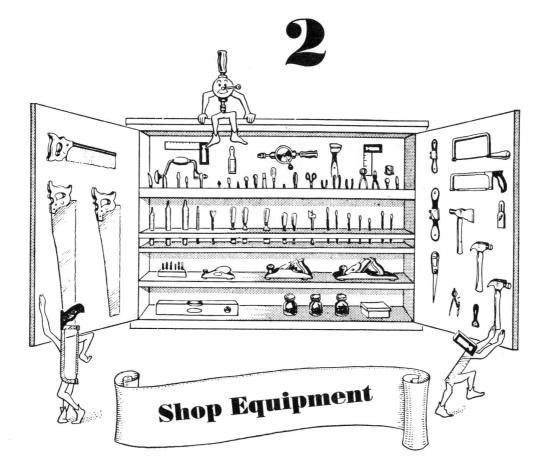

Shop Equipment

Designs by author

Workbench

No matter how modest or elaborate your woodworking ambitions may be, your first requirement of shop equipment is a good workbench. Obviously, your workbench should be sturdy. And it should be built heavy enough to withstand the impact of the constant buffeting, pounding, and lurching which are part of the woodworking process.

A good workbench is much heavier than an ordinary table. The top should not be resilient and the entire structure should be solid enough to hold the floor and not jounce around while work is being processed. It needs a thick pounding surface. But since some work may require your moving the bench, it is not too desirable to have it secured permanently to floors or walls.

Workbenches like the one pictured above, and the working design shown with construction details on pages 144-146, illustrate features which will facilitate your shop work. For instance, all parts are fitted flush, providing a smooth, neat appearance and an area easily brushed to keep your work surface tidy. Front edges of the top overlap for attaching vises and clamps. The vise on the bench illustrated is fitted with an "adjustable dog" — a protruding metal lip that can be moved up and down. This holds work flat on the bench top when pressed against a movable bench stop which fits into the holes bored at intervals across the top.

Since most woodworkers prefer to build their own workbenches, a sturdy build-it-yourself design is presented with working drawings on pages 144 and 145. This is built of stock materials — two by fours, plywood, and heavy planking. All parts are bolted and glued together to assure durable construction.

Tool Board

As your woodworking tool requirements increase, you will need a place to put them. They can be kept within easy reach and constant view with a tool board like the one pictured below.

Pegboard with its assorted metal fittings of prongs, loops, and eyes offers the ideal solution to tool board arrangements. Indeed, the adaptability of pegboard provides neat containment of large and small collections of tools — and since the hanger fittings can be instantly rearranged, you can always make room for additional tools. Plans for a tool board that fits over the workbench are shown on page 145.

Supply Cabinet

Going hand-in-hand with your workbench and tool board, a cabinet should be built to contain your working materials and supplies. Construction details appear on page 146.

Woodworking Tools

You don't *have* to know the name of every woodworking tool in order to use it successfully. Still, it is rather a good idea to get acquainted with these names, and probably as your interest in the subject grows, you will become naturally curious about all names and terms.

To "humanize" the subject in caricatured categories, the following pages group and describe woodworking tools in natural relationship. Thus, to get acquainted with them, it may only be necessary to read the following paragraphs which picture, name, and describe the various tools. (This should serve as an interpreter between you and your hardware dealer.) After studying these pages you won't be satisfied going around just calling a saw a saw, a chisel a chisel, or a file a file. You will discover there are many different types of saws, as there are of chisels and files and other tools — and each *type* has its own name.

Tools courtesy Millers Falls Co.

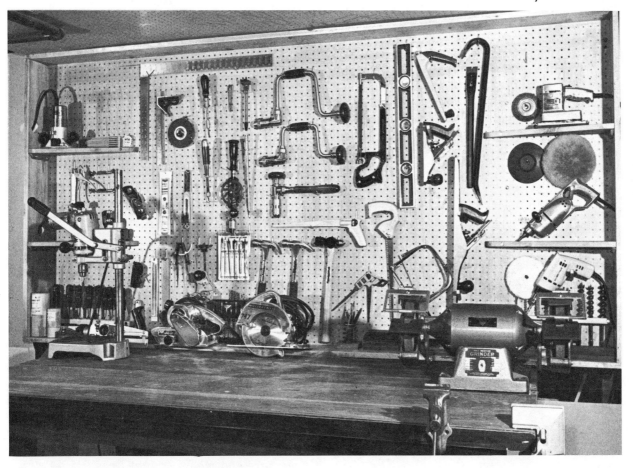

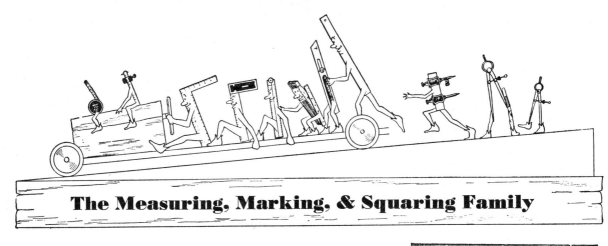

The Measuring, Marking, & Squaring Family

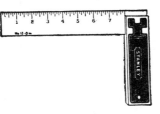

Try Square

This little tool is as important to the woodworker as the compass is to the mariner. Using it as a check and a guide, you can always tell if you are right or wrong. It is used for marking lines square across the work — a very important function in woodworking. It is equally as important in checking the squareness of boards and construction.

As shown, the try square consists of a metal blade, fitted so as to form a perfect right angle to the straight edge of a heavier piece of wood or metal. The blade is usually stamped in one-inch graduations and their fractions, which makes the try square a measuring tool as well as a squaring tool.

Framing Square (Steel Square)

Like the try square, the larger framing square is fashioned in an L-shape with one arm forming a perfect right angle to the other. It is also used for marking lines and for checking the accuracy and squareness of work.

The carpenter greatly depends upon this type of square when he is building a house. He uses it for laying out angles, foundations, and framework. The two arms of the framing square are stamped in various fractions of an inch. They are also marked with computing tables, which are used by the carpenter in many different phases of his work.

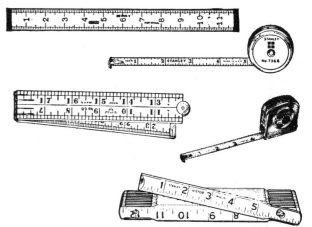

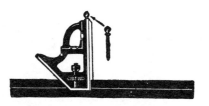

Combination Square with Level

This very useful tool serves three purposes: (1) That of a straightedge ruler; (2) a marking and gauging square; (3) a level. It is especially useful in carpentry work where joining parts must be tested for *level* as well as for *square*, and for a 45° bevel. A small pointed scribe used for marking accompanies the model shown.

Rule and Ruler

An important item in any shop is a good quality straightedge bench rule. These rules are manufactured of either wood or metal. They are used to check work for *straightness* and to measure and mark straight lines.

Included in the other types of rules used in shop work are the *folding two-foot rule;* the *pull-push rule,* made of steel tape and usually six feet long; the wood or metal *zigzag rule* which likewise unfolds to a six-foot length.

Bevel Gauge

The bevel gauge is used to mark and check angles. The blade can be adjusted and set to any desired slant. When being used it is held against the work like a try square.

Tape Rule

For measuring longer distances, the tape measure, commonly available in lengths of 50 to 100 feet, is indispensable.

Compass and Dividers

Dividers serve the same purpose as compasses, only they are made entirely of metal and their pointed ends scratch the marking rather than penciling it. Dividers are also used for dividing lines into equal parts and for setting out or measuring distances.

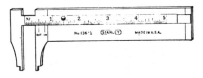

Caliper Rule

This is used to make accurate *inside* and *outside* measurements. While the caliper rule is especially necessary for taking inside and outside measurements of circular cutouts and turned work, it is also generally useful for precise measuring.

Stanley "All-In-One"

This combination tool performs the functions of a *square, level, compass,* and *marking gauge.* As illustrated, it is used to scribe lines, mark circles, gauge sizes of nails and screws, and also act as a precise square. As well as this it gauges inside measurements and has a built-in level for checking horizontal and perpendicular alignments.

Straightedge

This very necessary tool is made either of wood or metal and ordinarily varies in length from one foot to three feet. Usually it is not stamped for measuring and, therefore, is used exclusively for marking straight lines and for checking the straightness and accuracy of work.

Marking Gauge

The marking gauge is used for making lines at a uniform distance, in from the edge of a board or piece of work.

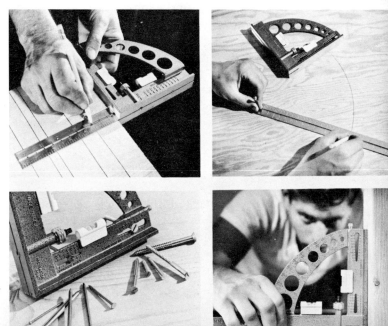

The Saw Family

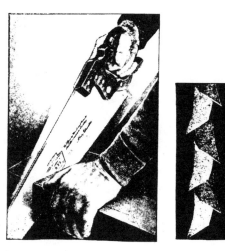

Crosscut Saw

The crosscut saw is one of the "old reliables" of the woodworking shop. As the name indicates, it is used for cutting across the grain of the wood.

The saw teeth are set alternately to the right and left. The illustration shows how they are shaped so as to form sharp cutting points along the outside edge. Saws of this type are made in various sizes. The fineness or coarseness of the cutting edge is determined by the number of teeth per inch.

A number of other saws, bearing different names, have teeth which are shaped for crosscutting.

Ripsaw

In the language of the woodworker, when a piece of wood is sawed with the grain it is *ripped*. The ripsaw has teeth which are especially shaped to perform this particular type of

cutting. The illustration shows the way in which each tooth is shaped so that it is perpendicular at the front, and sharpened to an even edge at the cutting point. When being used, these teeth bite into the wood with the cutting action of a series of small chisels.

Ripsaws are made in different sizes; their teeth vary in coarseness for either fine or rough cutting.

"Teflon" Coating

Saws and other cutting tools are now being treated with "Teflon S" coating, which provides a slippery surface with minimum binding. Because of "wood-pinch" binding, in the past it was often necessary to oil the saw blade. This had the undesirable result of soiling the wood with oil residue. Now, however, "Teflon S" does the lubricating job of oil, but with a dry surface. The chemicals are baked into the steel and the coating is claimed to remain effective for the life of the tool. Saws, like the Disston model shown here, are Teflon-treated and may be recognized by their distinctive blue color.

Backsaw

As the name indicates, the backsaw is made with a rigid steel reinforcement attached to its top edge to form a "back." The teeth of the backsaw are shaped like those of the crosscut saw. Having a thin blade and fine teeth, it is well suited for accurate and precise cutting.

Cabinet Saw

This saw bears some resemblance to the backsaw but lacks its rigidity. It can be used to cut entirely through a piece of wood. Saw teeth on opposite edges are sharpened for different cuts. The handle is adjustable for position, when either edge is being used.

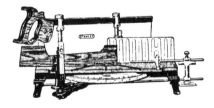

Miter Saw

The miter saw is simply an oversized backsaw. Ordinarily, however, it is only used in a *miter* box for special, accurate cutting. The miter box illustrated may be set for cutting at various angles. It holds and guides the miter saw so as to insure accuracy, even for the inexperienced woodworker.

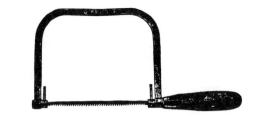

Coping Saw

Coping saws are used for cutting curves, roundings, and special shapes. There are two distinct types, namely: the *wire frame* coping saw and the *rigid frame* saw. Each of these types may be fitted with either fine or coarse blades. The ends of the blades are made with pin fittings, loops, or lock loops, which hold them in place in the frame.

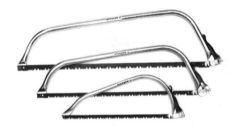

Bow Saw

While they cannot be regarded as *precise* woodworking tools, bow saws find many uses in the workshop and around the home. They are particularly good for "roughing" lumber to length when the operation is followed by more precise cutting. For sawing heavy timbers they offer advantages over conventional saws because the narrow blade is less apt to bind in thick wood.

The Disston bow saws illustrated offer the additional advantage of being Teflon-treated. Thus they cut through heavy planks with exceptional ease. As indicated, they come in various sizes. Blades are removable and may be purchased separately.

Dovetail Saw

This little saw is closely related to the backsaw. It is lighter, however, and possesses a thinner blade and finer teeth. The handle is round, to provide a delicate grip for fine cutting. This saw is used where absolutely precise and delicate cutting is required.

Compass Saw

With a blade resembling the beak of a sword-fish (the shape incidentally which was probably used when saws first originated) this type of saw is commonly used for making "cutouts" on the inside surface of a piece of work. A hole is first bored inside the portion which is to be cut out. The pointed compass saw is pushed into the hole to start the sawing operations.

Keyhole Saw

Although it is smaller in size, the keyhole saw is used in the same manner as the compass saw. For this reason it is generally employed for finer work where the compass saw would be too big and clumsy for the job.

Hack Saw

While essentially designed for cutting metal, this tool comes in for a variety of uses in the woodworking shop. The hack-saw frame is designed in a number of different ways, some with pistol grips, others with handles similar to those used on a conventional saw, others with turned handles. Blades are detachable and can be obtained with teeth of varying coarseness.

Sawing Operations

In sawing, the saw handle should be grasped lightly and easily, with the forefinger extended along the side. The general tendency when first using a saw is to hold it too tightly and to depend too much on the muscles of the arm to give it movement and direction. As the saw cuts while it is being pushed away from the workman, the tendency at first is to press the teeth forcibly into the wood during this part of the movement. This pressure is unnecessary, as it does not increase the cutting speed and makes it difficult to guide the saw properly. By grasping the saw lightly, in fact, in what seems at first to be a loose manner, and putting no more pressure on the teeth than comes naturally with the back-and-forth movement of the body, the best results in the way of speed in cutting and guidance are obtained.

Before the cut is started, a line is marked on the wood with a lead pencil to serve as a guide, and the cut is started by drawing the saw toward the operator, as this gives a groove of sufficient depth to keep the saw in place. The cut is made along the waste side of the marked line, and just away from it.

At times, the saw may tend to run off the line, in which case the blade should be twisted gently, so as to change the course to the proper one. It should be noted that the more nearly the line of the saw teeth is perpendicular to the face of the work, the fewer are the teeth that are actually cutting and the smaller is the effort required to do the work. This is true of both the rip and the crosscut saw. By lowering the handle and putting more teeth in action, the workman will find that his labor is increased, as the effect is then the same as if he were cutting through thicker stock. In general, the more nearly upright is the position of the saw, the less will be the effort required to do the work. An angle of 45 degrees with the surface of the work may be taken as a good angle for rip saws.

The Plane Family

There are various sizes of planes: little planes, big planes, and medium-size planes. There are also many different types of planes and each type is used for its own special work.

All planes are assembled of a number of different parts. Each part serves to make the plane cut smoothly and efficiently. Most types of planes may be adjusted for a desired depth of cut. The cup which is adjusted over the cutting edge of the blade provides a smooth and even cut, and prevents the blade from sticking and roughing the work.

Jack Plane

The jack plane is so named because the woodworker uses it in a variety of ways, especially for rough or preliminary work. While there are actually forty-six different parts to this plane, the worker need only become acquainted with the working or regulating parts. These are: (1) The *cutting blade* or plane iron; (2) the *adjusting nut*, which is turned to raise or lower the blade; and (3) the *adjusting lever*, which regulates the blade so as to make possible an even or slanted cut.

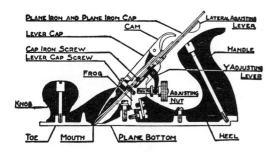

The cutting blade or *plane iron*, as it is usually called, is guarded with a metal cap which is adjusted on top of the blade to within about $\frac{3}{32}$ of an inch of the cutting edge. As already noted, this cap eases the cutting action by curling and breaking off the wood shavings evenly, thus preventing splitting or splintering of the wood.

Smooth Plane

This useful little plane is somewhat smaller than the jack plane, measuring between 6 and 10 inches in length. It is a fine utility tool, especially useful for planing end grain, chamfers, and other edge shaping.

Jointer Plane

When a fairly long board must be planed absolutely straight and square along the edge, it is easier to obtain a straight and level surface with the jointer than with any other type of plane. All planes when set for a small cut and pushed evenly along the edge of a board, cut so as to make that edge straight and even. However, the longer the plane, the easier it is to produce an exactly level edge. While sizes vary, the most popular type of jointer plane is 24 inches in length.

21

Fore Plane

This plane may be aptly referred to as a "junior" jointer plane. Measuring 18 inches in length, it is slightly shorter than the conventional jointer plane. It is used principally for planing edges of medium length.

Block Plane

The little block plane is particularly useful in planing end grain, inasmuch as its blade is tipped at a lesser angle for this type of cutting. It is also well adapted to small work where precision is essential. The popular type of block plane is 6 inches in length. It is held in the palm of the hand.

Router Plane

Having two knob handles, the router plane hardly resembles a plane. However, it is listed under this heading and it is used for routing out grooves in the surface of a board. It is especially useful in making dado joints and small panels.

Circular Plane

This tool was especially devised for shaping round edges. Its shape adapts it for planing either convex or concave surfaces. This plane may be adjusted so that the flexible bed will conform to circles of various sizes.

Rabbeting Plane

If the edge of a piece of board is to be rabbeted, this type of plane may be used. The side guide and the cutting blade may be adjusted so as to cut rabbets of varying widths and depths. The plane is useful, as well, for various types of edge shaping.

Plane Gauge

The plane gauge, which may be fastened to any standard size of plane, is very helpful, especially for the beginner. It is used to hold the plane for cutting at any desired slant and thus greatly helps the accurate cutting of bevels and chamfers. When set at right angles to the bottom of the plane, it can be used as a guide for straight cutting.

Combination Plane

This interesting type of plane, with its many adjustments and its variety of cutters, may be used to produce a great number of edge shapings. In fact there are well over 100 different shaped cutters which may be used with a plane of this type.

The Boring Family

Brace

The brace is a crank-shaped tool which is used to hold various types of boring and utility bits. Some braces are made with a *ratchet* attachment which permits use of the brace in a confined space or position, where a complete revolution of the brace is impossible. A knurled ring on the crank permits the use of the brace in either direction.

The Stanley corner brace, at left above, is very useful for working in tight corners or confined places which do not allow the cranking space required by a conventional brace.

Drill
(Hand Drills and Automatic Push Drills)

The hand drill works on about the same principle as the household egg beater. The action of cranking a geared side-wheel causes the drill to revolve and to drill holes.

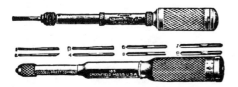

The push drill, illustrated above, turns automatically when being pushed into work. When

it is released and drawn away from the work, the drill revolves backward. This type of drill is especially useful when a number of small holes must be made.

Auger Bit

Auger bits are commonly made in sizes ranging from $\frac{3}{16}$ inch to $1\frac{1}{4}$ inches. The size of the bit is stamped on the square end (shank), which fits into the brace. All size graduations are based on the $\frac{1}{16}$-inch fraction, the size being stamped in the numerator of the fraction.

Bit Gauge

The bit gauge regulates the boring of auger bit holes to specific depth.

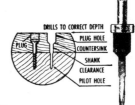

"Screw-Mate" Drill Bit

Stanley "screw-mate" drill bits perform the triple function of *drilling* holes of specific required sizes for each of a variety of standard flathead wood screws, and *countersinking* and *counterboring* in the same operation. Another type of "screw mate" regulates uniform countersinking by omitting extension of the counterboring shank.

Forstner Bit

The Forstner bit is especially useful for boring into end grain, and also when a hole already bored is to be made larger. This bit can also be used to bore a hole along the edge of a piece of stock where a portion of the bit is not working in the stock, or to bore two holes that partly lap or cut into each other.

The fact that this bit lacks a pointed spur is indeed a help when holes are to be bored *almost* through the stock. Like the auger bit, the Forstner bit is graduated in size by sixteenths of an inch.

Expansive Bit

Expansive bits are obtainable in two separate sizes. The smaller and lighter size is fitted with a cutter which may be adjusted to cut holes from 1 inch to 2 inches in diameter. The larger size bit is fitted with cutters which bore holes up to 3 inches in diameter.

Hole Saw

While designed primarily for use with an electric drill, the Arco hole saw cuts holes graduating by $\frac{1}{4}$ inch from 1 inch to $2\frac{1}{2}$ inches through wood, metal, and plastics. Blades for each diameter of hole are secured in tool head with safety lock screw. One-quarter inch drill makes pilot hole.

Countersink Bit

When a "pilot hole" has been bored to receive the unthreaded stem (shank) of a flathead screw, something must be done so that the head of the screw will "seat" evenly into the hole.

For this purpose the countersink bit was invented. It chamfers the hole opening to receive the screw head.

Bradawl

This handy tool is used for piercing small holes. It can be used for making pilot holes for smaller sized screws.

Bit Extension

As the name indicates this implement is simply an extension rod which fits into the brace to extend the regular length of the boring bit for especially deep boring.

High-Speed Power Bit

High-speed power bits are designed for boring larger-diameter holes with an electric drill. Sizes range by $\frac{1}{16}$-inch graduations from $\frac{3}{8}$ inch to 1 inch for drills with $\frac{1}{4}$-inch chucks and up to $1\frac{1}{2}$ inches for $\frac{3}{8}$-inch chucks.

Screwdriver Bit

When steady pressure is to be applied, especially on larger sized screws, the screwdriver bit is the answer. Used with a plain or ratchet brace, this bit provides for a degree of driving pressure that would otherwise be impossible to obtain. Like standard screwdrivers, these bits may be obtained in various sizes.

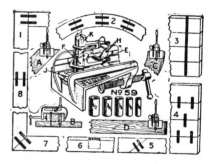

Doweling Jig

The doweling jig is an extremely important device to have on hand when absolutely straight and accurate boring must be accomplished. As the name implies, it is especially useful for boring holes for dowel joints.

The File Family

History of Files

The file is one of the oldest tools.

To abrade, or file, ancient man used sand, grit, coral, bone, gritty woods, and stones of varying hardness in connection with sand and water.

Crude as were these abrading instruments, and slow and laborious as must have been their use, they nevertheless served primeval man well throughout the Stone and Bronze Ages. Up to the time of the discovery of iron, natural abrasives were used extensively. Copper, and later bronze, did not permit of sufficient hardening to be used as a material for the making of artificial files, although attempts were made to use both for that purpose.

Among the earliest known examples of artificially made metal abrading tools, for which a date can be fixed, is a bronze file which was dug up in Crete by an expedition from the University of Pennsylvania and is now in the Museum at Candia. This prehistoric file believed to have been made about 1500 B. C. possesses an astonishing likeness to the half-round file of today. The Egyptians are also known to have made small rasps of bronze, about 1200-1000 B. C.

Cut of Files

The cut of files is divided with reference to the *character* of the teeth, into *single, double, rasp* and *curved;* and with reference to the coarseness of the teeth into *rough, coarse, bastard, second cut, smooth,* and *dead smooth.* Single-cut files are used with a light pressure to produce a smooth surface finish; or they may be used to produce keen edges on knives, shears, saw teeth, or other cutting implements.

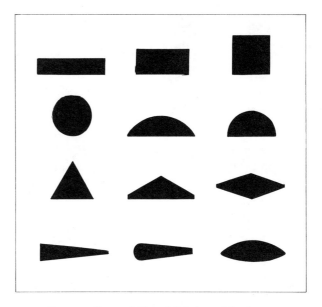

Cross-sections of files. *Nicholson File Co.*

Double-cut files are usually used under heavier pressure, for fast metal removal where rougher finish is permissible.

The rasp cut consists of a series of individual teeth produced by a sharp, narrow, punch-like cutting chisel. It is an extremely rough cut and is used principally on wood, hoofs, aluminum, lead, and other soft substances for fast removal of material. Rough, coarse, and bastard cuts are used on heavier classes of work, and the second-cut, smooth, and dead-smooth files for finishing on more exacting work.

Files are just as useful in woodworking as they are in metal work. They are used in the smoothing steps which follow after a piece of wood has been roughly cut. There are a number of different sizes and shapes of files. Their surfaces vary in texture for different kinds of use.

Single-cut   Double-cut   Rasp-cut   Curved-tooth

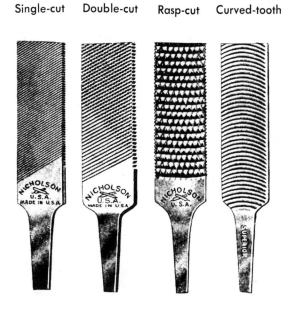

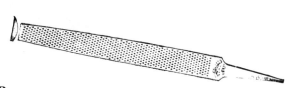

Rasp

Strictly speaking, the rasp does not belong to the file family. However, it is shaped and used like a file. The triangular shaped projections or teeth which appear on its surfaces cut into the wood. It is used only for rough shaping.

Triangular Tapered File

This type of file is really more of a metal-working tool. However, it comes in handy around the woodworking shop, especially for cutting nails and sharpening certain tools.

Auger Bit File

This tiny file is indispensable for sharpening auger bits. Each end is especially shaped and provided with teeth cut for the job.

Files should be well taken care of; should be kept in a dry place to avoid rust; and should be brushed and cleaned frequently with a file card. Different types of files are illustrated and their use explained.

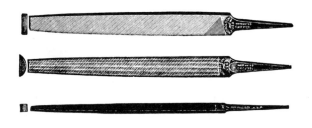

Flat and Half-Round Files

Each of these files has its specific uses. The half-round file is used for work that curves inward, and the flat file for work that curves outward, as well as for straight work.

Round or Rat-Tail File

The round or rat-tail file is used for shaping curved parts, or in holes and indentations where the flat file could not be used.

File Card

When files become clogged with wood dust, there is nothing more useful than a stiff wire brush for cleaning them. The *file card* is especially designed for the job. It should be kept handy when files are being used.

Other Abrasive Tools

During recent years many new and effective abrasive tools have appeared on the market. Some of these do the job originally performed by files, while others promise some improvement over traditional methods of sandpapering.

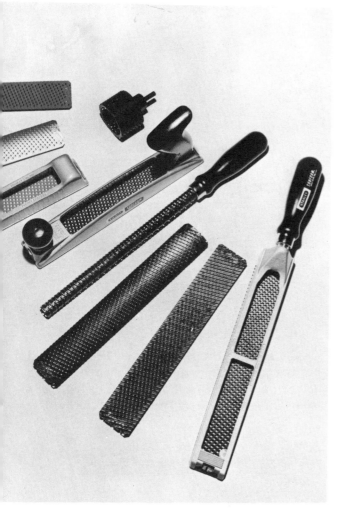

inch in thin sheets of steel. Each hole produces a five-sided burr which causes a mild cutting action like that of a scraper. This material is said to be five times more effective than sandpaper for certain types of work.

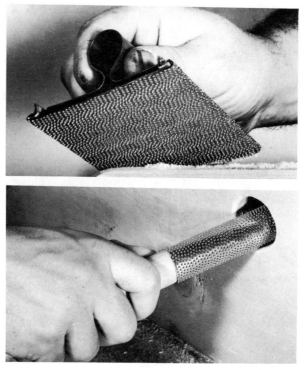

"Dragon-Skin" comes in $4\frac{1}{4}$" x 5" sheets to fit the regular Red Devil sandpaper holder or may be purchased in full sheets measuring 9" x 11" to be cut to desired sizes for making abrasive devices, as illustrated.

Stanley "Surform"

One of the most effective new abrasive tools is the Stanley "Surform." As illustrated, it is made in a variety of types and shapes. It is also made as a spindle accessory for use with power drills. The "Surform" cutting surface of Sheffield tool steel is made of hundreds of tough, razor-sharp teeth which effectively abrade wood and other materials. The cutting edges are spaced to prevent clogging. Four different blade cuts are available: *regular, half-round, regular fine cut* and *half-round fine cut*.

Red Devil "Dragon-Skin"

This remarkable steel abrasive material serves the purposes of both file and sandpaper. It is made by punching 150 holes per square

Millers Falls Hand Sander

This handy sandpaper holder, designed to hold tungsten carbide lifetime abrasive, is widely used both for shaping and smoothing wood. A $\frac{1}{8}$-inch felt pad, between block and steel plate, distributes the sanding pressure evenly.

The Pressure Family

When making articles out of wood, it is often necessary to press and hold together the different parts for a certain length of time. The gluing together of a piece of furniture calls for the use of clamps to hold the parts together while the glue is drying. Likewise, it is often desirable to hold a board in a special manner while the work is being done. For all of these purposes, clamps are very necessary in the workshop.

amply strong, the woodworker should avoid putting too much pressure on the screw or there may be a tendency to warp or "spring" this part. They vary in size from 3 to 12 inches.

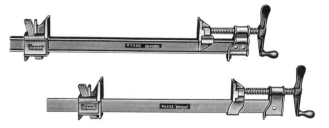

Adjustable Bar Clamp
(Cabinet Clamp)

The long, crank-handled, adjustable bar clamp is another of the woodworker's standbys. It is used to join boards together, or to obtain even pressure over broad surfaces. Clamps of this type are obtainable in sizes ranging from 2 feet to 8 feet. Of course, each size of the clamp may be adjusted to any spread less than its total length.

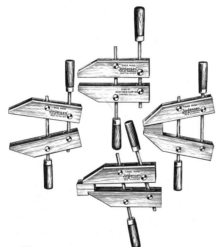

Handscrew Clamp

Here is a type of clamp that fulfills a countless number of purposes in the woodworking shop. As shown in the illustration, it is adjusted with parallel screws. The handscrew clamp serves to apply pressure on even or uneven surfaces. In use, the object is to obtain pressure with leverage from the back screw. These clamps vary in size from 4″ to 24″.

"C" Clamp
(Carriage Clamp)

This type of clamp serves in a number of ways around the shop. While the "C" part is

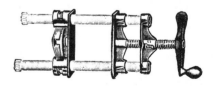

Double Bar Clamp

Like the cabinet clamp, this clamp is used principally for joining boards together. The double bars straddle the connecting boards and thus an even pressure may be applied along each surface of the board. This pressure helps to prevent the boards from buckling when pressure is applied, an advantage that the single cabinet clamp lacks. These clamps vary in length from 2 feet to 5 feet.

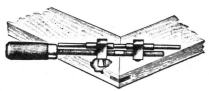

Steel Pipe Clamp

This clamp differs from the standard cabinet type only in that a steel pipe forms its backbone as shown. The adjusting parts consist of an adjustable end stop, and a crank screw which is fastened to the opposite end. These parts are attached to standard plumbing pipe of any desired length. This type of clamp is particularly handy for the workman who needs clamps of varying lengths and who does not want to purchase a number of different size cabinet clamps.

Miter Clamp

Miter clamps find their principal use in applying pressure to miter joints. They are especially

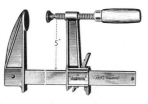

helpful in the construction of various types of frames where even corner pressure is essential.

Steel Bar Clamp

This clamp is most effective for applying "inside" pressure — where surfaces must be

pressed a distance in from the edge. Throat depths range from 2½″ to 5″ with lengths extending from 6″ to 36″.

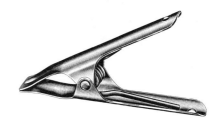

Spring Clamp

For fast clamping of many kinds of work nothing is more adaptable than spring clamps. They range in sizes from 4″ to 12″ with their pressure proportioned to size.

Band Clamp

When even pressure must be applied around the perimeter of the work — as is necessary for drawing together four sides of a frame or for box construction — nothing does the job better than band clamps. The web bands literally "strap" the work together. They are tightened with a screw crank or ratchet device.

Special Application of Clamps

As illustrated on the next page, clamps are of various types to suit different kinds of jobs. It is important that the proper type of clamp is selected, especially for production woodworking, in which case the quality and efficiency of assembling operations often depends on the use of exactly the right clamps.

This illustration demonstrates the proper use of "I" bar clamps and short steel bar clamps.

"Deep-reach" bar clamps apply pressure inside the perimeter of work.

Band clamps are used to press curved parts together.

Press screws can be used to make your own surface pressure jigs.

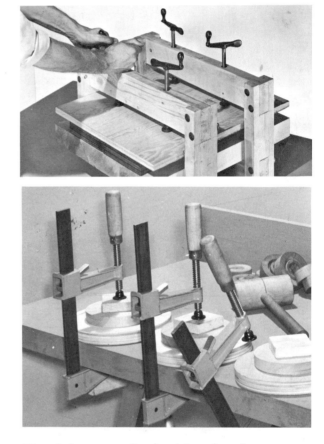

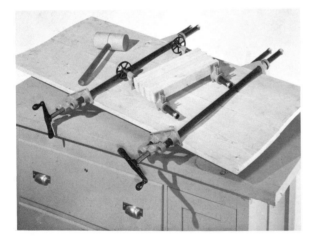

Double pipe clamps join larger boards, while short pipes hold small pieces.

Hinged clamps expedite the gluing of small parts.

Spring clamps are quickly applied to many assemblies.

A combination of large and small bar clamps, supplemented by edge-clamp screw fixtures, secures this assembly.   *All photographs: Adjustable Clamp Co.*

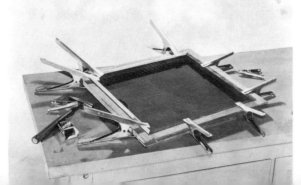

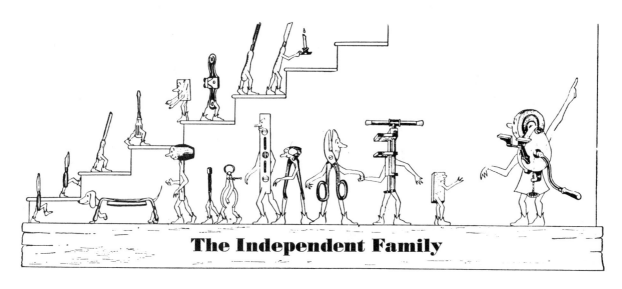

The Independent Family

While the tools which follow are listed as being "independent," they all form part and parcel of the essential group of hand woodworking tools.

They are placed separately, however, because in most instances each particular tool is in a class by itself and, therefore, is not a member of any of the foregoing families.

Chisel

Chisels are among the most necessary tools in woodworking. They are commonly made with either wooden or composition handles. The widths of the blades range from 1/8″ to 1″ by eighths, and from 1″ to 2″ by fourths. There are two types of construction employed in the making of chisels, namely, the *tang* and the *socket* types. The tang chisel is made with a tanged, or pointed end which pierces into the handle. The socket type reverses the process by having the handle fit into the socket collar on the blade.

It will also be noted that the chisel blades vary in shape, some types being beveled along the sides as well as the cutting edge. Mortise chisels, used in making mortise joints, have perfectly flat blades usually a trifle thicker than the other ordinary types. Of course, the blades of all chisels are sharpened on a bevel from one side only.

It is a very good idea to use two hands when using a chisel. The work should be held securely in a vise or with clamps so that both hands of the worker are free to handle the chisel.

Gouge

Gouges are sharpened in two different ways, either from the outside edge or from the inside. They range in size from 1/8″ to 1″ by eighths, and from 1″ to 2″ by fourths. While the standard types of gouges are manufactured with straight shanks, there is a separate type made with a bent, "gooseneck" shank. The latter is more practical for deep cutting.

Spokeshave

This tool is used primarily for shaping and smoothing edges. As the name implies, it was originally designed to make oval-shaped spokes for wagon wheels.

As indicated in the illustration, spokeshaves are made in a number of shapes, sizes, and designs. They are obtainable in straight, hollow, and convex forms. Some types provide for adjustment of the blade in a manner similar to that of the plane blade.

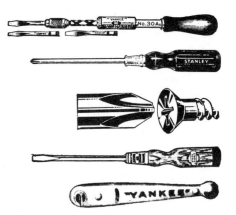

Cabinet Scraper

There are several distinct types of cabinet scrapers. The experiencd craftsman often prefers to use the scraper blade alone, without a handle. Three different types are illustrated.

Screwdriver

The hand automatic screwdriver, illustrated at top, drives screws with a *pressing* action. Phillips head and regular screwdrivers are made in an infinite variety of shapes and sizes, each having a special purpose. The Stanley *offset* screwdriver, illustrated at bottom, is most useful where leverage is required at close quarters.

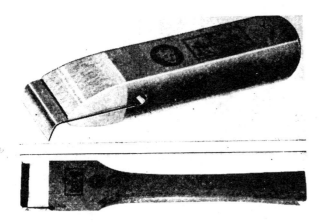

Utility Scraper

There are many different types of scrapers that are used to advantage in and about the woodworking shop. Each is designed to perform a specific job.

Those illustrated above are a small scraper for use in tight quarters and a long-handled type for heavy work where extra leverage is needed. Other common scrapers include the wall type, with its flexible wide blade, and painters' tools with interchangeable blades for scraping molding and unusual shapes.

Knives

The sloyd knife, illustrated at top, originated in Sweden, where it was used by the founders of the Sloyd school. The Stanley utility knife (center) accommodates blades of various types which are inserted, interchangeably, in a protective blade guard handle. Red Devil linoleum knives, shown at bottom, are ideal for cutting softer materials.

Glass Cutter

While obviously not a woodworking tool, a good glass cutter is a necessary addition to the operations of most woodworking shops.

Draw Knife

This type of knife is generally used for cutting wood roughly to size, and since it is not a precision tool, its use must necessarily be restricted to rough cutting only. Caution should always be observed to avoid drawing the blade in such a way that it may slip and cut into parts of the body.

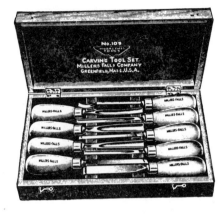

Carving Tools

As illustrated, carving tools are made in varying shapes. Like the instruments of the dentist, or the clubs of the golfer, each separate carving tool has been designed for a specific type of cutting.

Hatchet

Both inside and outside of the woodworking shop the well-known hatchet is one of the most useful implements. As a woodworking tool, it serves for the roughest sort of shaping.

Hammer

The hammer hardly requires any introduction — most of us have been familiar with it since infancy. However, it is interesting to know that hammers may be purchased in varying sizes ranging in weight from 7 to 20 ounces. There are two working parts to the hammer, the head for driving nails, and the claw for pulling them.

Mallet

This handy tool is used most frequently for striking chisels or gouges. It is also used to tap parts of a project together during the assembly process. Mallets are made in various shapes and sizes. Those of more recent manufacture have heads made of hard composition rubber, thus to protect the work or tools.

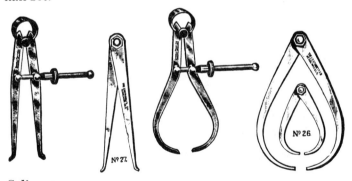

Nail Set

In order to drive the heads of nails below the surface, it is necessary to use either a *nail set* or a slightly larger size nail. Finishing nails of recent manufacture have small indentations on the head which provide for the use of a pointed nail set.

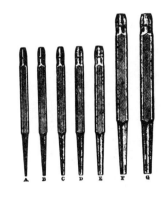

Calipers

The round or turned parts of wooden articles are most easily measured with calipers. In wood turning, it is necessary to use calipers frequently when turning or shaping wood to a desired diameter. In use, the arms of the calipers, at the curved tips, are pressed lightly against the wood at the point being measured. The separation between the tips is then measured. *Inside calipers* are used to gauge the size of inside surfaces.

Spirit Level

If you were to take a bottle or test tube of water and fill it so full that the water came to within a small space of the cork, and were then to place this bottle on its side, you would find a small *unfilled* space gliding along the top. Regardless of the position of the bottle the unfilled space would always remain on top. It is on this principle that the carpenter's level depends. Instead of employing a bottle, a small glass tube partly filled with alcohol and sealed is inserted in a metal or wooden mounting and the unfilled part of the tube, or "air bubble," indicates the level qualities of the object being checked.

Pliers

Like saws and some other categories of hand tools, there are dozens of different types of pliers — and each type is almost indispensable for performing certain types of work. While the general utility, combination pliers illustrated below are a household necessity they may be inadequate for special holding operations. And when an extra powerful grip is required, larger specially shaped pliers like the "Channellock" and "Griplock" hold more firmly than conventional types.

Illustrated and described here are some of the pliers constantly used in the workshop. If more specialized types are required there are dozens of others from which to choose.

Combination Pliers

Combination pliers have many general uses in the shop. The slip joint permits two positions.

Round Nose Pliers

Pliers with round jaws are used for forming loops of wire. They are also used in radio repair, reed, and upholstery work.

Side Cutting Pliers

Side cutting pliers are used for cutting wire and removing cotter pins. This tool is also used in electrical construction work and for miscellaneous purposes.

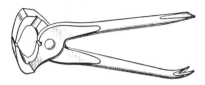

Carpenter Pincers

Carpenter pincers are found to be very valuable in removing brads and small nails. Usually one of the handles is formed in the shape of a tack puller and the other handle is shaped in the form of a screwdriver, making the carpenter pincers a very valuable utility tool.

Channellock Pliers

These slip-lock pliers may be adjusted to grip objects of various shapes and diameters. With strong leverage exerted direct on sharp-toothed jaws, they are virtually slip-proof. Channellocks may be purchased in several sizes.

Griplock Pliers

Powerful pliers, designed to grip firmly and lock to the work with a holding device, exert maximum pressure on any object that has to be held or turned. Griplocks come in various sizes.

"Pop" Rivetool

This is one of the greatest inventions to appear in the hand-tool line in several decades. The "Pop" Rivetool is indispensable for attaching hardware in "blind" positions — where you can't get at the back of the work to which the

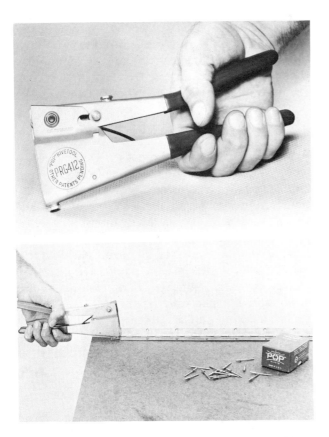

attachments are being made. Also it is excellent for fastening things to thin hardboard and composition materials.

Simply explained, with the Rivetool you bore rivet-sized holes through the pieces which are to be fastened together. Then, from the outside, you insert the rivets and draw up the stems with the riveting pliers. The action of the pliers spreads and "bunches" the inside end of the rivet and draws the bunch tight against the outside rivet collar, thus securing the fastening on both sides.

"Pop" rivets are available in various sizes. As illustrated above, the Rivetool can be used most effectively to fasten hardware to hardboard and thin plywood.

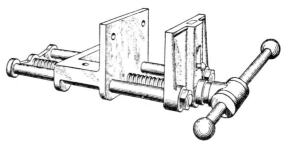

Adjustable Wrench

No workshop can function without a wrench — or a number of them. The adjustable wrench is well adapted to requirements. It can be purchased in several sizes.

Scroll Pivoter

The scroll pivoter operating on the pivoting principle enables one to cut intricate shapes out of sheet metal, such as circles, scrolls, or squares, as easily as cutting along a straight line.

Vise

The vise is a very necessary article in woodworking. Work must be held and the vise is the instrument that holds it. There are several varieties of vises, each possessing its own particular merit. One of the common types is illustrated above.

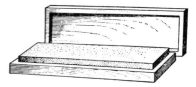

The new Stanley L-shaped, *portable* vise can be clamped to workbench, table, or sawhorse to hold objects *vertically* as well as horizontally.

Oilstone

Sharp tools are essential in woodworking. The oilstone serves this purpose. Ordinarily it is made in rectangular shape, having one coarse and one smooth side. Another form of oilstone, called the *gouge slip,* is used for sharpening gouge chisels and other curved cutting edges.

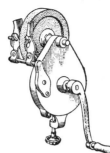

Tool Grinder

The tool grinder is used for grinding edges of cutting tools in the first steps of sharpening. Such grinding is necessary to remove nicks which would otherwise remain after the ordinary process of sharpening.

Automatic Stapling Tacker

For certain types of woodworking and composition-board construction, the Bostitch stapling tacker speeds work by automatically "shooting" staples ranging in size from $5/32$ inch to $9/16$ inch. Its trigger action not only simplifies the job but takes only a fraction of the time required to drive tacks or nails by hammer.

X-Acto Precision Tools

For the craftsman who does precise work — or for the general woodworker who often needs tools capable of almost surgical accuracy — the X-Acto kits pictured here offer unique advantages. They contain small, interchangeable, razor-sharp knives of various shapes and sizes. Fitting to the same handles are delicate little saws, routers, and gouges. There are also tiny planes, tweezers, punches, vises, clamps, pliers, sanders, drills, and other items. All tools are of miniature size and as precisely made as surgeon's instruments. As well as the complete kits pictured here, most X-Acto tools may be bought individually.

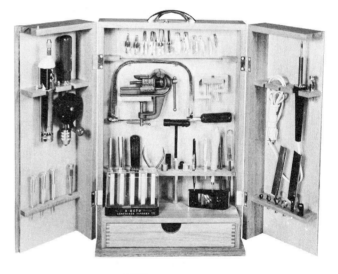

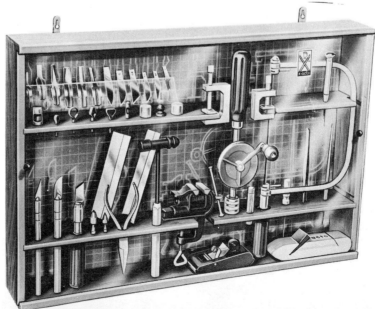

3

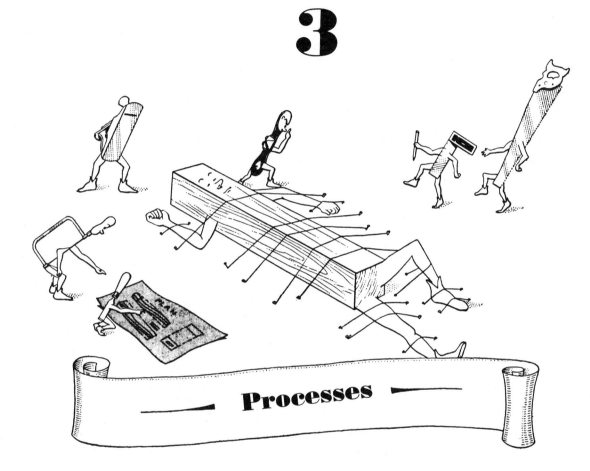

Processes

Let's Go to Work

One of the most important things in woodworking, as in any other endeavor, is a proper knowledge of *how to get started*. The beginning woodworker, finding himself in a fully equipped shop, is apt to become confused by all the tools and materials and finished work which confront him. Indeed, he may even become a little bit discouraged. After examining the work of the experienced craftsman, he may be inclined to wipe his forehead and say, "Whew! I could never do work like that!"

However, the beginner really need not become discouraged, because after he gets acquainted with the work he is bound to find that all those things which seem so difficult and confusing at first are actually quite simple. In order to get started all he needs is the ambition to make something out of wood.

It is always advisable to start on a simple type of project, something that does not involve the more complicated woodworking processes. Plans and working drawings of many simple "easy-to-make" project ideas can be found in the last section of this book. In order to get started on one of these projects, it is first necessary to know how to read a working drawing.

Reading a Working Drawing

Before doing anything or making anything, it is necessary to have a plan. If you were to start out on a long automobile trip, you would probably figure out the way you were going to go before you started. You would consult a road map and this would give you a *plan* of your route. In like manner, the company that builds a skyscraper, a steamboat, an airplane, or anything else, must have a plan to work by before any of the actual construction takes place. So too, the woodworker must first have a plan of the article that he is going to make. In woodworking, the plan is usually referred to as a working drawing.

The woodworker's working drawing shows all the dimensions as well as the construction of the article being made and, by studying it, the worker can determine, ahead of time, what the thickness, width, and length of each part of the article should be. Also, he can decide upon a method of attack for making the article; what parts to make first, what parts to put together first, and other important information of this nature.

A plan known as an *orthographic projection* is used in the preparation of working drawings. By this method three separate views of the article are drawn, namely, the *top view, front view,* and *end view*. Ordinarily these three views are drawn at right angles to each other; the top view occupying the top left corner of the paper, the front view immediately below it, and the end view in the right-hand lower corner. In instances where the article being made is identical in appearance when looked at from both front and end, the end view is not drawn.

The illustrations on the next page show the method whereby working drawings are prepared. In the working drawing, the *top view* of the five-board stool is shown as though the actual top were X-rayed, revealing the dimensions and construction of the parts below the top. Similarly, the front view reveals the sizes and hidden construction of the front. Likewise, in the end view all of the end construction is shown. In this way both the size and the shape of every piece of wood used in making the article are accurately revealed.

It will be noted that all hidden construction, joints, and pieces that lie beneath each view of the article are shown with dotted line. Moreover, the dimensions of each piece are clearly indicated with arrows and figures. Even the position and size of every nail and screw are given.

Not only does a good working drawing show full dimensions and construction of every piece in the article, but it also shows the shape of curved and scrolled parts. This is generally done by "graphing out" the scroll; which simply means that lines are marked in the manner illustrated for the curved edge. From this a full-size pattern is laid out in squares of the size indicated. The points where the line of curve crosses the lines of the squares are spotted off on the pattern and thus the curved line may be accurately drawn.

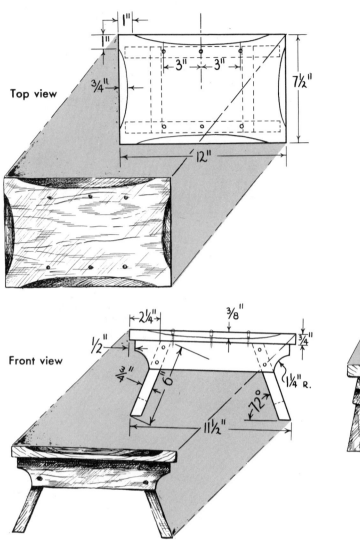

Top view

1"

1"

3" 3"

3/4"

7 1/2"

12"

Front view

2 1/4"

3/8"

1/2"

3/4"

3/4"

6

11 1/2"

72°

1 1/4" R.

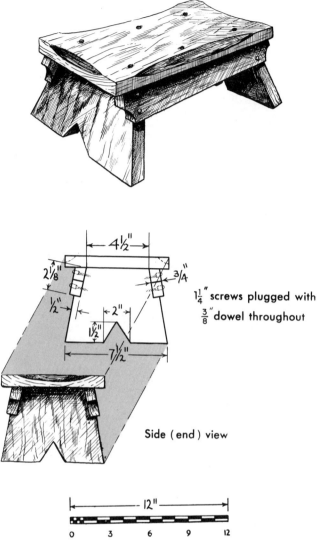

4 1/2"

2 1/8"

1/2"

3/4"

2"

1/2"

7 1/2"

1 1/4" screws plugged with
3/8" dowel throughout

Side (end) view

12"

0   3   6   9   12

How to Saw Lumber to Size

It is wise at the start for the beginning woodworker to use a soft, even-textured species of wood. A good grade of white pine serves admirably. This, and similar softwoods, cut and shape easily. The end of a board will often be found to be slightly damaged. Therefore, assum-ing that the long edge of the board is perfectly straight, the very first job is to mark a line square across the end of the board so as to margin off the damaged portion.

The original squared line serves as a starting point. A rule is used to measure off from this line the length of the required board. A line is

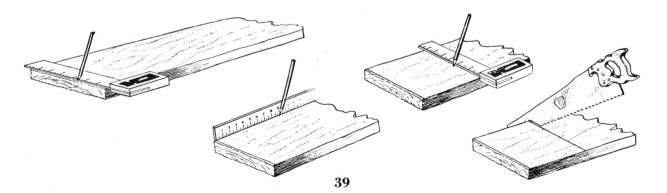

39

1   Marking square line to length for sawing.

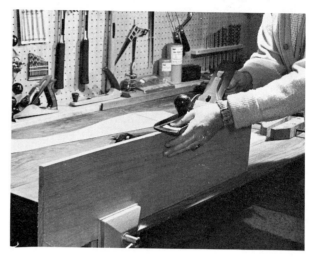

2   Planing edge straight and square.

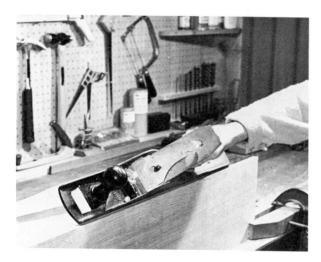

3   Checking straightness of planed edge.

4   Checking squareness of planed edge.

5   Planing ends to squared lines.

6   Checking squareness of ends.

then marked across the board at the required length.

The sawing is performed slightly outside the squared line with a crosscut saw. It is easier to guide the saw if the board is held flat. In sawing, it is good practice to hold the thumb lightly against the side of the saw. This will prevent the saw from jumping back, which might injure the hand or mar the work. Saw with a slow, even drive. When the end of the cut is reached the board must be supported so that it will not break off and splinter.

After the piece of lumber has been sawed slightly outside the squared line on both ends, proceed with the following steps.

Squaring a Board to Exact Size

Assuming that the face of the board is smooth and level, the first job will be to plane one of the edges perfectly straight and square. Using a jack plane, the blade is set for a shallow cut, and the plane is driven evenly along the edge.

After this, one end of the board must be planed square to the first edge and square to the face. Right here the special job of planing end grain will be met. However, this is not too difficult to perform if the plane is set for a shallow grazing cut. Extreme care must be practiced to avoid splitting the end grain. The plane must not go all the way across the end in one cut, but from both edges toward the middle.

However, if the board is extra wide, so that some of the width will later be taken off to make the board the proper width, a corner notch can be made on the further corner of the end. This notch makes it possible to plane the end all the way across in one direction without splitting.

With one edge and one end planed true and square, the other end may be planed square to the first edge, and to the face, and to the exact length required.

The final step in squaring the edges is to plane the opposite edge to the exact required *width,* straight and square.

Chamfering and Beveling

When the chamfer is planed along an edge that runs *with the grain,* it is only necessary to set the plane to a small cut, and holding it on the angle of the chamfer, to plane along evenly until the desired portion of the edge has been removed. It is extremely important that the plane blade be perfectly sharp.

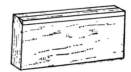

Guide lines for chamfering

Planning chamfer with grain of wood

Planning chamfer on end grain

Use of spokeshave for cutting stop chamfer

Use of block plane for cutting center portions of stop chamfer

The chamfering of *end grain* requires a special technique. The plane must be held in a paring position so that it will shear off the wood partly with the grain, and not splinter the grain at the end of the stroke. This type of chamfering is most successfully performed by working from both sides toward the middle so that the plane blade never actually passes entirely across the edge. The small block plane is favored for end-grain chamfering, especially when there is a narrow edge to be planed.

Rounded Edges and Corners

When a half-round is required it is first necessary to mark the amount of rounding. This marking is done by making pencil lines along the center edge of the board and along each opposite face, equal distances in from the edge. With these lines as guides, the work is proceeded with in two steps.

The first step involves the cutting of a regular straight chamfer at *half* of the span of the final rounding. With the plane set for a very small cut, the final rounding is accomplished in a series of graduating *rounding* cuts to the line of marking. The edge, which is now roughly rounded, is further smoothed with a wood file and is then sanded to a smooth, perfect rounded edge.

Rounded corners are first marked with a compass or are traced from circular templates. A coping saw, bandsaw, or scroll saw may then be used to remove the excess portions. The work is then planed, filed, and sandpapered to the final shape of rounding.

How to Bore Holes

While the action of the brace and auger bit is more or less self-explanatory, still there are many people who experience difficulty in using these tools properly. In the first place, the bit should be placed in the brace in such a way that it is held firmly and securely. This means that the end of the bit should be inserted into the chuck or holding part of the brace, *as far as it will go.* When the bit is in action, and if a hole is to be bored entirely through the wood, the worker should stop turning when the point, or spur, of the bit appears through the opposite side of the board and then re-bore from the opposite side to finish the hole. Otherwise, the board may splinter on the opposite side.

For straight boring, the brace must be held so that the bit is perfectly perpendicular, and at right angles to the wood. The knack of holding it in an accurate position is soon acquired. However, it is well at the start to test the position of the bit with a try square, as the work progresses.

When boring holes of a diameter greater than 1″ the expansive bit is generally used. After it has been adjusted to the required size, the boring continues in the manner already described. However, when using an expansive bit to bore a large hole, it is sometimes advisable to use the ratchet adjustment on the brace, making part turns with the ratchet. Otherwise the resistance to the wide spread cutter would make steady and accurate work difficult.

Likewise, when the screwdriver bit is used, the ratchet attachment assists greatly. Small turns on the brace make the driving of large stubborn wood screws possible, after all other methods have failed.

Chamfers cut for half rounding

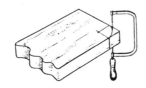

Rounding off chamfer with plane

Filing and sanding to final half rounding

Use of compass to mark corner rounding

Cutting rounding with coping saw

Use of block plane for finishing rounding

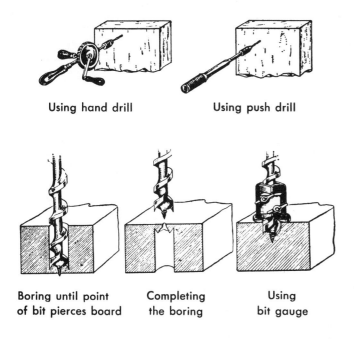

Using hand drill   Using push drill

Boring until point   Completing   Using
of bit pierces board   the boring   bit gauge

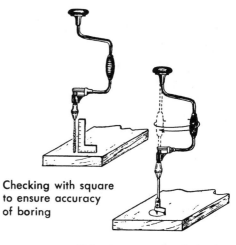

Checking with square
to ensure accuracy
of boring

Using brace ratchet in boring
with expansive bit

Using the Bit Gauge

When holes of an exact required depth must be bored, the bit gauge comes in very handy. This little device which is attached directly to the bit, permits the bit to enter the wood to the adjusted depth. Care must be taken, however, to watch the gauge so that it does not scratch or mar the wood after the required depth has been reached.

Marking and Cutting Curves and Scrolls

Ordinarily a *template,* or "pattern," is used to mark scrolls on a piece of wood. In making a template, first lay out squares on a piece of bristolboard or similar material, as shown in the illustration. These squares should correspond to the size indicated in the working drawing. The exact line of the desired curve is transposed from the working drawing and "spotted off" on the squares of the template. After this operation, the several points are connected by a free flowing line representing the desired curve. The bristolboard template is then cut out with a pair of scissors, a sharp knife, or razor blade.

After the template has been made, it is used to mark the scroll on the work. In the absence of a machine bandsaw or jig saw, the actual cutting is performed by hand with a coping saw, turning saw, compass saw, or keyhole saw. Each of these is well adapted for its own particular job.

Turning saws are admirably suited for the type of scrollwork wherein long deep curves are to be cut. Because of its wider and coarser

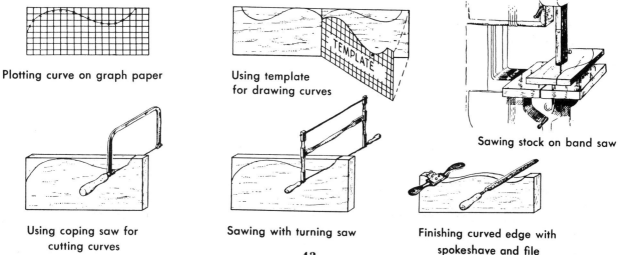

Plotting curve on graph paper

Using template
for drawing curves

Sawing stock on band saw

Using coping saw for
cutting curves

Sawing with turning saw

Finishing curved edge with
spokeshave and file

43

blade, however, it is impossible to obtain as fine a cut with the turning saw as with the coping saw. Therefore, provision must be made in cutting for final working and smoothing to the desired scroll.

The coping saw is probably the most popular of the saws used for cutting curves. While using this tool, the work should be clamped in position so that the blade may at all times cut absolutely perpendicular to the surface. By maintaining an evenness and uniformity of cutting thrust, keeping the saw blade absolutely straight and level at all times, the resulting cut will be perfectly square and very little dressing up will be required. All sawing should be carefully performed just at the outer edge of the desired line, thereby preventing any change of the pattern curves. This method also eliminates a great deal of the work involved in finishing off curved work with other tools.

As shown on the preceding page, a spokeshave of the straight or convex type, a file, and sandpaper are indispensable in finishing curved areas. Sharp edges should be avoided. A rounding of at least 1/16 inch tends to soften the curved lines.

Incised Cutting

It is often necessary to cut out spaces and curved shapes *inside* the edge area of a piece of wood. Cut-out handles and other incised decoration call for this type of cutting. There are various ways of going about this job. Sometimes it is desirable to bore out a handle shaping by making a series of holes of the required width which eclipse each other to remove the center stock. Following this operation, the inside handle may be chiseled and shaped to exact requirements.

In other cases the power scroll saw or coping saw may be "threaded" through a hole which has been bored within the cut-out area. The stock is then sawed out in regular fashion from this starting hole. Turning saws may likewise be taken apart so that the blade can be threaded through an inside hole. This saw is especially helpful for such cutting in heavier stock, or where the margin between the edge of the stock and the cut-out is greater than can be normally spanned by a coping saw.

Keyhole and compass saws are especially designed for inside cutting and can be used to very good advantage where holes and shapes are to be cut out in central areas of broad surfaces. Of course, these saws are apt to make a rough cut, but they are invaluable where the span or the spread of work is so great as to prevent the use of a loop frame type of saw. This is especially true on work which has already been constructed and where the tool must be brought to the work rather than the work to the tool.

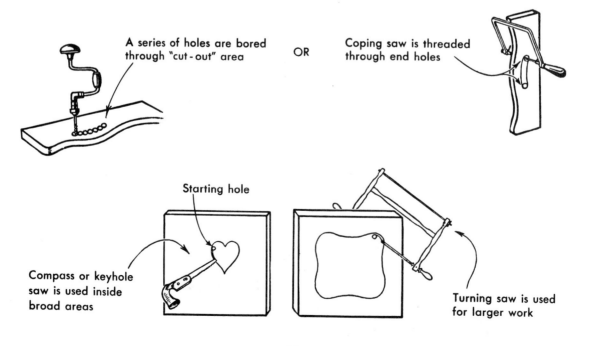

A series of holes are bored through "cut-out" area

OR

Coping saw is threaded through end holes

Starting hole

Compass or keyhole saw is used inside broad areas

Turning saw is used for larger work

1
Place hinge in position
and mark outline

2 (a) (b)
Marking gauge is used
to scribe cut, (a) width
and (b) depth of area

3
Make series of chisel cuts to
depth slightly greater than
thickness of hinge leaf

4
Clean out
cut area

5
Leaf of hinge fits
slightly beneath
adjoining surface

How to Fit Butt Hinges

In attaching butt hinges it is necessary to inset each leaf to a thickness equaling one-half the thickness of the hinge knuckle. These cut-out insets are called *gains*.

Gains are cut in both of the pieces that are to be hinged together. Proceed first to determine the position of the hinge. Then mark out the position of each gain by holding the hinge in place and marking along each end with a sharp pencil or knife. Then mark the depth of the area to be cut out, which is equal to slightly more than the thickness of the hinge leaf. This is marked on each of the pieces that are to be hinged together.

In cutting out the gain, the chisel is placed in an upright position on the line which locates one end of the hinge. The mallet is then used to drive the chisel as deep as the line which marks the depth of the gain. Next, a series of chisel cuts is made within this area, as shown in the illustration. After these cuts have loosened up the area to be removed within the gain, a sharp chisel is used to clean out the area. The gain is cleaned so that the hinge leaf fits within it snugly and evenly. The hinge should not be forced into the cut-out area.

Holes for the hinge screws are drilled as described for driving screws. As a rule, it is advisable to drive only one screw in each hinge leaf, so that the fitting of the hinge may be tested. If the fitting functions properly, the rest of the screws are driven. If not, the depth or position of the hinge leaf is adjusted before driving the remainder of the screws.

How the Legs of Tables and Chairs are Shaped

Legs of chairs and tables are shaped in three general ways, namely, round (turned), curved (cabriole), square (straight or tapered). Obviously the square type is the easiest to make, although frequently the least desirable. However, there is no difficulty attached to the making of any of these types, provided, of course, that they are devoid of elaborate decoration and carving.

The perfectly square leg is simply cut to length, planed to the required thickness, thoroughly sanded, and thus considered complete.

The *tapered leg*, however, requires additional treatment. In most cases the taper, or slant, is cut on two sides of the leg only. Thus the leg is first pencil-marked on one side to the desired amount of the taper. A ripsaw, or better still, a band saw, may be employed to remove the extra wood outside of the taper line. A plane is then used to smooth the tapered side down to the line.

When one side has been finished, the adjoining side of the leg is marked. This side in turn is carefully sawed and planed. It will be noted that in assembly, the two tapered sides generally remain on the inside, to improve the appearance of the article and to give it a splayed effect.

Square top line of taper

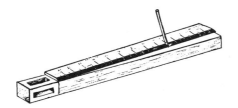

Marking taper on one side

Marking tapered side for second taper

Turned legs are made on a lathe. Naturally, the work involved may be simple or difficult depending on the type of design and the skill of the worker at lathe work. Turning is explained in the section on lathe work (page 96).

Cabriole legs, because of their appearance, seem hard to make, yet when it comes right down to the actual work of making them they are not at all difficult. A template, or pattern, is first made of the curved cabriole shaping. This pattern is carefully marked on the two opposite faces of the square piece of wood from which the leg is to be made. The leg is then cut outside the marking and smoothed down with a spokeshave, and sandpaper to the cabriole marking. After this primary shaping, the pattern is again marked on the two opposite sides of the leg that have already been shaped. The cutting and smoothing is performed as in the primary step and thus the cabriole shaping is accomplished.

Often, however, the cabriole shaping must be further shaped and rounded. This operation is performed with a sharp spokeshave, file, and sandpaper.

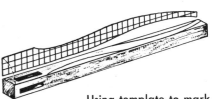

Using template to mark cabriole shaping on square stock

Half cut cabriole leg being marked for final shaping

Finishing second taper

Finishing cabriole leg with spokeshave and file

Leg being turned on lathe

A variety of edge shapings

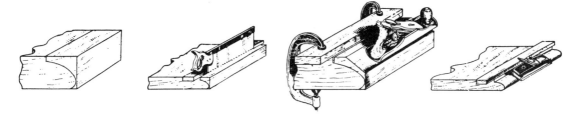

Marking the "thumb edge"   Sawing shoulder cut   Planing off rough stock   Finishing with rabbet plane

Simple Edge Shaping

The tops of tables, chests, and stools are generally embellished along the edge with some special type of treatment. This treatment may vary from simple rounding or sandpapering of the edges, to involved and elaborate carving and scalloping.

One of the most common of these treatments is referred to as the "thumb edge." As indicated in the illustration, the usual thumb edge requires a straight top cut, or shoulder, and a gently sloped and rounded edge. If the worker decides to make this edge by hand he should proceed in the following manner.

First mark a marginal line at the required distance (usually as deep as the thickness of the wood) in from the edges that are to be shaped. Proceed then to saw along this line, on the surface, to a depth of ⅛ inch or slightly less. This process is most easily accomplished by first placing a board on the line and securing it in place with a clamp. This board then acts as a guide for sawing the shallow shoulder.

After the shoulder cut has been accurately made, several additional saw cuts should be made to the necessary depth, on the portion of the edge which is to be rounded off later. With a sharp plane, preferably a rabbeting plane, the stock outside of the shoulder is then leveled off. Following this operation, the edge is pencil-marked to the required amount of sloped rounding and either a rabbet plane or block plane is used to make the rounding. In doing this, the edge is first chamfered and then rounded off. The opposite, or bottom, edge is then given a ⅛-inch rounding. A wood file and sandpaper are used to give the thumb edge its final shape

and smoothness. A rabbet plane may also be used to make the shoulder cut, as shown.

Of course, if the thumb edge is made on a circular saw, the work is greatly simplified because the primary shoulder cuts may be machine-made and all the excess stock be removed by making a number of trips across the circular saw. Only the finishing work need be done by hand.

A typical assortment of edge moldings are shown in the accompanying illustrations. They may all be successfully shaped by hand.

Seat Weaving

The fibers commonly used for seat weaving are of two basic types: *Round cord,* referred to as *rush;* and *flat cord.* Natural rush fibers are obtainable in round cord — although both types are usually made of compressed paper.

Flat cord comes in ¼" widths. The first step in its application is to tack one end beneath the top rail of the chair or stool to be covered. Then, using opposite rails as a reel, wrap the fiber tightly, in successive strands, across the open seat span. Be careful to avoid twisting and see that it is flat-wrapped with each successive strand drawn snugly beside the one that went before. With completion of preliminary wrapping, tack the terminal end of fiber beneath the rail.

The weaving steps follow: Start by cutting off about 10 yards of flat cord. Tack one end beneath the side rail, snugly beside the leg. Be sure there are no twists in the fiber. Start the weaving by going over and under five strands at a time. Repeat the process over and under the bottom strands. The second — *and all succes-*

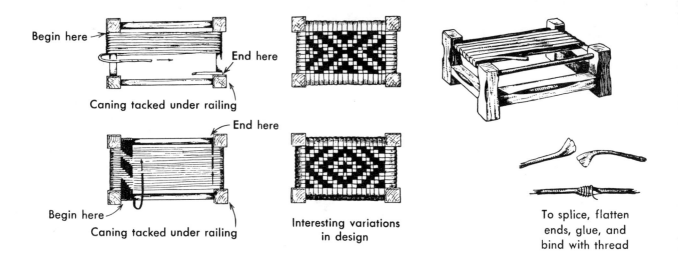

Begin here → ← End here
Caning tacked under railing

End here →
Begin here → Caning tacked under railing

Interesting variations in design

To splice, flatten ends, glue, and bind with thread

sive — strands are also woven over and under at five-strand intervals. But, in order to produce a diagonal woven pattern, each strand "steps in" at one strand less than the line that went before.

After the 10-yard length of fiber has been woven, splice on another length with glue and thread and conceal the splice inside the bottom strands. The in and out process continues until the top has been completely woven. The terminal end of the cord is then tacked beneath the rail. (See accompanying sketches of variations of flat cord weaving designs made by similar process.)

For *rush weaving,* take the hank of rush fiber and tack one end under the *left end* of a top rail. As sketched below, the cord is (1) tacked beneath the rail, (2) it passes over the top of the

rail directly opposite, (3) down under it, and (4) up over the end of the other rail attached to the same leg. This process is repeated on the remaining three sides. It is then continued until the diagonal corner lines meet snugly in the center.

In a rectangular stool the width will naturally be completed before the length. This remaining area is then filled in by simply passing the round fiber back and forth, over the side rails. Be sure that the cord is kept taut at all times and that the work is carefully done, so that the diagonal corner lines will be straight and neat. After the weaving process is completed, adjust the woven surface carefully with a pointed stick or screwdriver so as to make the cords line up in an orderly fashion. Sitting on the newly woven top helps to pull the strands

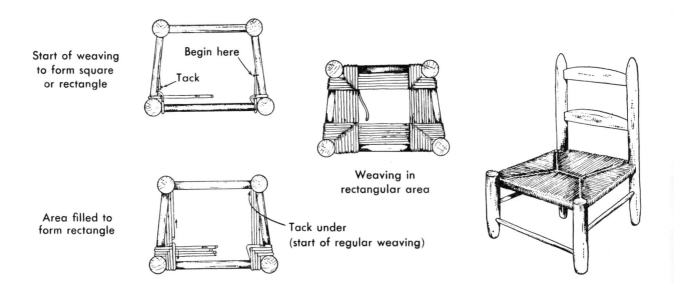

Start of weaving to form square or rectangle

Begin here

Tack

Area filled to form rectangle

Tack under (start of regular weaving)

Weaving in rectangular area

into their required positions. In order that there may be less sagging, soft paper is sometimes carefully packed beneath the layers during the weaving operation.

The weaving of an irregularly shaped seat requires the weaving in of the wide area so as to form a regular square or rectangle. This weaving in is easily done by tacking the round fiber to the inner edge of the side rail, near the widest part, weaving across the wide area to the other side and then securing the remaining end to the inner edge of the other side rail. Then weave another strand across the wide part — and another — and another — until the remaining area has four right angles. The regular opening is then woven just as any other square or rectangular area would be woven.

For several reasons, the woven seat should be protected with a suitable preparation. Because these materials are relatively porous, thin clear glue is frequently used as the sizing, or priming coat. This may be applied with a brush just as a coat of varnish is applied. The sizing provides an excellent base for a coat or two of white shellac or clear varnish.

Veneering

The art of veneering dates back many centuries. But the techniques involved have never been so easy for the nonprofessional to perform as they are today.

Originally, in order to veneer successfully, it was necessary to employ elaborate equipment, including veneer presses and special clamps. This was because glues were slow-drying and veneers had to be held down during the drying period. Now, however, with the instant adhesion of *contact cements* and self-sticking vinyls, there is no waiting. The job is completed as quickly as the veneers can be applied.

Self-adhesive vinyl veneers, like *"MACtac,"* shown at the right, are available in a variety of simulated wood grains as well as colors and patterns. They are made with waxed paper backing printed in 1" squares to facilitate measuring and cutting. The paper back seals the adhesive. As the paper is peeled off, the exposed sticky back is pressed to the surface. The resulting bond is instantaneous and enduring.

Wood Veneers

Solid wood veneers come in many rare species and exquisite grain patterns. They may be pur-

Vinyl veneer is made with waxed paper backing, grid-marked in 1" squares to facilitate measuring and marking.

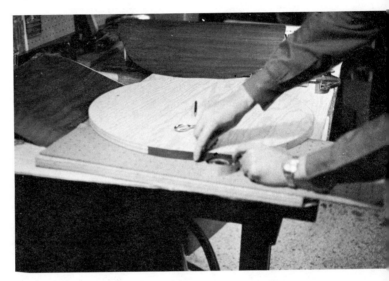
Edges are covered first with rolled strip of self-adhesive veneer.

As vinyl is applied, waxed paper backing is gradually peeled off while exposed adhesive is pressed evenly to the surface.
All photographs: "MACtac" by Morgan Adhesives Co.

1 Flexwood veneer comes in sheets measuring 4' x 8'. Lines are squared to mark size of required section.

chased from woodworking supply houses. With *contact cements* they can be applied almost as easily as the self-adhesives. The only drawback is that such veneers are not commonly available in broad widths and must be joined along the edges when wide surfaces are covered.

However, the edge-joining problem has been solved with an excellent natural-wood veneer called *Flexwood*, which is produced by U.S. Plywood-Champion Papers, Inc. Flexwood comes in large sheets measuring 4' by 8' and may be obtained in a variety of handsome woods — walnut, teak, mahogany, rosewood and many others. Since the wood is backed with tissue, Flexwood isn't nearly so fragile as the conventional veneers.

For best results, Flexwood is also applied with contact cement. This provides an absolute and everlasting bond. But it is a bit tricky to use. For this reason the correct procedures are detailed in the accompanying step-by-step instructions.

2 Razor-blade knife and steel straightedge are used to cut veneer accurately to the required size.

3 Contact cement is applied to tissue backing of Flexwood and allowed to set for 30 minutes.

4 Contact cement is also applied to surface which will receive the veneer.

All photographs: "Flexwood" by U.S. Plywood-Champion papers, Inc.

5 After contact cement has become dry to the touch (approximately 30 minutes), a paper "slip-sheet" is inserted between veneer and bonding surface. As sheet is gradually removed, impregnated veneer is pressed down to contact one edge and then, with even pressure, is bonded to entire surface. *Once contacted the veneer cannot be lifted.*

Inlaying

Many types of work require the use of inlays as part of their decorative treatment. Ordinarily, inlaying is not too difficult a process, but, because it is one of the finer practices of woodworking, it demands strict adherence to the rules of precision and accuracy. Sharp tools are, of course, a primary requisite in the performance of this work.

The straight inlay is first marked out with a sharp pencil and straightedge, as shown in the first illustration. Care must be taken to inscribe the exact location and width of the inlaid portions. Straightedges are then fastened along the inscribed lines. Several perpendicular cuts are made along each edge with a sharp knife. By grooving out the section between the straightedges with a sharp chisel, to a depth which corresponds to the thickness of the inlay, the channel is finished and the edge guides may be removed.

After the channels have been made and the strips of inlay cut to the desired length, thin glue is spread on these strips and they are lightly tapped into the groove with a small hammer or mallet. It is unnecessary to use clamps if grooves are cut with absolute precision. When the glue has set, the entire surface should be thoroughly sanded.

How to Bend Wood

Most types of wood when cut into thin strips may be bent to some extent without treatment. Some woods — notably *white oak, yellow birch,* and *white ash* — can withstand relatively sharp curves without breaking. But when severe curvature is required or when wood must retain a bent shape without support, special bending procedures must be employed.

It is common industrial practice to steam-treat the wood and then press it into shape in large hot-plate presses. The wood dries between the heated plates and retains its curvature after drying.

For bending flat surfaces such as ski tips without special industrial equipment, the best procedure is first to make a curved form shaped to the desired bend. This can be cut and smoothed to exact shape by using a single block or laminated assembly of boards. It serves as a *jig,* or mold, for the bending process.

The wood to be bent must be thoroughly steamed. An old oil drum or metal container,

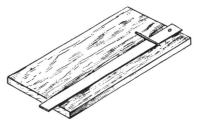

Marking out area to be inlaid

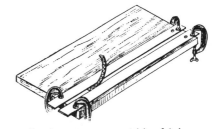

Clamping straightedges to exact width of inlay

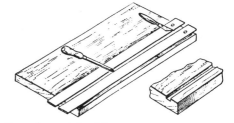

Cutting shallow channel for inlay

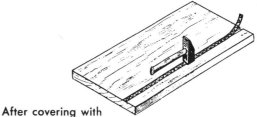

After covering with
thin coat of glue, tapping inlay lightly in place

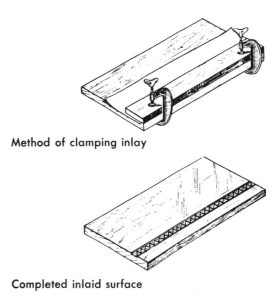

Method of clamping inlay

Completed inlaid surface

Set of carving tools

Design drawn
on paper

Use of carbon paper for transferring design

Incising outline of design with "v" or veining tool

Scooping design with gouge for finished effect

large enough to immerse that part of the wood which is to be bent, is filled with water and brought to a boil. The wood is then placed in the boiling water and steamed for at least two hours. By this time it is sufficiently pliable to be clamped securely over the curved jig.

To control the bend so that it doesn't continue into any part of the wood which must remain straight and flat, clamps or heavy pressure must be applied exactly and evenly at each end of the curve.

This method may also be applied to the shaping of long bent parts, such as boat rails, by contriving a steaming receptacle of long sections of large-diameter metal pipe, such as drain pipe, with a watertight stopper at one end.

When strips require only slight bending and are to be fastened down to other construction, it is only necessary to keep them wrapped overnight in water-soaked rags.

Simple Carving

Carving is fun. It is not difficult to learn and yet it provides an excellent opportunity for self-expression. Like all other phases of woodworking, successful carving is largely dependent upon sharp tools. The variety of carving tools has already been noted. They form part of the craftsman's kit.

A typical example of simple carving is shown in the illustration at right. This type of carving is performed by first making a pattern of the desired design. The outline of this design is then marked on the wood. The design can easily be transferred through the use of carbon paper. The design is lightly incised with a V-cut carving tool. The inner portions are scooped out carefully with a sharp round-nosed carving tool. Care must be exercised to cut from alternating ends of the scooped out portions.

Simple carving of this type is suggested as a beginning step. Other elaborate forms may be attempted as the skill of the worker increases.

Upholstering

When you stop to consider the procedures involved in traditional upholstering of furniture, you will agree that the new materials and techniques used to create soft, contemporary seating come as a blessing. For while it was traditionally maintained that you could not produce comfortable upholstery without introducing bulk quantities of springs, burlap, feathers, horse-hair, and padding, the contemporary designer eliminates all this and still produces lounge seating of luxurious comfort. To accomplish this he discards the heavy and bulky materials and uses in their place, lightweight and efficient cushioning of urethane or rubber foam on resilient platforms made of elasticized webbing or rubber stretch panels. And the resulting upholstery is not only as comfortable as before, it is also far more durable and easier to maintain. No longer do burlap tacks come loose in the bottom platforms of easy chairs to cause sags and spill padding. With stretch-web platforms, there are no springs to work loose and stab through covering materials. And the hourly chore of "plumping up" feather, down or kapok cushions is eliminated entirely when foam-fillings are used, for foam retains its shape without "plumping."

But one of the chief appeals of the new upholstery is that it provides comfort without excessive weight. You don't have to struggle with heavy and bulky chairs and sofas when it's time to vacuum under and around them.

As an example, the sectional seating-unit illustrated here, while providing a maximum of softness and comfort, actually weighs less than twenty pounds. The resilient seat platform is made with an Acushnet "Elastaseat" stretch-panel, while the cushions are of light-weight du Pont derivative, urethane foam. This seating unit is used to make luxurious chairs and sofas.

Other types of light-weight resilient seat platforms are made with the "Pirelli" and "Diatex" strap webbing shown on page 54. This is manufactured of a tough, rubber composition. It is stretched to form lattice-like platforms of various shapes. Strap webbing is installed either with metal end-clips, which fit into beveled

All photographs: "Elastaseat" by Acushnet Process Co.

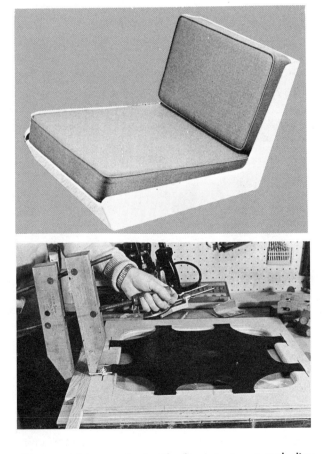

Urethane foam and covering fabric are components of cushions at left.

"Elastoseat" is stretched with clamp to insert end clips in beveled slots of seat platform.

Assembled seat platform is ready to be attached to seating unit.

grooves of the frame, as sketched below, or with screw-on clamps as pictured at the bottom right. It can be purchased at houseware or upholstery shops.

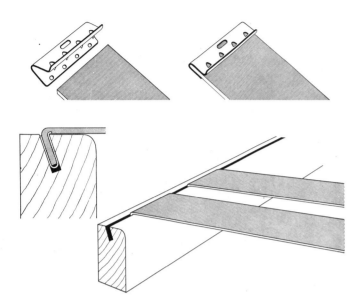

Beveled groove secures metal end clips of "Pirelli" webbing. *General Foam Corporation.*

Even the effects of "heavy" upholstery are now obtained with platforms of resilient webbing and lightweight foam cushioning and padding. *General Foam Corporation.*

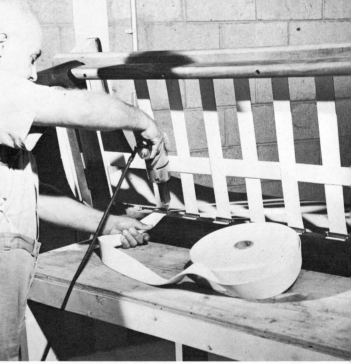

Press-on, clip webbing, combined with foam cushions, assures seating comfort of contemporary chairs and sofas. *Firestone "Diatex."*

Platform is attached industrially from roll of "Diatex" webbing. Screw-on clamps secure the ends under proper tension. *Firestone "Diatex."*

Simple Upholstery

With the introduction of foam materials the art of upholstery has become vastly simplified.

Following the procedures shown on this page, an effective upholstering (or, *reupholstering*) job can be performed, even by the amateur.

1 Foam upholstery materials may be purchased by the yard at department stores. Various types and thicknesses are available.

2 First a pattern is made of the chair seat or cushion you wish to upholster.

3 An outline of the pattern is traced on the foam with a ball-point pen; *allow ½-inch overlap on all edges.* The foam is then cut to the pattern outline with sharp scissors.

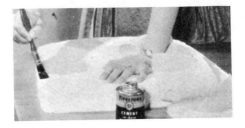

4 Cement is now spread 1 inch in from the edges on one side and also applied to strips of tacking tape.

5 Tape is then applied to one surface along the cemented perimeter of the foam.

6 Tape is now drawn over the cushion edges to the opposite surface and tacked or stapled to the ½-inch plywood seat base previously cut to the pattern.

7 The upholstered base is then placed in the seat cover, which is also tacked or stapled to the plywood.

8 The finished job. Foam upholstery is not only easy to make but is also comfortable and enduring. *All photographs: Firestone Tire & Rubber Co.*

How to Reduce Lengths of Flush Doors

1 Door is sawed to required length. Use fine-tooth crosscut saw.

2 Diagonal staves of hollow core appear in sawed-off section.

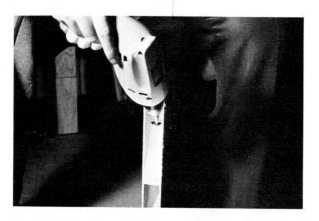

3 Drill is used to sever staves within margin of panel edges.

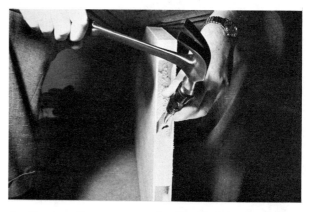

4 Stave ends are removed with chisel. Tap gently to avoid surface splitting.

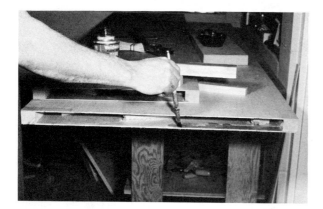

5 Glue is applied to inner surfaces of panels. Cover entire exposed area.

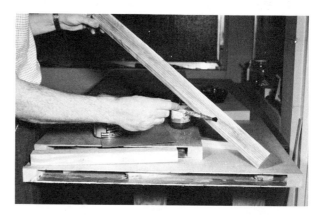

6 Edge stave is glued to insert between panels. Make new stave 1¼" thick on surface.

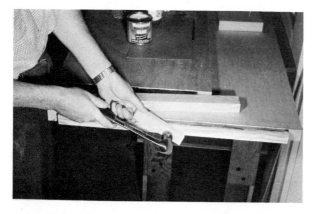

7 Glued stave is tapped into place. Piece must be exact thickness of inner staves.

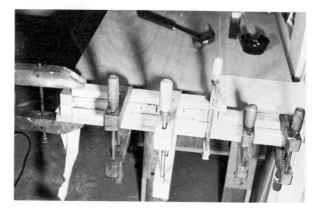

8 Reinforced end is clamped until glue dries and then planed flush.

How to Cut Glass

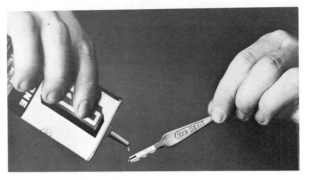

1 Wipe the glass free of all dirt and foreign matter which may obstruct the cutter and prevent a uniform cut.

2 To eliminate friction between glass and wheel, lubricate cutter wheel and be sure it revolves freely.

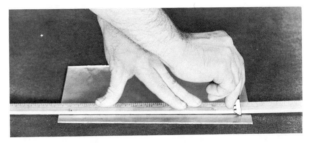

3 Hold glass cutter properly — between first and second fingers with thumb underneath. *Do not squeeze too hard.*

4 Use a straightedge rule or yardstick. Wet the underside to prevent slipping. Hold the cutter upright and draw it along the edge gently and firmly.

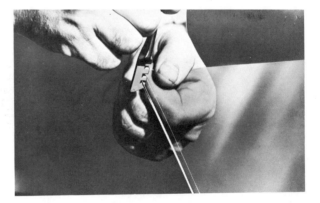

5 *Immediately after cutting, break the glass,* with a quick bending motion. Any hesitation permits the cut to get "cold," causing an uneven break.

6 For narrow marginal cutting, lightly tap the underside of the glass and bend it gently with the proper slot of the cutter.

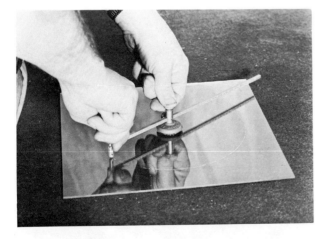

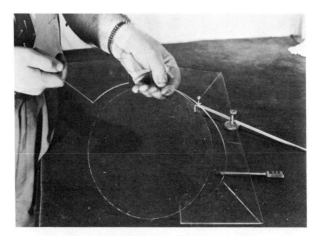

7 A circle-sweep glass cutter with rubber mat center base can be adjusted to cut the glass in circular shapes measuring from 2 inches to 24 inches.

8 After cutting the perimeter of the circle, the glass is removed with several straight cuts from circle to edge. *All photographs: Red Devil Tools.*

4

Joinery

What Is Meant by Joinery?

The common dictionary definition of the word "join" is set forth as follows: "To set or bring together; connect; combine." The term "joinery," as applied to woodworking, follows the same definition.

An article made of wood can be no stronger than the *joints* which hold it together. It is necessary, therefore, to secure all wood joints in the strongest possible manner. We cannot merely put wooden parts together and expect them to stay together, *if they are not fastened securely.* From the very beginning the worker should get the habit of making good, stout, secure joints. Actually, little extra effort is required to accomplish this end and the result may double or treble the life of the things you make.

Many sturdy pieces of Colonial furniture, dating back well over two hundred years, are still in use because of the excellent joinery employed by old-time craftsmen. We can profit by their work if we wish to produce articles of lasting sturdiness and strength.

There are many different types of joints, each adapted to certain specific needs. Frequently nails are used to make joints; sometimes screws. Other types of work call for glue, hinges, dowels, mortises, and tenons; or frequently a combination of several fasteners. Let us consider some of the general methods of joinery.

Nails

Nails are probably the most common and best known type of wood fastener. The relative strength of nails and the ease with which they may be used, accounts for their wide usage. They are most commonly used, of course, in carpentry and building where speed and strength of construction go hand in hand.

Nails range in size and style from the smallest of brads and tacks to the heaviest of railroad and construction spikes.

The subject of nails would not be complete unless a few words were said in regard to their sizes. Long years ago there originated the term "penny" to tell the sizes of nails. In its abbreviated form, it is marked by the letter "d." It is interesting to note that these terms still exist and that we speak of 6d or 10d nails. For regular usage, nails range in size from the tiny 2d nail to the huge 100d spike.

Many different types of nails are made from several kinds of metal; iron, copper, and steel. There are nails with galvanized coating to retard the destructive action of rust. There are nails bent in the shape of a "U" with both ends sharpened, which are known as staples. They come in a variety of sizes. There are shingle nails, roofing nails, casing nails, and cut nails. Even carpet tacks, upholstery tacks, lath nails, and shoe nails belong to the nail family and each is made for a specific use. All of these types are shown.

Brads may aptly be referred to as small finishing nails. They differ principally in size rather than in style or use. The small head found on finishing nails and brads tends to hold and yet minimizes the danger of splitting the wood when it is driven beneath the surface.

The nail most commonly used when it is not necessary to conceal the head, is the common wire nail. Usually the diameter of the head is approximately three times as great as of the nail itself. The enlarged head serves to prevent the head of the nail from being drawn through the board. Sometimes the large flat head is *set* and is then concealed just like a finishing nail. This type of nail eliminates the danger of a small head being drawn through a soft board. Securing soft cedar siding to the side of a house is probably one of the best examples of the use of common wire nails in which the heads are set and concealed.

For certain types of work, the heads of the nails are allowed to remain exposed; while in other instances they must be set beneath the surface. This practice permits them to be covered and concealed by putty and paint.

The finishing nail is easily set beneath the surface with a *nail set* or, sometimes, by using another larger nail. This latter practice is permissible when using finishing nails of the variety which have heads with depressed centers.

Nails driven in at a slight angle provide greater holding strength than those driven straight into a board. This is especially true when driving nails into end grain. The practice of sloping the nails is known as *toeing*.

An inexperienced person usually finds that some nails have a nasty way of creeping out through the side of the board when nailing into thin stock. This fault is caused by incorrect aiming when driving the nail. Sighting along a nail is similar to aiming a rifle. Always be sure to stand in a position which permits sighting carefully over the edge of the thin stock. Start the nail so that it will be in direct line with the center of the thin board. Except in rare cases of hard, sloping grain, the nail will then continue indefinitely through the center of the stock.

One mistake which is commonly made is to start the nail so that it is headed in the wrong direction. Even after the exposed part of the nail has been straightened, the remainder of the nail may follow the incorrect direction set by the point. The nail point then splits out through the surface of the board.

For certain types of fastening, especially in rough work, it is necessary to drive a nail clear through the joining pieces of stock and to bend over the point on the opposite surface. This is known as clinching. Thus with the head on one end and a bent-over point on the other, the nail resembles a small bolt or rivet in its holding strength.

Use of the Hammer in Drawing a Nail

It is well to remember when attempting to draw or pull a nail with a claw hammer that a block of wood placed beneath the head of the hammer not only protects the surface of the board, but also provides greater pulling leverage, and thus makes the operation much easier.

Making a Nail Joint

When making a joint with nails the following considerations should be kept in mind. The application of glue before assembly tends to strengthen the joint. Nails placed directly in line with the grain and close together tend to split the board. Whenever possible, stagger the nails. When large nails are used near the end of a board or when the wood is extremely hard, drill holes (slightly smaller than the nail) to prevent splitting. Use judgment in deciding upon the sizes of nails to be used.

Correct method of holding
nail and hammer

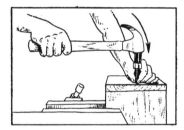

Setting nails with a nail set

Sighting nail to exact
center of edge

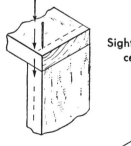

Nails toed at angle for
greater holding strength

Pressing fill substance with thumb
and planing off with putty knife

Correct method of
drawing nails

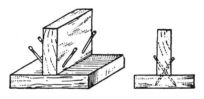

Toenailing an end fastening

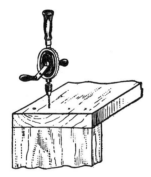

Drilling hole in hard wood
to prevent splitting

How to clinch a nail

Wood Screws

In many instances screws are used for the same purposes as nails. However, they are threaded metal fastenings which offer distinct advantages over nails. By using screws the strain caused by heavy hammer blows is eliminated. Screws have much greater holding power than nails, they may be removed with greater ease, and frequently they are needed to harmonize with cabinet hardware and special fittings. Their chief disadvantage lies in the fact that they are more expensive than nails and require more time and effort to apply.

Screws come in a variety of styles and sizes, and are made of several types of metal. The one style most widely used is the *flathead bright screw*. In addition to this well known type, we have the *roundhead, oval head, and square head* (commonly known as the *lag screw*.) Unlike the other types which require the use of a screwdriver, the lag screw has a square head which requires the use of a wrench. This head permits greater ease in driving extremely large screws.

To meet the many needs, screws are also manufactured in a variety of finishes: galvanized, nickel-plated, brass and bronze finishes, blued, japanned, the common bright finish, and even the tinned finish for ease of soldering. Obviously, solid brass and bronze screws are indispensable for wet fittings in that they defy rust. Other types of finishes tend to resist rust.

Wood screws are also made in various lengths and diameters. Inasmuch as screws are made from wire of graduating gauges, the gauge of the wire used determines the diameter of the screw.

The *Phillips screw*, a comparatively recent development, differs from the conventional screw in that the center of the head is slotted crosswise. Its advantage lies in the fact that it may be readily driven without fear of "burring" or breaking the head. Likewise, the appearance of the cross-slotted head makes it suitable for exterior or exposed use.

Rivets and Bolts

For sturdy construction, rivets and bolts far surpass the strength of nails and screws. In using them, it is necessary to drill a hole corresponding in size to the diameter of the rivet

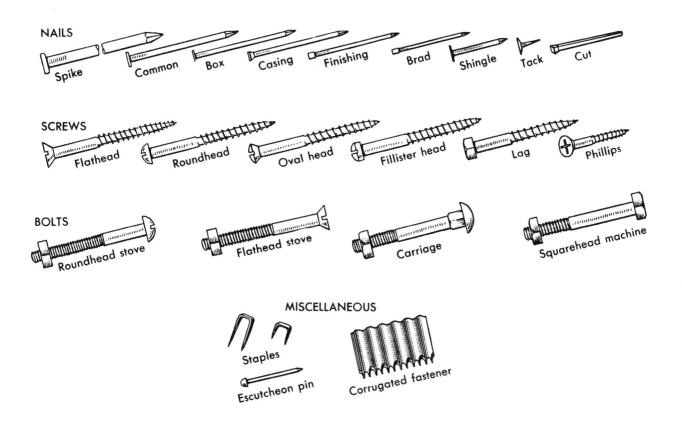

NAILS
Spike Common Box Casing Finishing Brad Shingle Tack Cut

SCREWS
Flathead Roundhead Oval head Fillister head Lag Phillips

BOLTS
Roundhead stove Flathead stove Carriage Squarehead machine

MISCELLANEOUS
Staples
Escutcheon pin Corrugated fastener

or bolt all the way through the connecting pieces of wood.

The rivet and bolt differ principally in that the rivet is held in place with a washer and a burred end, whereas the bolt requires a conventional nut and washer. Consequently, a bolt can easily be removed by merely unscrewing the nut; but to remove a rivet it is necessary to file or grind off the rivet burr.

Rivets are manufactured in a variety of styles and sizes and are usually made of relatively soft metal, so as to permit the making of a flattened, or clinched end. Copper rivets (which, of course, do not rust) are used in the construction of boats. The rivets used for wood construction form an interesting contrast to the large metal rivets which are used in building skyscrapers and huge bridges.

To meet the many needs which arise, bolts of several types are available in a variety of lengths and diameters. The types most commonly used are *machine bolts*, *stove bolts*, *machine screws* (with round and flat heads), and *carriage bolts*. They range in length from tiny bolts and machine screws which are but a fraction of an inch long to those which are measured by the yard.

Likewise, they are made in diameters which fit the most exacting engineering requirements.

Corrugated Fasteners

Corrugated fasteners are often used for rough work and for concealed construction. Among their many uses, we find that of making plain butt joints and miter joints, especially when one has to perform an adequate job in a short time.

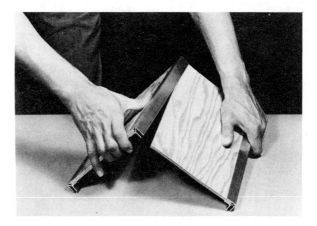

Aluminum corner posts are a new product for joining panels at right angles. *Reynolds Metals Co.*

These metal fasteners come in a variety of sizes. The one edge is sharpened (either with a plain edge or with a saw edge) to facilitate their being hammered into the wood. Also, they are produced with tapering or parallel corrugations. Those of the former type tend to pull the boards firmly together, thereby making a tight joint.

The worker should be careful to see that the adjoining boards are in correct position before driving this type of fastener. Once driven into place, the fastener is hard to remove without breaking off the adjoining sections of wood which it secures. For fine cabinet work, the corrugated fastener is rarely used. Many other methods of joining are preferable.

Attaching flush butt hinges.

Hinges

There are numerous types and kinds of hinges. Most of them are designed for special use. Some of the decorative types in use today date their origin back several centuries. Most common of all hinges is the *butt* type. These hinges are used principally for attaching doors and table leaves. They are manufactured in two types, namely, the *fast-pin butt hinge* and the *loose-pin butt hinge*. The loose-pin type is commonly used for attaching doors. After this hinge is attached, the pin may be removed and the door detached.

How to Drive Screws

Driving small screws in soft wood is an easy job. A light tap of the hammer starts the screw and the screwdriver then drives it home. For larger screws and for harder wood the process becomes more involved. Frequently three operations are necessary to avoid splitting the wood or twisting off the screw. First, a hole should be drilled to accommodate snugly the shank, or unthreaded portion of the screw. Next, the edge of the hole should be *countersunk* to accommodate the head of the flathead screw. Lastly, a small pilot hole should be drilled to receive the threaded portion of the screw.

Using a lubricant on screws greatly expedites the work of driving them into place. Various types of waxes, oils, and special mixtures are frequently used. The lubricant can best be applied by simply dipping the threaded section of the screw into the preparation.

COMMON TYPES of HINGES

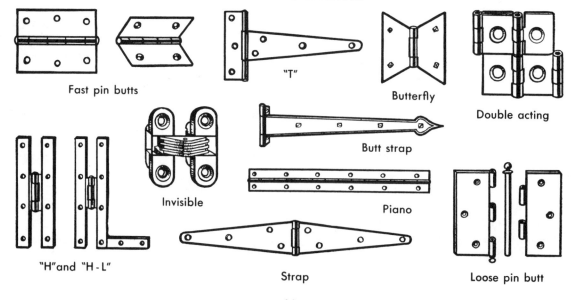

Fast pin butts

"T"

Butterfly

Double acting

"H" and "H-L"

Invisible

Butt strap

Piano

Strap

Loose pin butt

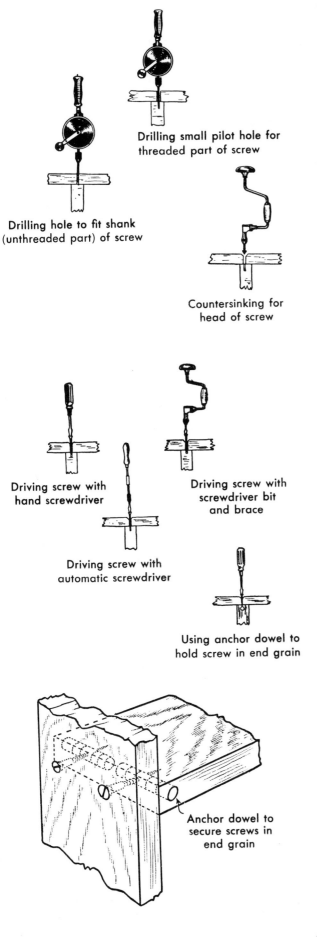

Drilling small pilot hole for threaded part of screw

Drilling hole to fit shank (unthreaded part) of screw

Countersinking for head of screw

Driving screw with hand screwdriver

Driving screw with screwdriver bit and brace

Driving screw with automatic screwdriver

Using anchor dowel to hold screw in end grain

Anchor dowel to secure screws in end grain

Counter Boring and Plugging

In most cases it is desirable to conceal the heads of screws. This is readily done by counter boring, that is, drilling a hole approximately halfway through the board with a bit, large enough to accommodate the head of the screw. After securing the screw, it may then be concealed, or covered over with a wooden plug. After the counter boring is finished, the respective holes are drilled for both the shank and the threaded part of the screw.

Now let us consider the plugs which are used to conceal the screw heads. For ordinary shop use we might list them in the following manner: First, there is the *boat plug*, or *surface grain plug*. When it is cut from the same type of wood with a special cutter, the wood grain can be matched so as to make the plug almost invisible, after the sanding operation.

Next, there is the *end grain plug*, cut from an ordinary dowel, which when sanded level gives an interesting effect. The end grain of the plug usually absorbs a little more stain than the surrounding area, causing the small decorative plug to be slightly darker. This gives the piece of furniture the interesting effect of being "pegged."

Third, we have the protruding end grain plug, again cut from an ordinary dowel. The plug is cut long enough to extend approximately one-eighth of an inch above the surrounding surface. It is inserted after the surface of the article has been thoroughly sanded. This protruding end is then nicely decorated by cutting the edges irregularly with a sharp chisel. Quaint pegged effects are likewise obtained by using the square or irregular plug. These plugs should be cut to fit snugly within the bored area.

Wood plugs should always be glued securely in place.

Glue and Cement

Of the many different kinds of glues and cements now on the market, one of the most notable is the relatively new "Epoxy" adhesive. The powers of Epoxy are so remarkable that feature news stories have been written about it. This adhesive, now sold under various trade names, comes in two separate containers, the contents of which are mixed together to form Epoxy immediately prior to application.

An Epoxy bond is absolutely waterproof, and since this adhesive does not dry like ordinary

Assorted adhesives. *The Borden Co.*

Parts bonded with Thermogrip electric glue gun are held about 20 seconds while glue sets. *USM Corporation.*

glue but "cures" by catalytic action, it can actually harden under water. It provides a firm, rubber-like grip which expands and contracts with the joint but is virtually unbreakable. Moreover, it may be applied effectively even without clamps. Because of its strength, durability, and waterproof qualities, the chemical ingredients of Epoxy are now also used in the manufacture of special protective paints and patching materials.

Waterproof resorcinol glue, also marketed in two separate containers to be mixed just before application, furnishes an extremely strong, 100 per cent waterproof bond. This glue is sold under trade names of *Weldwood Waterproof Resorcinol Glue* and *Elmer* (Borden) *Waterproof Cascophen Resin Glue.* It is widely used in boat building and for other exposed outdoor construction.

Plastic resin glue, which comes in powdered form to be mixed in water, is highly water *resistant* and provides an extremely strong bond which can be protected by varnish or paint for construction exposed to water.

Casein glues, which also come in powdered form for mixing with water, have long been popular for general use. For indoor work, casein is both economical and highly effective. It also *resists* moisture and can be used for outdoor work when adequately covered with protective coats of waterproof finishing agents.

Animal glue, as the name implies, is made from the gelatine of various animals. It is sold in flake or granulated form and must be soaked in water and heated in a double-boiler glue pot or other suitable receptacle. This is the type of glue one usually finds in the familiar glue pot of the school shop or of the woodworking plant. It congeals rapidly, and therefore no time must be lost in placing the glued articles in clamps. This glue is affected by the presence of excessive moisture and is not waterproof.

Many different types of cements and "instant" ready-mixed glues may be purchased under a variety of trade names. The new *contact cements,* used for veneering, provide a strong and enduring bond.

Applying Glue and Cement

Regardless of the kind of glue or adhesive used, there are a few simple directions which must be followed in order that a secure joint may be made. First, make sure that the surfaces to be glued together fit perfectly and that they are free of grease, wax, dirt, or any other foreign matter which might weaken the holding strength of the glue or cement. After applying a thin layer to both surfaces to be glued, the pieces should be pressed securely together with suitable clamps. This process tends to force all excessive glue or cement from the joint and holds the joint until the glue has dried and gained full strength. It is always well to allow ample drying time before removing clamps.

Glue must always be of correct consistency. If it is too thick it will not readily penetrate the pores of the wood, and if too thin it will be absorbed and thus leave a dry joint with little

strength. The wood should not be too cold or certain kinds of glue will be chilled, thereby causing them to congeal. This chilling greatly impairs their penetrating powers. Also, place the work in clamps as quickly as possible after applying the glue, before the glue has started to congeal. Good glue properly used makes a tremendously strong joint.

Regardless of the kind of glue or cement you have selected for the job, *don't spread it over the outside surfaces of the finished article.* Smeared glue or cement is very difficult to remove. It mars the wood and spoils what might otherwise be a perfect surface.

Applying glue to edges of board for butt joint

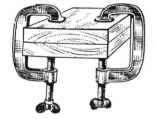

note: glue is applied to both edges

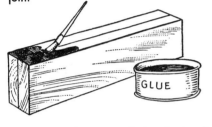

Use of "C" clamp in gluing blocks together

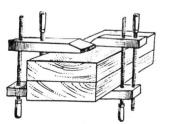

Use of hand screw clamps

Use of adjustable bar clamps for edge gluing

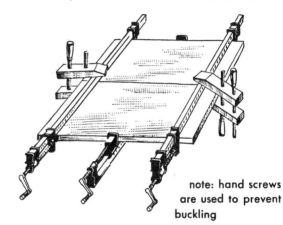

note: hand screws are used to prevent buckling

Assembly of rails and posts, properly clamped

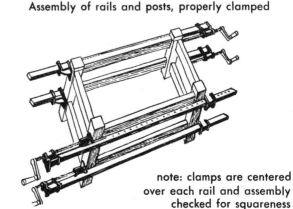

note: clamps are centered over each rail and assembly checked for squareness

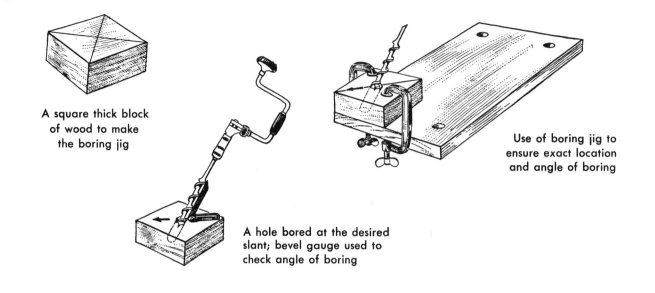

A square thick block
of wood to make
the boring jig

A hole bored at the desired
slant; bevel gauge used to
check angle of boring

Use of boring jig to
ensure exact location
and angle of boring

Peg-Leg Construction

The use of "peg-leg construction" provides an extremely strong and effective means of securing legs of stools, tables, and kindred articles. The results are pleasing and usually very secure.

The job of boring the holes for the legs is extremely simple. In order that it may be done accurately, prepare a jig by boring a hole of the desired size through a small block of wood. Bore at the proper location and hold the brace and bit so as to bore at the desired slant. A bevel gauge may be set to the desired angle and used as a guide. This block of wood then becomes the "jig" and can be clamped upon the board for boring each of the required holes. In this manner the jig guides the bit so as to ensure identical locations and splays for each of the legs.

The legs are then shaped. Next, the top of each leg (the section which is to become the tenon) is made to fit the prepared holes. The tenons may be made to fit the borings either through the use of a lathe or simply by whittling carefully with a knife. A file may be convenient for the final fitting. Be sure that each tenon fits snugly within the hole.

If a tenon wedge is to be used, run the saw down the center of the tenon, lengthwise, to about two-thirds the length of the tenon fitting. This permits spreading the tenon to receive the wedge. It is always well to make the saw kerf, or cut, so that all the wedges line up nicely in a position across the grain of the adjoining board.

After the wedges have been prepared, place glue upon the sections to be fastened together. Tap the legs into position and then drive the wedges securely into place. The protruding ends of the legs and wedges may then be cut off and sanded flush with the surface of the board. Otherwise they may be allowed to protrude slightly, and then decorated by making irregular cuts with a sharp chisel. This is known as a through, or open, tenon.

Sometimes it is desirable to make a hidden, or blind, tenon instead of the usual through type. In this case, the holes must be carefully bored so as not to extend through the top. After the fittings and hardwood wedges have been made, apply glue and assemble. The wedge, which is placed at the mouth of the saw kerf, is pushed into place as the leg itself is forced into the mortise. Obviously, the wedge causes the tenon to spread and assume a slight fan shape. For a secure fitting, it is customary to enlarge slightly the inner part of the mortise to permit wider spreading of the tenon.

Sometimes holes are bored through the edge and hardwood pins are glued and driven through the completed wedged tenon joint so as to provide even greater strength.

Dowel Joints

Dowels are small round sticks made of hardwood. They are used in a variety of ways. Usually they are produced in lengths of three feet and in various diameters to meet their many needs.

Dowels are commonly used to reinforce butt joints. Also, they are frequently used as a substitute for mortise-and-tenon joints. Dowels may be also used to strengthen miter joints, to secure legs and other fittings to turned columns, for strengthening square, circular, and irregular forms, and for numerous other purposes.

The correct use of dowels may be explained under a few simple headings. First and most important of all, *be sure that the location of dowel holes, of one member, match identically the location of the dowel holes of the corresponding member.* To insure accuracy in this respect, it is only necessary to place the pieces to be joined together, side by side, and then carefully measure and square off identical points. When the squared points match perfectly, it is obvious that the drilled holes must also match perfectly.

Next in importance is the problem of drilling *straight holes* so that the dowel will not be forced into a bent position when the boards are drawn together with clamps. To assist in accurate drilling, a *doweling jig* (an adjustable metal holder for guiding the bit) offers a great deal of help. However, if a jig is not available, stand directly in line with the edge of the board, sight the bit just as you would aim a rifle, and drill carefully. It might be well to stop drilling now and then and look at the job from different angles in order to be sure that the bit is held perfectly straight.

After the holes have been correctly drilled to the required depth, cut the necessary dowels approximately one-eighth inch shorter than the combined depths of the corresponding holes. This process permits a slight clearance and thereby prevents the danger of having the dowels jam. It is advisable to cut or file a small glue channel or spiral extending the full length of the dowels, especially when the dowels are an extremely tight fit. Dowels may be purchased which are prepared with a spiral glue channel. Otherwise, if the excessive glue and air cannot escape, the dowel may act like a tightly fitting piston and thus jam while being forced into the hole.

Location of dowels on connecting parts

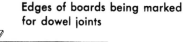

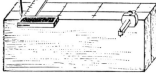

Plain dowel

Round at ends

With spiral glue groove

Edges of boards being marked for dowel joints

Note: Marking gauge used for locating exact center of edges

Connecting parts being held evenly together for accurate marking

Boring dowel holes: bit gauge regulates depth of hole; direction of boring is checked with square

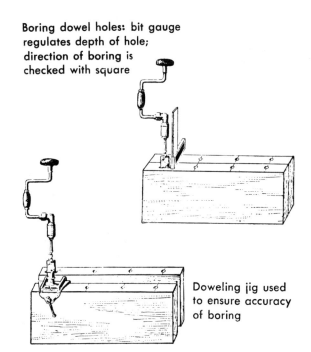

Doweling jig used to ensure accuracy of boring

When gluing a dowel joint, be sure to place a thin layer of glue over both edges which are to be joined, over the entire surface of the dowels, and also inside the holes which are to receive the dowels.

Lap Joints

In construction work it is frequently necessary to have two boards cross each other on the same plane so as to form an even surface. To do this, it becomes necessary to cut away the upper half of the stock from the one member and the lower half of the stock from the other member, at the point of intersection. Then, when these two lapped pieces are put together, the upper and lower surfaces fit perfectly flush.

Lap joints, as such, are very easy to make. Probably the most important detail to stress is that all measurements be carefully made and that cutting lines be sharp and accurate. This is really half of the battle. Before proceeding with the cutting operations, always hold the members together in order that the accuracy of the lines may be checked. It is then merely a matter of removing carefully the stock within the area of the lines so that the members may cross to form a snug joint.

The lap joint may be cut in several ways. A series of saw cuts extending in depth to the center line may be made within the limits of the side lines. The opening is then carefully dressed to the required lines with a sharp chisel. The sawing should be performed with either a hand saw or by making several cuts on a circular saw which has been set to the correct depth.

Several types of end laps may be cut directly by using the saw for cutting, both from the surface and from the end. In other cases the stock may be removed with bit and chisel, depending upon the nature and location of the joint. There is hardly one set rule for performing this operation, inasmuch as each craftsman follows his own particular rule for getting the greatest degree of accuracy with the least amount of unnecessary effort.

An error to guard against in this type of construction is that of making the opening too large, thereby causing a loose and sloppy joint. As long as the fitting is too tight it is a simple matter to enlarge gradually the opening with a chisel, until a perfect fit is made. But when the cut has been made too large, the best thing to do is discard the work and start again.

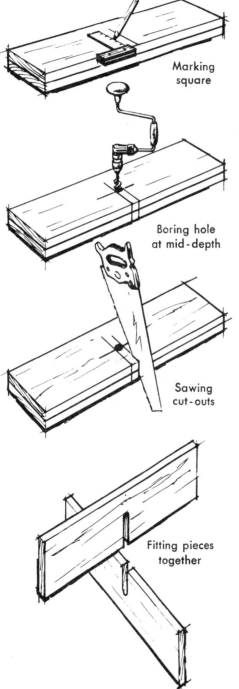

Marking
square

Boring hole
at mid-depth

Sawing
cut-outs

Fitting pieces
together

Lap joints are made in a variety of styles. There is the *center lap* where the members intersect each other at the centers; the *cross lap* when they cross somewhere between the center and the end; and the *end lap* where the ends are lapped over each other. These types are also combined in several different ways. In addition, there are *dovetail halving* joints of several varieties which are described with dovetail joints. Lap joints and dovetail halving joints are usually secured with glue, but concealed screws may also be used when additional strength is required.

Dovetail Halving Joints

This type of joint provides extra strength at a middle lap point of construction. It has an advantage over the conventional middle lap joint, in that it offers greater resistance to pulling strain. Moreover, it is quite easily made.

The work is started by marking out the cut-out part of the joint. This marking is done with a bevel gauge and square. After the cut-out has been marked, it is carefully sawed with a sharp backsaw. The cutting should be kept inside the marked lines. A number of saw cuts should be made within the marked area. The part that has been sawed is then carefully removed with a sharp chisel and the walls of the cut may be pared off until they are clean and even.

In making the end dovetail which fits into the cut-out, the joining piece is accurately marked at the end to the same dimensions as the cut-out. It is then sawed to the half thickness indicated by the marking. The final step is to make shoulder cuts at the base of the dovetail marking, and to saw the dovetail shaping. It is then finished with a sharp chisel and assembled to the first piece. The final fitting of the joint is made with thin cuts to avoid marring the corners. A tight fit is recommended, even though the joint is further held by glue or screws.

Grooved Joints

There are several different types of grooved joints, some running with the grain and others extending crosswise, either directly or on a slant. In some instances, certain of these joints are concealed, while others may remain exposed. As shown in the accompanying illustrations, good craftsmanship demands the frequent use of grooved joints in a variety of ways.

Pieces held side by side for marking center cross-lap joint

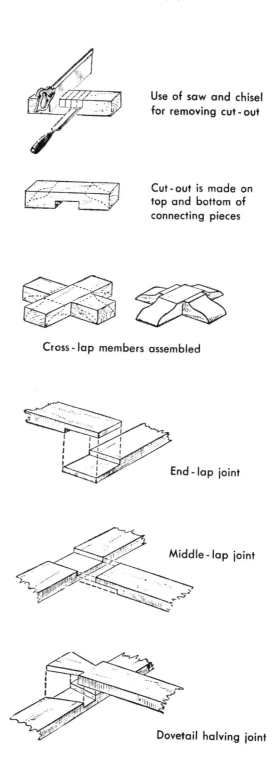

Use of saw and chisel for removing cut-out

Cut-out is made on top and bottom of connecting pieces

Cross-lap members assembled

End-lap joint

Middle-lap joint

Dovetail halving joint

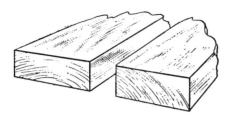

Butt

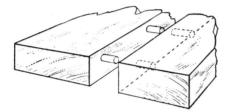

Dowel

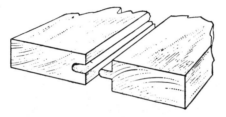

Tongue and groove

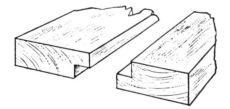

Rabbet

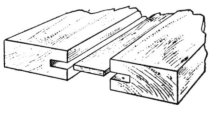

Spline

Let us first consider the simple *rabbet joint*. This joint is the square-edge cutting found usually on the backs of picture or mirror frames. It is put there so that the glass and other necessary fittings may be recessed into the frame. This is probably the most common of its many uses. Obviously, the rabbet should be carefully marked off and cut before assemblying the various parts.

The process of cutting a rabbet is very simple indeed. Actually, only two cuts across a circular saw, which has been set to correct depth, with the ripping fence set to the proper width, will perform the job in the shortest possible time. Also, routers and shapers are frequently fitted with blades and may easily be adjusted for the rapid cutting of rabbets of varying sizes.

Then again, clamping a straightedge board to the desired lines (one at a time) will serve as an excellent guide for the backsaw in making the necessary rabbet cuts. For small rabbets which are to be made in soft wood, one can easily make the cuts by tracing the two respective lines of the rabbet with a sharp, thin-blade knife, until the perpendicular cuts meet at the inner edge of the rabbet. Marking gauges which have been sharpened to a razor edge are also efficient for cutting rabbets in soft stock. A sharp chisel is used for making the rabbet smooth and accurate.

Next in order, let us consider the regulation groove joint. This joint is the type of recess needed to accommodate the tongue of the board in "tongue-and-groove" fittings; as a fitting into which panels are set; as the groove into which drawer bottoms are placed; and as a fitting for the use of splines and other interesting types of construction. The tongue-and-groove joints of flooring boards, sheathing boards, and other kinds of stock lumber have probably been noticed.

The groove itself, regardless of whether or not it is to be centered on the edge of the board, can be made with a dado head circular saw, a shaper, a router, or a simple tongue-and-groove plane.

Cutting a groove requires several trips across a circular saw, properly set, to remove the stock within the marked portion. Shapers, routers, and tongue-and-groove planes (combination planes) may be adjusted for grooves of the specified width and depth. A rabbet on each side of the piece will form the tongue.

Groove cut along
length of board

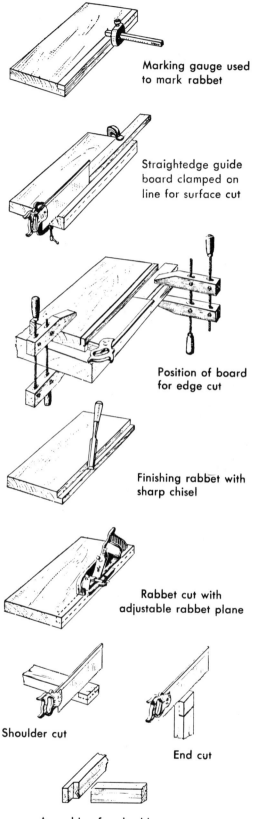

Marking gauge used
to mark rabbet

Straightedge guide
board clamped on
line for surface cut

Position of board
for edge cut

Finishing rabbet with
sharp chisel

Rabbet cut with
adjustable rabbet plane

Shoulder cut

End cut

Assembly of end rabbet

When it is necessary to make short grooves without this special equipment, the job may be done with ordinary shop tools. A saw, a sharpened marking gauge, a knife, and a small chisel may be used for the job in much the same manner as that outlined for the hand-cutting of rabbets.

Cutting Dadoes

Dadoes are grooves cut *across the grain* of the board. They may be either visible or concealed in the finished article. The former are generally known as "open," or "through" dadoes; whereas the latter are placed under the heading of "blind," or "gain" dadoes. The grooves into which the shelves of bookcases and cabinets are ordinarily fitted, constitute the most common use of the dado joint.

The first step in the making of an open dado is to measure carefully and mark clearly the section of stock which is to be removed. Check the accuracy of all measurements. A few cuts across the circular saw, properly set, will automatically remove the stock to form the required dado. Otherwise, several careful cuts with a small hand saw, to the prescribed depth, make it easier to trim the dado to the exact size with chisel and router. In this latter practice, a wooden straightedge, clamped to either side of the dado measurements, guides the saw and prevents it from slipping beyond the limits of the dado. For shallow dadoes in soft wood, a sharp knife can easily be substituted for the small hand saw in making the necessary cuts.

The process of making a blind dado is not quite as simple. Here, inasmuch as the groove does not extend entirely across the board, the

Measuring and marking the dado

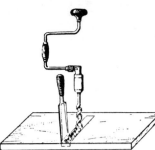
Blind dado roughly cut to size with brace and Forstner bit

Use of router plane

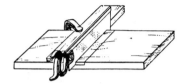
Use of saw and straightedge for cutting dado

Finishing dado with chisel

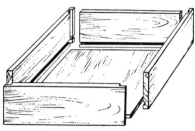
Common drawer construction showing assembly of dados, grooves, and rabbets

use of a circular saw or a hand saw is somewhat limited. In wide stock, they may still be used for cutting part of the distance in much the same manner as for a through dado. Boring a series of holes which correspond to the width and depth of the desired groove, is quite effective in removing the bulk of the surplus stock. The chisel is then the most effective tool for trimming it to exact size. Routers and router planes of various types greatly facilitate the task and permit speedy and accurate cutting.

Miter Joints

Diagonal joints, which are commonly used for fastening together the strips of wood used in making picture frames and mirror frames, are known as miter joints. This type of joint is also basically used in the application of different kinds of trim and moldings, for cove and quar-ter-round fittings, and in many other cases where no end grain is to remain exposed at the joint.

In order that the strength of miter joints may be increased for greater structural support, various methods of reinforcement are used. Of these, some may be easily reproduced by craftsmen, while others call for complicated cuts which can be performed only through the use of special machines and cutters. Blanket chests and cedar chests of the commercial type are often constructed in this manner. Let us consider a few of the miter joints most frequently used by craftsmen.

First, and the simplest type to make, is the plain miter joint, which is secured in not too sturdy a fashion simply through the use of glue and a nail or two.

The cutting of the joint should be performed on an adjustable miter box of the conventional

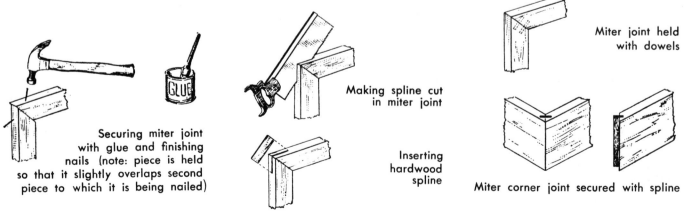

Securing miter joint with glue and finishing nails (note: piece is held so that it slightly overlaps second piece to which it is being nailed)

Making spline cut in miter joint

Inserting hardwood spline

Miter joint held with dowels

Miter corner joint secured with spline

type or, if none of these is available, on a handmade miter box. This simple device can be made by fastening two hardwood side boards to a bottom board; and then carefully measuring and cutting saw kerfs at the required 45-degree angle, down through the side boards. These saw kerfs may then be used to guide the saw for subsequent miter cuttings. The accuracy of the miter joints which are cut on this device depends a great deal upon the accuracy of the guiding saw kerfs and the construction of the miter box.

Not all miters, however, are cut at the same angle. A 45-degree saw cut is necessary for making a four-sided mitered frame, a 30-degree saw cut for an hexagonal frame or column, and a 22½-degree angle for preparing an octagonal fitting.

The ordinary miter joint can easily be strengthened by the use of a slip-feather; thereby producing a *slip-feather miter joint*. This contrivance is nothing more than a thin strip of hardwood which is inserted in a saw kerf, across the outer edge of the joint. When properly glued into place, the joint will withstand far more hard use because of this reinforced fitting.

Long miters, which are frequently used in constructing chests, columns, and similar articles, are reinforced with a spline. These joints are referred to as *spline miter joints*. This thin spline of hardwood, with a grain which extends across the joint, is inserted in prepared saw kerfs extending all the way down the center of the miter length.

Solid miter joints are fairly difficult to make and consequently require good workmanship. Various types of clamps and clamping devices are available to facilitate the task of assembly. When these devices are not available, small strips of wood may be nailed at right angles on a board or on a bench top to accommodate the frame after the miters have been treated with glue. The frame may then be wedged into place and should be allowed to remain in this position until the glue has set. In this practice, a saw kerf can then be made after the assembly, in order that the miter joint can be strengthened with sturdy slip-feather construction.

Mortise-and-Tenon Joints

The mortise-and-tenon joint is one of the most commonly used joints in woodworking.

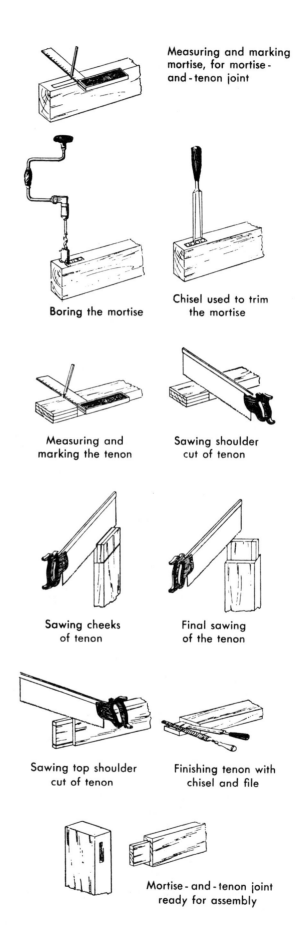

Measuring and marking mortise, for mortise-and-tenon joint

Boring the mortise

Chisel used to trim the mortise

Measuring and marking the tenon

Sawing shoulder cut of tenon

Sawing cheeks of tenon

Final sawing of the tenon

Sawing top shoulder cut of tenon

Finishing tenon with chisel and file

Mortise-and-tenon joint ready for assembly

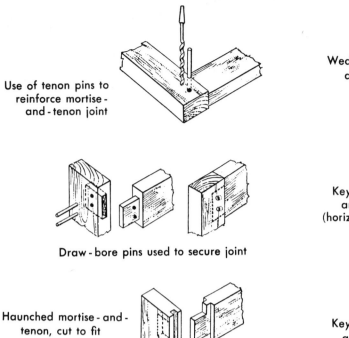

Use of tenon pins to reinforce mortise-and-tenon joint

Draw-bore pins used to secure joint

Haunched mortise-and-tenon, cut to fit panel groove

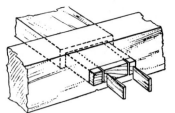

Wedged mortise-and-tenon

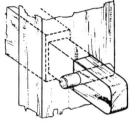

Keyed mortise-and-tenon (horizontal wedge)

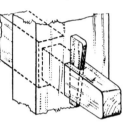

Keyed mortise-and-tenon (vertical wedge)

It is the type of construction generally used for fastening rails and aprons to the legs of tables, stools, cabinets, and benches. Such joints when properly made with full snug fittings, wedged and pinned, represent construction of the strongest and best type.

Mortise-and-tenon joints, like many other types of joints, may be made in a variety of interesting styles. The *blind* and *through* mortise-and-tenon joints, the *pinned* and *wedged* types, the kinds which are keyed with an exposed wedge (either vertical or horizontal), in fact, even the *slip joint* is a close relative of this family.

Marking off the stock and making the necessary cuttings for mortise-and-tenon joints requires no great skill. If a circular saw and a machine mortiser are available, the task is especially easy.

The first step is to mark off carefully the exact size and location for each mortise. Check so as to avoid an error either in size or location. This being done, take a brace and bit which correspond to the width of the mortise and bore a series of holes so as to produce the exact length, width, and depth of the mortise. A bit gauge, properly clamped to the bit, will assist in boring to the correct depth. This boring operation should actually remove all the rough stock. It is then merely a matter of trimming out the mortise with a sharp chisel so that it will be exactly true and square.

The machine mortiser, or drill press, fitted with a hollow chisel mortising bit, simplifies the work. With this equipment it is only necessary to punch out the mortises.

Having completed the mortise we are now ready to cut the tenon. To begin this process, carefully mark off the depth, length, and width of the required tenon. Hold the markings against the mortise and check the accuracy of the proposed cuts. Then with a saw make the necessary cuts, one by one, on each of the two edges and the two surfaces.

Certain types of tenons require less than the usual "four cuts." Obviously, several movements across the bed of a properly adjusted circular saw will remove the required stock in a speedy manner. *Always cut slightly outside the lines* so that the tenon will be slightly oversize. Then with chisel, carefully work the tenon down until it slides snugly within the mortise.

Mortise-and-tenon joints may be pinned in either of two ways, that is, the pin may be applied after the assembly, or during assembly by the regular draw-bore pin method. In the former practice, the hole may be bored right through the center of the mortise-and-tenon joint after the project has been assembled and the glue has set. It is then merely a matter of applying glue and driving in the pin. In this case the pin reinforces the glue in maintaining rigid construction.

However, in following the *draw-bore pin*

method, the holes must be drilled separately in both the mortise and the tenon, before the joint is assembled.

The hole in the tenon should be approximately one-sixteenth inch nearer the tenon shoulder than the corresponding boring through the mortise. This arrangement causes the tenon to be pulled snugly into the mortise when the pin is driven home, eliminating the need of clamps in the gluing operation. In fact, this type of construction was used long before glue came into use. Round, square, or irregularly shaped pins are used to provide an interesting effect.

For certain types of construction, the tenon is made to extend not only clear through the stock, but to protrude some distance beyond, in order that it may be secured with a decorative wedge. These wedges are made in a variety of interesting styles and are both the horizontal and vertical types. The hole which is to receive the wedge is really one form of a through mortise. It is made in exactly the same way as the original mortise-and-tenon joint which it secures. The wedge is merely a thin piece of hardwood which is fitted so as to provide maximum strength to the joint. Be sure that the wedge is not too thick or else it will tend to split the extending section of the tenon.

Mortise-and-tenon joints are also secured with *blind* and *open tenon wedges*, just as the tenon wedges described in the section devoted to peg-leg construction (page 68). However, due to the fact that a mortise-and-tenon fitting is usually rectangular in shape, two wedges are generally used; one near each end of the mortise. By slightly lengthening the inner edge of the mortise, the wedges impart a noticeable "fan-shape" to the tenon and insure a very strong type of construction.

Finger Joints

Finger joints are frequently employed in corner construction. Sometimes this type of joint is used as a wooden hinge. Its construction resembles, to a certain extent, that of the open dovetail joint. Like the open dovetail, the ends of two adjoining boards interlock.

In making this joint, the ends of the two boards that are to be joined are first marked with a line square across the boards, at a marginal distance from the end corresponding to their thickness. This marking is squared off around the entire end of each board.

Following the initial marking, the width of each "finger" is spotted off on the marginal line of marking. Ordinarily each finger is made of equal width. They are marked with square lines from the end of the board. Alternating spaces between the fingers are checked for cutting. After these checked portions have been cut away, the ends of the two boards interlock.

The cutting operation is performed either with a sharp fine-toothed saw, or a backsaw. Of course, the work is simplified when performed on a power saw. Extreme care must be taken not to cut below the depth marking. A number of saw cuts are made between each finger. After the sawing has been completed, the excess material is carefully chiseled away at the depth lines with a sharp chisel. Each finger is evenly cleaned along the cut edges to assure perfect fit. The success of the job is determined by the precision with which the two pieces interlock after the cutting has been completed.

Boards clamped together
for measuring and
marking fingers

Series of sawcuts to
ease removal of stock

Trimming fingers to
exact size with chisel

Completed finger joint,
ready for assembly

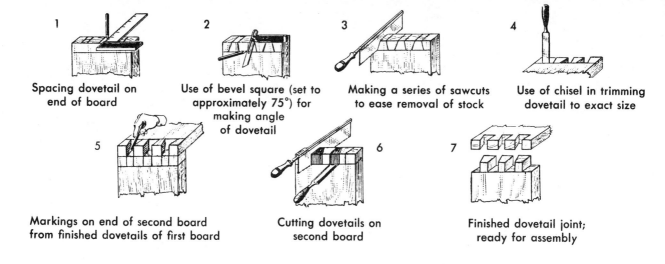

1. Spacing dovetail on end of board

2. Use of bevel square (set to approximately 75°) for making angle of dovetail

3. Making a series of sawcuts to ease removal of stock

4. Use of chisel in trimming dovetail to exact size

5. Markings on end of second board from finished dovetails of first board

6. Cutting dovetails on second board

7. Finished dovetail joint; ready for assembly

Dovetail Joints

Dovetail joints have long been a favorite of the woodworker. They are strong and dependable and will hold over an indefinite period of time, where all other types of construction might fail.

There are, however, many different dovetail joints, and their common resemblance is limited solely to the fact that they all bear the shaping of the "dove's tail." In fact, this family is extended to several common groups which are known individually as *open dovetails, sliding dovetails*, and *dovetail halvings*. Moreover, each of these different types is shaped and fashioned in its own peculiar way.

The *open dovetail*, which is, possibly, the most elementary of the group and the least difficult to make, is fashioned in the following manner. It is first necessary to square lines around the two adjoining pieces, a distance in from the ends equaling the thickness of each piece. This is the *depth line* of the dovetails. This depth line is then marked at intervals, on *one* board to indicate the width of each dovetail. A bevel gauge is then set to an angle of approximately 75 degrees and a series of *alternating* bevel lines are scribed extending from the depth line to the end of the board.

The position of the gauge is then reversed to mark the opposite (alternating) side of each dovetail. Each marking is then squared across the end of the board and scribed with a bevel on the opposite face.

The open portion of the dovetail is checked and sawed with a sharp backsaw or dovetail saw. Additional saw cuts may be made within the waste portion to facilitate the job of removing it with a chisel. Extreme care must be exercised to chisel evenly and squarely along the depth marking.

After the first board has been carefully dovetailed and cleaned, it is held in position over the *end edge* of the board to which it will be attached. Each finished dovetail is carefully marked on this end. For the sake of precision, this end marking should be re-marked with a bevel gauge. A square is then used to carry the lines from the end to the depth lines on both sides of the second piece. These dovetails are then carefully sawed and chiseled and the first piece is fitted into place.

The sliding dovetail functions in much the same manner as a dado joint. It is, however, a much stronger type of construction. In order to make this joint it is first necessary to cut a dovetail groove. A groove of this type is narrow on the surface of the board and spreads, or dovetails, out to a wider width at the depth.

First mark the groove carefully on the board, using a bevel at the edges to mark the angle of the cut. For accuracy of cutting, it is well to clamp a straightedged piece of wood along the marking and with this as a guide, and holding the saw on the proper slant, saw evenly to the depth mark. Sawing is repeated on the second line and a third straight cut is made in between to facilitate chiseling out the inside portion of the groove. After the sawing has been completed the inside of the groove is carefully cleaned with a sharp chisel.

The dovetailed tenon which slides into the groove is made by marking a line square across the board, the same distance in from the end of the second board as the depth of the groove. This line is carried entirely around the end of the board. The shape of the dovetail tenon is marked on this end section. Again, using a sharp saw, and a wooden straightedge for accuracy, the shoulder cuts are made on each side of the tenon. The dovetail shape is made with

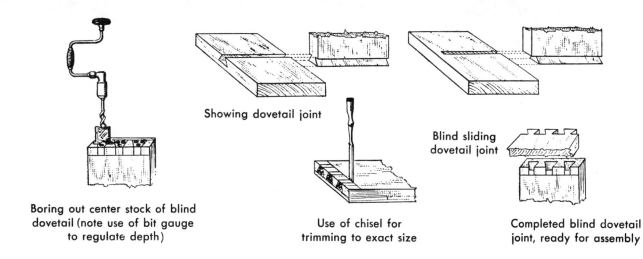

Boring out center stock of blind dovetail (note use of bit gauge to regulate depth)

Showing dovetail joint

Use of chisel for trimming to exact size

Blind sliding dovetail joint

Completed blind dovetail joint, ready for assembly

a sharp chisel. This tenon is then ready to be slid into the dovetail groove.

Blind Dovetail Joints

The blind dovetail joint is commonly used in drawer construction where the sides of the drawer are dovetailed in the front. It differs from the open dovetail joint in that the connecting parts do not entirely overlap each other. In fact, only one piece is openly dovetailed, and this laps part way across the edge of the piece to which it is connected.

The part of the joint on which the open dovetail is cut (in drawer construction the side) is first marked and cut in the manner already described, for the primary cutting of open dovetail joints. When this piece has been cut, the dovetails are held in place over the edge of the front piece. This permits marking on the sec-

ond piece. The dovetails should lap about three-fourths of the way across the edge. The edge of the front piece is marked from the side piece and the cut-out portions are removed. This operation is most easily performed with a boring bit and sharp chisel. The dovetailed pieces are then ready to be joined together with glue.

Stem-Leg Assembly

At first glance it appears quite difficult to assemble a cluster of curved legs to a central table stem. As a matter of fact, this process is by no means simple, but, like many another complicated process, it may be accomplished by careful adherence to a few fundamental directions.

When the mortise-and-tenon joint is employed for this construction, very little pressure is needed to hold the members together. One

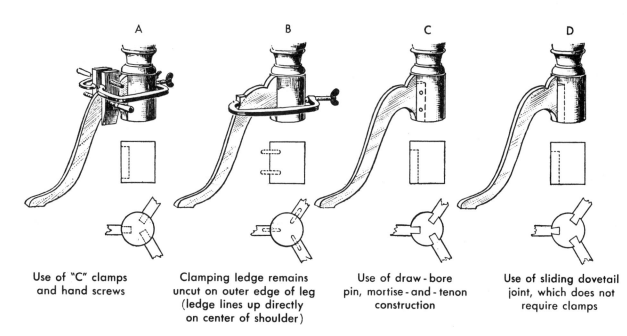

A — Use of "C" clamps and hand screws

B — Clamping ledge remains uncut on outer edge of leg (ledge lines up directly on center of shoulder)

C — Use of draw-bore pin, mortise-and-tenon construction

D — Use of sliding dovetail joint, which does not require clamps

After applying glue to all joining edges, assembly of laminated strips is clamped together for overnight drying.

When glue is dry, clamps are removed and surfaces are planed and belt-sanded.

Final smoothing of laminated surface is obtained by hand sanding or with fine-grit orbital sander. Laminated plank is then squared or cut to desired shape.

method of obtaining this necessary pressure is provided with the use of an ordinary hand screw applied to the leg in a parallel position to the stem. The two jaws of the hand clamp, *A* on page 79, will serve as ledges for pressure clamping. Another method is to leave a small shoulder, cut square and parallel to the tenon, and in line with the center of the tenon, on the otherwise shaped leg. This shoulder serves as a clamping jig and after the leg has been glued into place it may be easily removed with a coping saw. When either of these methods are employed by the amateur in assembling tripod legs, each leg in turn should be glued, clamped, and allowed to dry.

The use of clamps in assembling stem legs may be eliminated by following through with the drawbore-pin-and-tenon assembly, or by using a sliding dovetail joint. The sliding dovetail joint, shown at *D*, requires some degree of craftsmanship in its execution, but provides a splendid method of construction.

Laminated Construction

Many interesting effects may be obtained by *laminating* — or gluing together — narrow wooden strips of contrasting color. Since a secure gluing job can produce a bond between pieces of wood which is actually stronger than the wood itself, it is only necessary to square the edges of the strips to be joined and after applying glue to *both* joining edges clamp them together until the glue dries.

While butt joints made with good glue are amply strong, some may prefer to dowel or tongue-and-groove the strips as described in previous paragraphs.

The sturdy cutting board, illustrated above, was fashioned from the laminated stock shown in process at the left. It consists of alternating strips of walnut and maple wood. After dressing down and sanding, the laminated assembly is handled like a single board and may be squared or cut to any desired shape.

When laminating utility boards which are exposed to moisture it is advisable to use *water-resistant* or, preferably, *waterproof* glue. The current popularity of laminated articles — for table tops as well as utility items — suggests use of the process in constructing some of the projects presented in Chapter 9.

Pictorial Summary of Typical Joinery Methods

The following series of photographs shows how wood joints are actually made. The three types of joinery pictured here — *doweling, dovetailing, and mortise and tenoning* — are most commonly used and require cutting and fitting skills typical of other wood joints previously described.

It should be noted that the woodworker has several options of tools for cutting these joints. For example, holes can be bored with a brace and bit as well as a power drill — and for hand-tool operations a doweling jig can produce just as accurate results as a drill press. Also, tenons can be precisely cut by hand or with a circular saw.

Because dovetail joints seem to fascinate the average woodworker — and because they are somewhat more complicated than other types — the next two pages detail twelve steps of their cutting and assembly.

Doweling

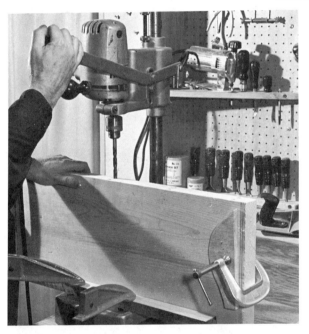

1 Dowel holes are bored on drill press; they can also be hand-bored with doweling jig.

2 Glue is applied inside holes and to dowel pegs, which are then inserted.

3 Joining edges of boards and protruding dowels are brushed with glue.

4 Doweled boards are clamped together until glue dries.

Dovetailing

1   Bevel gauge is used to mark dovetails.

2   Series of saw cuts are made to strips clamped at shoulder depth of dovetails.

3   Dovetail cutouts are removed with sharp chisel.

4   Dovetails are dressed with file.

5   Side dovetails are marked on end of joining board.

6   Dovetail edge marking is squared to depth lines.

7 Connecting dovetails are sawed to depth strips.

8 Dovetail shoulder cut is made with backsaw.

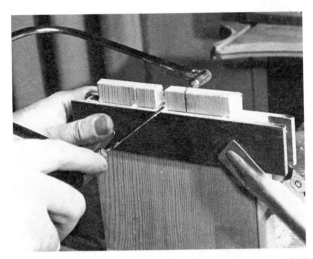

9 Inner dovetail cuts are made with coping saw guided by depth strips.

10 Finished dovetails are dry-fitted together.

11 Dovetails are glued and clamped for final assembly.

12 Protruding ends of dovetails are sawed off and sanded flush.

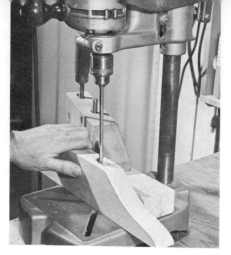

1 Mortises can be bored by hand or on drill press, then squared out with sharp chisel.

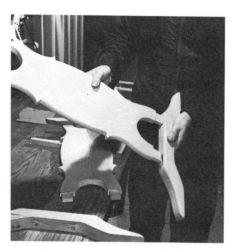

3 Mortises and tenons are dry-fitted before gluing.

5 Glue is applied to inside walls of mortises.

Mortise and Tenoning

2 Tenon edges can be trimmed with saber saw after shoulder cuts have been made on circular saw or with back saw.

4 Glue is applied to cheeks and edges of tenons.

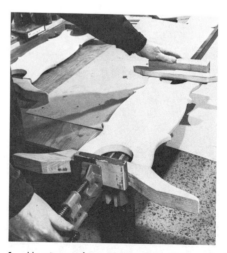

6 Mortise and tenon joints are clamped while glue dries.

5

Woodworking Machinery

Rockwell Mfg. Co.

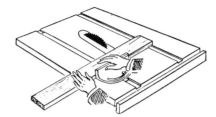

Crosscutting with circular saw

Arbor of saw tilted for end-bevel cutting

Ripping with circular saw

Circular Saw

The circular saw is one of the most important power machines used in woodworking. It is used for ripping, cross-cutting, shaping edges, cutting moldings, cutting dadoes, grooves, tenons, and various other woodworking processes.

Circular saws are adjusted in various ways. Some types are made so that the cutting blade itself may be raised or lowered, while with others the blade remains stationary and the table is moved up and down. Likewise, with one type of saw, the table is tilted on an angle for slanted or beveled cutting, while on other types, of the tilting arbor variety (two examples of which are illustrated), cutting is performed by tilting the blade.

Some very excellent circular saws have been introduced during the past few years. Most of these are light in construction, yet may be accurately adjusted for the many cutting operations. They serve the needs of the average woodworker; performing all the jobs of heavy duty equipment, lacking only its ponderous size. Moreover, these light machines are very easy to set and to adjust for various woodworking operations.

The principal uses of the circular saw are outlined in the following paragraphs.

Arbor of saw tilted for ripping edge bevel

Crosscut feed set for cutting miter

Cross-cutting. The blade of the circular saw is set slightly deeper than the thickness of the wood to be cross-cut. Press the wood firmly against the cross-cut carriage and slide it with even pressure through the revolving blade. The ripping fence should never be used as a measuring gauge during cross-cutting operations. Otherwise the cut-off section may bind between the revolving blade and fence, causing a "kick-back." Be sure to follow through evenly and avoid jerky motions.

Ripping. When ripping boards to width, the ripping fence should be set so that the distance between the fence and the revolving blade will correspond to the desired width of the board. With the fence accurately set, the wood is driven into the blade, pressing it against both the table and the ripping fence. In ripping narrow strips, a small notched stick is generally employed to push the final end of the stock through the blade.

Beveling and Mitering. In order to cross-cut the end of a board at a prescribed angle or miter, the cross-cutting carriage is adjusted to this angle.

End Bevels. Chamfers and bevel cuts which extend across the end of a board are cut by adjusting the saw blade so that it forms the desired cutting angle to the saw table. If the saw has a stationary blade, the table is tilted to form the necessary angle.

In order to cut a bevel, miter, or chamfer along the length of a board, the saw is again adjusted so that the blade and table form the desired angle. The work is then fed along the ripping fence.

Dadoes. For an open dado, the board is first marked for the dado, care being taken to square the lines across the edges as well as the faces of the wood. The saw blade is then set for the required depth of cut and the wood is fed across the blade so that the actual cutting is performed *inside* the dado lines. Ordinarily several inside cuts are made between the outer dado cuts. This method makes it much easier to remove the remaining stock within the dado. Special dado cutters, *dado heads,* which cut the entire dado in one operation, do away with the necessity of making a series of saw cuts.

Blind Dadoes. After the dado has been marked, the work is held above the revolving blade. It is then carefully pressed down on the blade and fed across the wood as far as the marked width of the dado. Then it is carefully lifted off the revolving blade. Care must be ex-

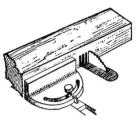

Cutting dado by making several trips across revolving blade

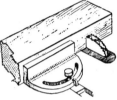

Outside cutter   Inside cutter   Assembled dado head

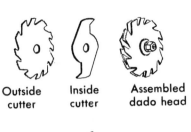

Using dado head for cutting to desired width - note dado head also used for plowing groove

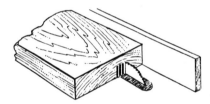

Cutting grooves by adjusting ripping fence for each successive cut

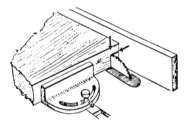

Rabbeting a board by sawing edge and surface to required depth

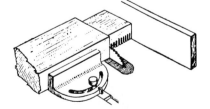

Cutting a tenon by making several trips across revolving blade

ercised not to go too far across the wood and thus exceed the marked bounds of the blind dado. This mistake may be avoided by marking lightly with pencil or crayon, the "span" of the dado, on the saw table, and using these markings as a gauge when cutting.

Grooves. After marking the groove along the face of the board, the ripping fence is set so that the blade will make a *primary* cut of the required depth, just inside the marking of the groove. Then the ripping fence is adjusted for the other side of the groove. It is good practice to make additional cuts inside the marking if the width of the groove makes it necessary. The cut portions of wood, inside the groove, are then removed with a sharp chisel, that is, if all the waste stock has not already been removed by additional trips through the saw.

Tenons. After the tenon has been carefully marked, the cutting is performed in either of two ways, namely (1) the saw is set to the side depth of the tenon and an initial cut is made across the wood at this required depth to form the shoulder. The ripping fence is then adjusted and the piece is fed across the saw blade *end down* for the side cut.

A far safer and more practical method (2) is to make a series of cross-cuts, close together at the required depth of the tenon. The waste stock is then easily removed with a sharp chisel.

Blades. There are three distinct kinds of blades used with the circular saw, namely, (1) the cross-cut blade, (2) the ripping blade, and (3) the miter blade. A utility blade has recently been introduced which can be used successfully to perform a variety of operations. Blades of varying types for special cutting may also be obtained.

Rockwell Mfg. Co.

Band Saw

After the circular saw, the most important power machine used in woodworking is perhaps the band saw. The working parts of this machine consist of a flexible blade which moves with the same action as an endless belt, around two revolving wheels. The work is placed on a flat table which may be tilted for bevel cutting. While the band saw is designed primarily for curved cutting, it may also be used for straight cross-cutting and ripping. Most band saws are equipped with a cross-cut and ripping fence to guide accurate operation.

Operating the Band Saw. To obtain the best results in operating the band saw, the worker should first determine that the saw itself is properly adjusted and that the blade is adequately sharp. The guard should be lowered as far as possible so that only a slight clearance is

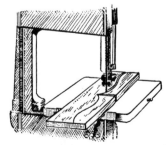

Cutting edge scroll on band saw
(note in-cut to ease removal of stock)

Bed of band saw tilted for
cutting bevels and miters

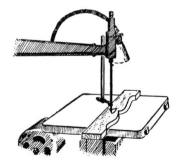

Cutting inside curve
on scroll saw

allowed for the stock to pass through. Actually there is no more difficulty involved in using a band saw than there is in cutting out a paper design with a pair of scissors.

At first the worker should proceed slowly, feeding the work toward the blade so that the saw skirts the outside of the marked line. Don't be afraid to steer the work gently at the curves, avoiding undue strain on the blade. Hold it flat and steady on the cutting table. Feed it along evenly and avoid jerky moves which might cause an uneven cut.

There is often an advantage in making a series of cuts leading into the curve, in order to keep the work clear of cut portions and to permit the cutting of sharp curves. Blades of varying widths are used with the band saw; the wider widths are used for heavy-duty work where sharp curves do not appear, while the narrower widths are kept for fine work where abrupt curves must be cut.

Some band saws are equipped with a cross-feeding device to help in accurate cross-cutting, and a ripping fence which may be attached to the table to facilitate accurate ripping. Likewise, the table of the band saw may be tilted for cutting bevels, miters, and large chamfers.

The band saw blade is difficult to handle when it is off the machine. To save the saw from damage and to save space it is rolled into a threefold circle. This can be done without injury to the saw.

To fold the saw, the operator stands with the blade in front of him, one hand on each side of the saw about one-third the distance from the top, as it stands in an oval position, as in the machine, the lower edge resting on the floor. The top is bent forward by twisting both hands so that the top bends out. One side of the saw is brought in back of the other, and the top continued down until it nearly meets the lower end of the saw about a foot off the floor. The saw then will naturally fall to the floor with a perfect roll or fold, and without a twist in it. The saw can then be hung on a hook, as it makes only a 16- or 18-inch circle.

Scroll Saw or Jig Saw

This type of saw is also designed for curved cutting. The fine blade of the jig saw with its up and down action makes possible the cutting of sharper curves than would ordinarily be attempted on a band saw. An added feature is the ability of the scroll saw to cut *inside*

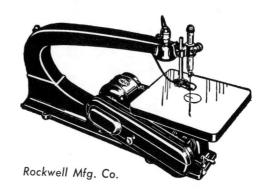

Rockwell Mfg. Co.

curves. This is done by threading the blade through a hole inside the marking.

Operating the Scroll Saw. The scroll saw is operated in much the same fashion as the band saw. The work is held flat on the table and fed evenly into the cutting blade. The action of the saw, together with the fineness of its blades, permits more delicate and precise cutting.

When the inside portions of a piece of work are being cut on the scroll saw, a hole is first bored along the inner edge and the saw blade *threaded* through this hole. After the blade has been re-attached the sawing is continued and, when finished, the blade is detached and the work removed from the table.

Radial Saw

The radial saw, or *slide saw* as it is sometimes called, cuts from *above* the wood rather than underneath it. Since the blade and motor are suspended above the work in cross-cutting operations, the blade slides out along an arm and is drawn into the work. Both blade and arm are adjustable and can be raised, lowered, turned, and tilted to make an assortment of cuts.

Radial saws are particularly well adapted to cross-cutting operations because this machine can be mounted on a broad counter surface which provides a stationary resting place for the work. Hence, as will be appreciated when cutting long sections of lumber, the saw blade itself is adjusted and moved into contact with the work rather than having to "juggle" the work into contact with the saw, as must be done on a circular saw. Moreover, sawing from above, as observed when using a hand saw, gives better visual control and thus assures greater accuracy.

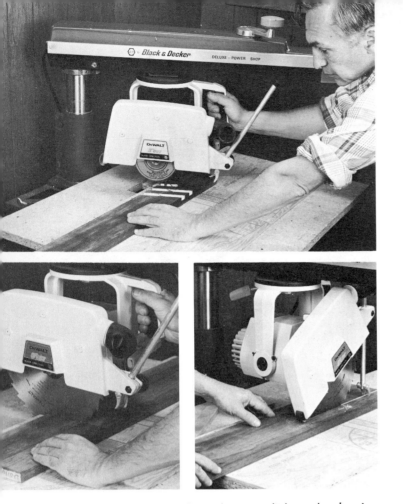

For *ripping*, however, the cutting head is turned to a position parallel to the stationary back rest. Then the work is pushed into the blade, as with the circular saw. The only difference is that the blade operates from on top of the work rather than underneath it.

The radial saw can do practically every type of saw job performed by the circular saw, adding a few operations of its own for good measure. As well as *cross-cutting* and *ripping*, it *miters*, *bevels*, *dados*, *plows*, *grooves*, and *rabbets*. For certain types of work — such as cutting *tenons*, *inside slots*, and *blind dados* — it offers the advantage of letting the operator bring the blade down upon the work for more positive control and accuracy.

The basic utility of the radial saw has been augmented in the DeWalt "power shop." This versatile machine comes with a variety of attachments which convert it into a shaper, drill press, drum, disk and belt sander, router, grinder, saber saw, and lathe. While some of these adaptations seem to overextend the fundamental functions of the radial saw itself and do not seem quite as well integrated as those of a true combination machine, they do provide greater latitude for the woodworker to improvise and thus perform a variety of operations with a single source of power.

Cross-cutting is performed on a radial saw by drawing the blade through the work. For ripping operations the work is pushed into the rotary. *Black & Decker Mfg. Co.*

Jointer

The labor of squaring the edges of boards is largely eliminated with the use of the jointer. The working parts of this machine consist of a *revolving cutter*, *adjustable fence*, and *table*. In operation, the work is pressed against the fence and driven across the cutter. Thus the work is planed square along the edge. Like most of the other machines mentioned in this text, the jointer is manufactured in both light- and heavy-duty types.

A variety of small bench jointers which mount on the regular work bench are becoming increasingly popular in small woodworking shops.

A revolutionary new type of jointer, called the *Uniplane*, was recently introduced by Delta-Rockwell. This machine, pictured at left, cuts from the side with a razor-sharp, rotary disk cutter. Its operation is much smoother than the conventional jointer — a precise shaving action for smoothing large and small pieces of wood. It can be used for beveling and chamfering as well as precise edge-jointing.

Rockwell Mfg. Co.

90

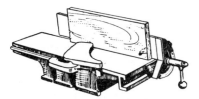

Jointing the edge of a board

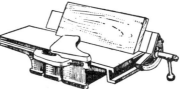

Fence of jointer tilted for
beveling edge of board

Surfacing board on jointer
(note use of pusher
for feeding stock)

Pusher

Planer

Because of the ever-increasing cost of finished lumber, many school and home workshops are finding it economically advantageous to install a planer and perform their own millwork. Rough, unfinished lumber can be bought much cheaper than surfaced stock. Hence, in shops where even moderate quantities of wood are consumed, the planer soon pays for itself. Moreover, the newer models of planers, as exemplified by the Delta *13 x 5* illustrated on this page, are compact and efficient and do not require an abundance of floor space.

The planer automatically surfaces the lumber to required thicknesses. These machines vary in size to accommodate stock measuring upward to 36 inches wide. The model shown above, as its name indicates, can take stock up to 13 inches wide and 5 inches thick.

In operation the stock is fed into the machine, which then feeds itself as its cutters revolve to smooth the surface of the wood. It is fully adjustable for large and small cuts. The newer models, as illustrated, are so thoroughly enclosed and well guarded that the operator is entirely protected from their cutting action.

As well as planing wood to exact parallel thickness, ranging from $\frac{1}{16}$ inch to 5 inches, with the model shown, this planer can be adjusted to *chamfer*, *bevel*, and cut *tapers*. Like the hand plane, the power planer produces the smoothest surface when adjusted for a light cut.

Before wood is run through a planer, the stock should be carefully inspected for concealed nails or other harsh matter which may nick the blades and thus cause a major blade-grinding operation.

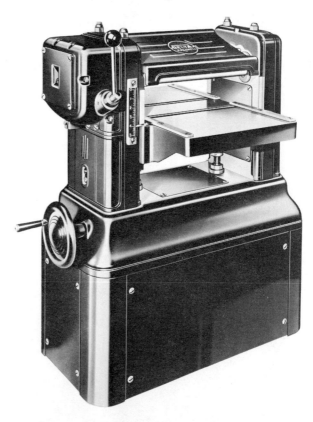

Rockwell Mfg. Co.

91

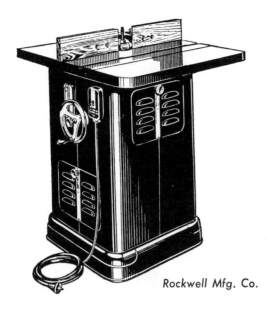

Shaper

While designed primarily for shaping wooden edges, the shaper can be adjusted for rabbeting, grooving, beading, and making various types of moldings. The action of this machine is provided by revolving knives which are shaped for desired types of cuts. The work is fed along a table which is equipped with an adjustable fence. The cutter is adjusted so that the blades revolve at the required distance *outside* the fence. Cutting knives revolve at very great speed and trim the edges of the wood, as it is fed into them. Even end-grain portions of the wood become smoothly shaped because of the high speed of the sharp cutter.

A portable shaper, of recent manufacture, while small in size, performs a variety of the processes ordinarily performed by the regular heavy-duty machine. The portable type may be removed from its regular mounting and taken to the job when necessary. It need hardly be emphasized that a shaper revolving at fast speed is an extremely dangerous machine. Every precaution should be observed in its operation.

Operating the Shaper. "Keep your fingers away from the cutter" are the key words of advice in regard to the operation of the shaper. The cutter on this machine revolves at very great speed and if the fingers get in the way, a most serious accident will result.

The shaping of end-grain portions is somewhat more difficult than with the grain. Unless the cutter is absolutely sharp, there will be a tendency for the work to vibrate or for the edge to burn as it is being cut.

The portable shaper, when it is mounted in its arbor, is operated in the manner already described. However, when it is removed from the arbor and used by hand, the technique is a trifle more difficult. While the cutter revolves at very high speed, the operator will feel the gyroscopic action of the little shaper as he holds it freely in his hand. Extreme care must be exercised to hold it *evenly* along the edge which is being shaped. Otherwise a wavering shape will result. Obviously, the shaper held free is an exceedingly dangerous tool.

Drill Press

The drill press is another important piece of power machinery. It is designed for boring holes. In line with this performance it can be used, with special equipment, for mortising. There are several different types and sizes of drill presses; some for heavy-duty work and

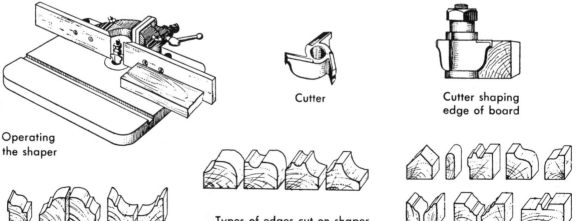

Operating the shaper

Cutter

Cutter shaping edge of board

Types of edges cut on shaper

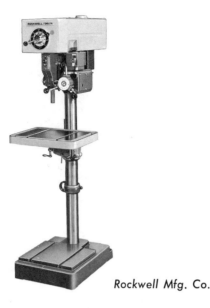

Rockwell Mfg. Co.

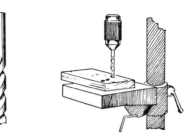

Boring wood with spur bit

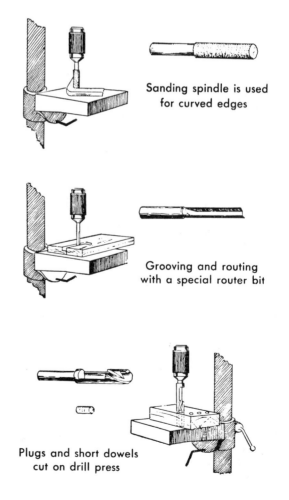

Hollow chisel mortiser
bit revolves inside chisel

Drill press used for mortising

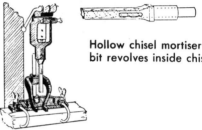

Sanding spindle is used
for curved edges

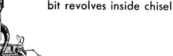

Grooving and routing
with a special router bit

Plugs and short dowels
cut on drill press

others of lighter variety. The portable power drill is included in this group.

While the drill press cannot be classed as an absolute necessity, still it is a very handy machine to own. The task of drilling holes, with exact precision, is accomplished with relative ease through use of this machine. Moreover the job of mortising, a somewhat difficult operation which requires a degree of skill, is greatly facilitated through the use of the hollow chisel and mortising bit.

Operating the Drill Press. The standard types of drill presses may be fitted with a hollow-ground chisel for mortising. They are operated with a lever which pulls the cutter and chisel directly *down* into the work. The mortising bit in this case revolves within the hollow chisel. As this assembly is pressed into the work, a square hole results. In mortising, however, it is first necessary to carefully mark the area to be mortised, on the stock. The work is then adjusted on the table of the drill press, so that the chisel drops into direct contact with the marked area. An elongated mortise is made by making a series of cuts with the mortising chisel.

Some drill presses are equipped with a foot lever controlling the up and down action of the drill. There is an advantage in this arrangement, because the operator is left with two hands free to hold the work. Still another type of mortiser is operated in horizontal position, the work being fed *against* the cutter, through lever action.

93

Sanders

Sanding is, of course, a common operation in woodworking. For this reason the craftsman is always looking for new and better ways of doing the job.

Rockwell Mfg. Co.

Combination Sander

Special sanding machines, as illustrated, incorporate the advantages of both disk and belt sanders in one convenient unit. These machines are equipped with an adjustable table and adjustable cross-feed device for sanding angles and bevels and to assure accuracy of work. To protect the operator from sanding dust, this unit comes with a dual dust collector which functions on the principle of a vacuum cleaner.

Many different types of sanding machines have been developed. Among these the *belt sander* is one of the pioneer forms. It consists of a long endless belt of sanding abrasive which passes over two large parallel wheels set a number of feet apart. This type of sanding device still retains much of its popularity, particularly in woodworking factories. In operating the belt sander, the work is placed beneath the middle slack part of the belt. As the belt moves, revolving about the wheel, the abrasive is pressed down upon the work. The work, placed upon a movable carriage, may be moved back and forth so as to produce a uniformly sanded surface. Smaller power sanders which operate on the same endless-belt principle are also available in both stationary and portable models.

Sanding surface of board with portable belt sander

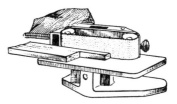

Portable sander mounted in arbor for stationary sanding

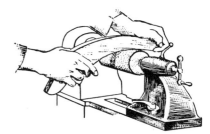

Sanding cylinder mounted in lathe for drum sanding

Disk sander attached to faceplate of lathe

Final shaping of curved edges finished on spindle sander

Disk Sander

The disk sander is likewise a stationary machine. It consists of a disk of abrasive attached to a face plate. This type of sander is often improvised on the face plate of the lathe. Like the drum sander, the disk type is used largely for the shaping and smoothing of small pieces of work.

Drum Sander

The drum sander consists of a cylinder to which abrasive has been attached. It is a stationary unit and the work is fed against the cylinder as it revolves. This type of sander is often used for shaping as well as for sanding. Small drum sanders of varying diameters may be made by attaching sandpaper to plain wooden cylinders. These abrasive cylinders may then be mounted on the lathe and used in much the same way as one would use a regular drum sander.

The various types of *portable power sanders* illustrated and described on pages 111–112 are extremely effective, particularly when the sander must be brought to the job.

Operating the Sanding Machine. In order to operate the sanding machine successfully, it is necessary, first of all, to be careful to select the proper grade of sanding belt. Coarse abrasive belts are intended for use where rough sanding is required. They cut quickly into the surface of the wood and, because of their rough texture, will wear down the thickness of a board in short order. On the other hand, the fine-textured belt does not leave any marks and serves only to smooth the surface of the work.

The worker should at all times take pains to handle the sander carefully. If it is of the portable type, it should be guided evenly along the surface. If it is tilted so that the edge of the belt comes in direct contact with the wood, it will leave deep ridges and scratches on the surface. It must, moreover, always be operated with the grain of the wood.

Power Grinder

While the hand-operated emery wheel meets the need for a grinding machine in the smaller woodworking shop, the electric grinder, complete with interchangeable abrasive wheels of varying coarseness, is by far the more useful sharpening device. Many electric grinders are so constructed that the revolving wheels are

Rockwell Mfg. Co.

lubricated from an oil reservoir for constant and uniform oiling of the abrasive stone. The speed of operation of the wheel is also variable. For the craftsman who insists on sharp tools (and what craftsman does not), the electric grinder is the answer.

Operating the Power Grinder. Ordinarily, edged tools such as chisels and plane blades require grinding only when the edges become nicked or rounded after repeated honing. Then it is necessary to *hollow grind* the edge in order to form a new cutting bevel.

Most grinders, like the one illustrated, are equipped with an adjustable guide for holding the tool to the proper slant during grinding operations. Moving the cutting edge from side to side, with the grinding wheel turning *into* it, a hollow bevel is soon produced. However, care must be exercised not to alter the slant during grinding operations. Otherwise many unwanted bevels will result. For this reason, if the grinder is not equipped with a holding guide, some degree of skill is required to get the knack of maintaining a uniform bevel.

Unless the power grinder is also equipped with a plate-glass guard, through which the worker looks while sharpening a tool, protective goggles should be worn while the work is in operation. Otherwise small fragments of ground metal or small chips from the stone, which are sometimes thrown by the revolving wheel, might prove injurious to the eyes.

Additional information on the proper use of the grinder is given in the chapter, "Tool Sharpening," which follows this chapter.

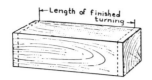

Wood cut square for turning

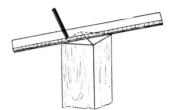

Marking diagonal lines to find exact center

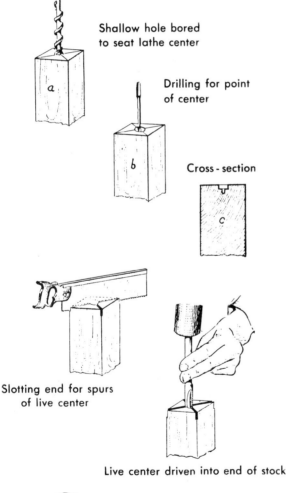

Shallow hole bored to seat lathe center

Drilling for point of center

Cross - section

Slotting end for spurs of live center

Live center driven into end of stock

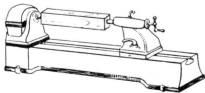

Stock mounted in lathe ready for turning

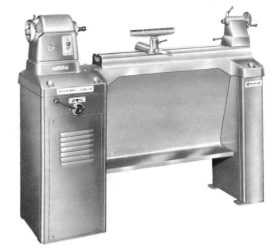

Lathe

The lathe is undoubtedly the most interesting machine used in the woodworking shop. Most amateur and professional craftsmen enjoy working with it. The lathe, of course, dates back many centuries. In its earliest form, it consisted of a crude mechanism operated by a treadle. Its function, then, as now, was to cause pieces of wood to revolve so that in the process the edges could be cut to form round pieces of varying diameters and shapes.

The modern wood-turning lathe is essentially a very simple machine. It consists of two centers between which the piece of wood being turned is mounted. One of these centers is attached to a motor and causes the work to revolve. This is the *live* center. The other center serves as a stationary bearing on which the work revolves. This is the *dead* center. As the work revolves between these centers it is cut with one of a variety of chisels or gouge-shaped turning tools. The tools are rested on a stationary tool rest which is adjusted to maintain proper clearance and position to the work.

Sketches at the left show how work is prepared for turning. Operations of the lathe are described and illustrated on following pages.

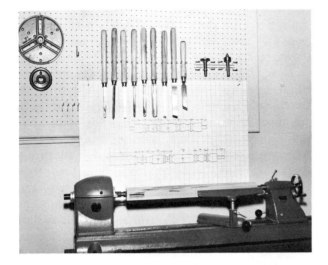

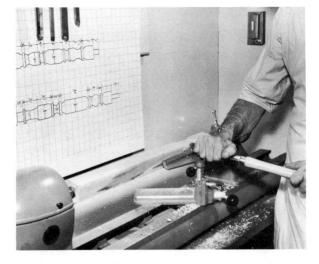

1 Squared stock is mounted in lathe preparatory to turning. Note assortment of turning tools and full-scale patterns of designs.

2 Gouge turning tool is used for "roughing" square stock to cylindrical shape. Note operator's firm hold on turning tool.

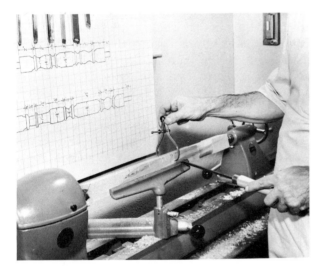

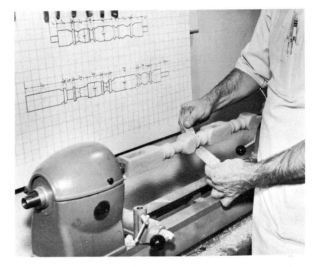

3 Parting tool is used to cut depth dimensions and mark spacing zones of turned designs. Other turning tools cut shapes.

4 Tool rest is removed for final sanding. Finished turning is then taken from lathe and trimmed to desired length. *All photographs: Black & Decker Mfg. Co.*

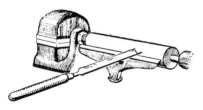

Use of large gouge for cutting stock to cylindrical shape

Making exact measurements of turned design by holding pencil against revolving cylinder

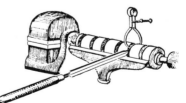

Use of parting tool and calipers to cut exact diameter

Wood-Turning Tools

The art of wood turning makes necessary the use of a variety of wood-turning tools. Like the wood carver who requires a separate tool for each type of cut, the wood turner also requires separate types of tools for each of the various turning operations. There are six distinct types of wood-turning tools. These are: gouge, skew, spear, round nose, square nose, and parting tool. Each of these tools serves its own distinctive purpose and most of them are manufactured in various sizes.

The large gouge seems to be best adapted for "roughing down" the square stock so as to form a rough cylinder. Grasp a large sharp gouge firmly in both hands and allow it to just touch the slowly revolving stock. The chips fly with amazing ease. By moving the gouge back and forth, the diameter of the spinning member gradually diminishes. Stop the lathe periodically, move the tool rest nearer the stock, and continue at increasing lathe speeds until the wood takes the shape of a completed rough cylinder.

To turn the cylinder to a given diameter, adjust the calipers slightly larger than the desired finished diameter. As the stock spins and the parting tool (which is usually held in one hand) touches the cylinder, it cuts a small channel wide enough to accommodate the calipers. The lathe is stopped, and when the calipers, usually held in the other hand, snugly slides across the stock, the right diameter has been reached. It is well to cut a series of these channels across the length of the stock, spaced approximately an inch apart. The depth of these tiny channels then serves as a guide for care-fully reducing the entire cylinder, with the tool you find most efficient, the square-nose chisel, skew, or the gouge.

Now, if a pattern is to be cut upon the plain cylinder, simply touch a pencil so as to mark the lengthwise measurements for each major change in diameter, while the cylinder is spinning rapidly. Then with a parting tool cut a channel to the required depth at each marking. These various spacings and diameters then serve as guides for producing each of the various shapes. Sanding is best performed while the stock is revolving, always being careful to first remove the tool rest from the lathe. This is done so as to prevent the possibility of accidents in catching the hands between the revolving work and the tool rest.

Turning a disk upon a faceplate follows much the same technique as that used for spindle turning. In this case the stock should obviously be cut to a circular shape and should then be mounted carefully and securely upon the faceplate. Due to the increased vibrations of large disks, make sure that the stock is accurately centered and turns at a relatively slow speed. Square-nose chisels and round-nose chisels of various sizes are used as the basic process tools. The measurements, shapings, and sanding operations are performed just as in spindle turning.

One danger found in large disk turning is that presented by the possibility that the faceplate will unscrew itself from the lathe, thereby releasing the combined disk and faceplate and permitting them to be hurled across the room with great force. This frequently occurs when shifting from a higher to a lower speed. The

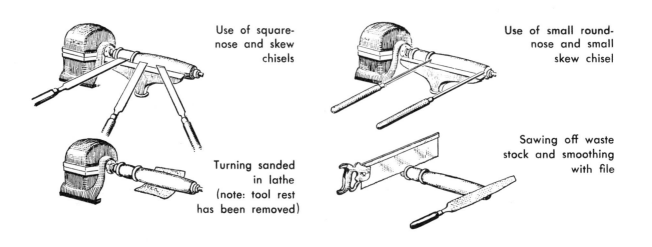

Use of square-nose and skew chisels

Turning sanded in lathe (note: tool rest has been removed)

Use of small round-nose and small skew chisel

Sawing off waste stock and smoothing with file

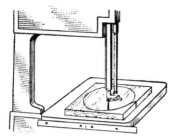

Band saw used to cut disk

Disk, carefully centered, mounted on faceplate

Cutting edge of disk to form perfect circle

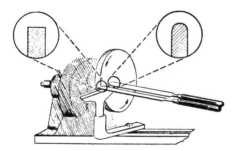

Face of disk worked to exact thickness

Pencil touched against revolving disk to mark design

sudden reduction in speed causes the momentum of the heavy disk to exert pressure in the direction which tends to unscrew the faceplate. Unless the lathe is equipped with a locking device, it is a sensible precaution to turn off the switch, thereby permitting the speed to slow down gradually.

There is also the interesting problem of split-turning a column or spindle which separates so as to form duplicating halves. To perform this operation, it is merely a matter of securing two perfectly fitting strips of wood together so as to form one square strip. These two strips are usually held together during the turning process with screws, driven through stock which extends beyond the required turning, at both ends. When the turning has been completed, the two temporary ends may be cut off, causing the finished spindle to fall into halves.

In preparing small split turnings, many workers prefer to place a piece of wrapping paper between the two strips of wood, before gluing up the stock. In this way the two halves may readily be separated after the turning has been completed.

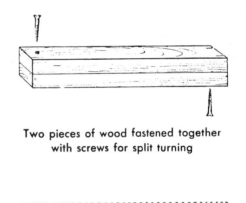

Two pieces of wood fastened together with screws for split turning

When turning is completed, cylinder separates into equal halves

Rockwell Mfg. Co.

Complete Power Shop

Pictured above is one of the newer lines of single-purpose power machines. An assembly of light and efficient woodworking units such as this can perform just about every job that may confront the home craftsman. Of course, in the average home, all these machines are not required. In fact, there's some redundancy in their operations. For instance, the band saw and scroll saw perform essentially the same functions of sawing wood into curved shapes.

Aside from their fine functional design another appeal of the new models of light woodworking machines is their mobility. Unlike the massive machines of old, these are equipped with retractable casters and can be wheeled about and then "anchored" wherever the work is to be performed.

Portable Light Combination

The light, multipurpose power tool, illustrated here, has been appropriately called "table-top workshop." For the Dremel *Moto-Shop* combines many tools in one. Identifying itself, basically, as a power jig saw, it also has a power take off which adapts it to the multifunctions of a light-duty *bench grinder, disk sander,* and *buffer.* Moreover, with its flexible shaft, it performs other craft operations such as *carving, drilling, routing, etching, engraving,* and *precision sanding.*

Light in weight, this convenient combination can be carried to the job and put to work even on a kitchen table or counter. With its rubber suction-cup base mounting, it grips any level surface and requires only a small amount of working space.

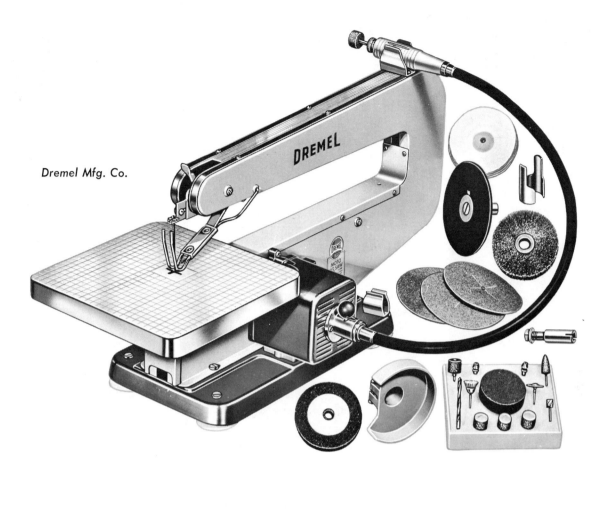

Dremel Mfg. Co.

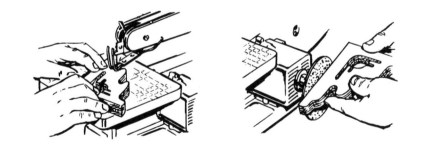

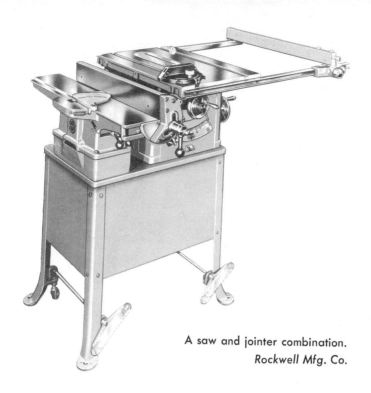

A saw and jointer combination.
Rockwell Mfg. Co.

Combination Power Tools

The primary appeal of the combination power tool is its compactness and economy. When two or more machines operate on a single source of power and are mounted on a single stand, economy is obviously effected in savings on the cost of maintaining motors for many single-purpose machines as well as in the amount of floor space needed.

Power combinations perform the operational functions of two or more single-purpose power units. Some provide added convenience, as the circular saw and jointer combination illustrated above. The most natural procedure, after ripping a board, is to plane the edge.

In the school industrial arts shop, combination power tools are frequently used as an auxiliary to the heavier single-purpose machines. But the multipurpose appeal of combination tools has attracted the "do-it-yourself" group. For while these combination tools are light in structure by comparison to heavy-duty industrial models, they can perform many jobs in the home workshop with speed and accuracy. Moreover, in the home workshop they provide the advantage of a number of expensive woodworking machines at only a fraction of their collective cost. Furthermore, they may be bought a unit at a time, as needed and as the craftsman's budget allows.

Pictures at the right show some of the combined functions of the DeWalt Power Shop.

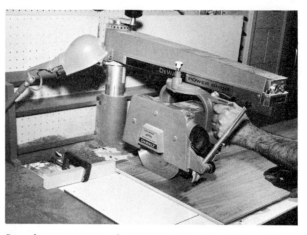

Boards are accurately crosscut on the DeWalt Power Shop with visual advantage of sawing from above the work.

Power head is swiveled to parallel position for ripping operations.

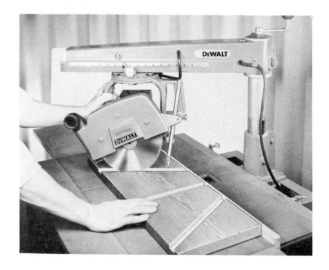

Radial saw is particularly adept at cutting square and angle dados.

Dado blades quickly remove cutouts of lap joints.

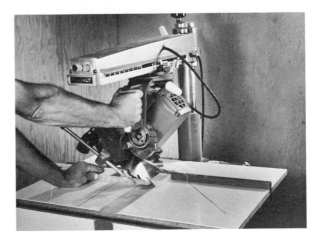

Bevels of end miters are accurately sawed with cutting head tilted to exact angle.

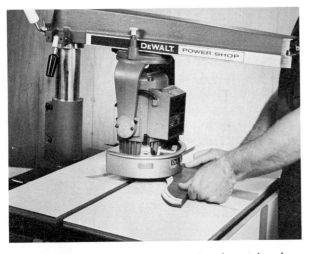

Shaper attachment is used for curved and straight edges. Other cutters are available for rabbeting and grooving.

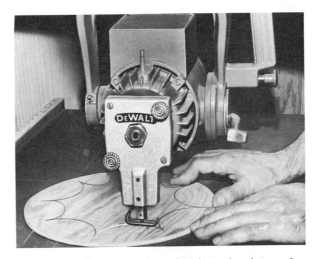

Jig saw attachment cuts curved and circular shapes. Saw pierces work for making inside cutouts.

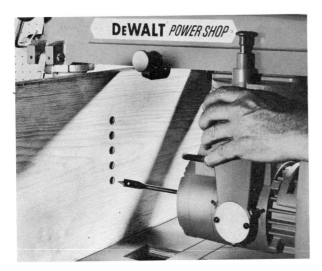

Horizontal drilling is accurately performed with drill chuck attached to motor spindle.

Disk sander is attached to power spindle for sanding and shaping of parts. *All photographs: Black & Decker Mfg. Co.*

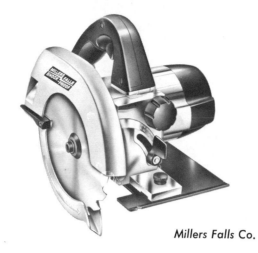

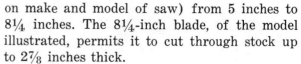
Millers Falls Co.

Portable Power Tools

The timesaving convenience of *taking the tool to the job* has advanced considerably with the introduction of an excellent variety of portable power tools. Many of these show real improvement in their design. And they perform jobs *in minutes* which heretofor have required hours of laborious hand work. Some, in fact, perform many of the operations of heavy stationary woodworking machinery.

Portable Power Saw

Portable power saws are fully adjustable for *depth* of cut. Blades range in size (depending on make and model of saw) from 5 inches to 8¼ inches. The 8¼-inch blade, of the model illustrated, permits it to cut through stock up to 2⅞ inches thick.

Since this type of saw must be exposed to the most rugged and prolonged use, heavy-duty models such as the one shown are powered by a 2 H.P., 13-amp, motor. This provides a margin of power for even the heaviest work loads.

The manufacturers of this model have installed extra precautionary features to safeguard the operator. It is double-insulated to prevent electric shock. A telescoping, spring-activated, *blade guard* encircles the saw blade and retracts only as the saw teeth enter the wood. It can be moved back, however, with a retracting lever when the saw is being used to make surface cuts where the guard may interfere. A Plexiglas *safety window* between the stationary guard and base shields saw teeth otherwise exposed on shallow cuts. This also deflects sawdust and chips.

Because of their excellent balance, portable power saws of this type are relatively easy to operate. Depth scales, calibrated in ⅛-inch graduations, assure accuracy of cutting depth, while angle scales, graduated from zero to 45 degrees, register precise bevel adjustments. A *microguide* provides an accurate sighting line for sawing, regardless of angle or depth of cut.

Cross-cutting lumber to size. Even the heaviest grades of lumber can be sawed rapidly with a portable power saw. *Millers Falls* Co.

"Pocket cuts," surface cuts, *inside* cutouts, and grooves are started from the surface by pressing the top lever, which retracts the blade guard. *Millers Falls* Co.

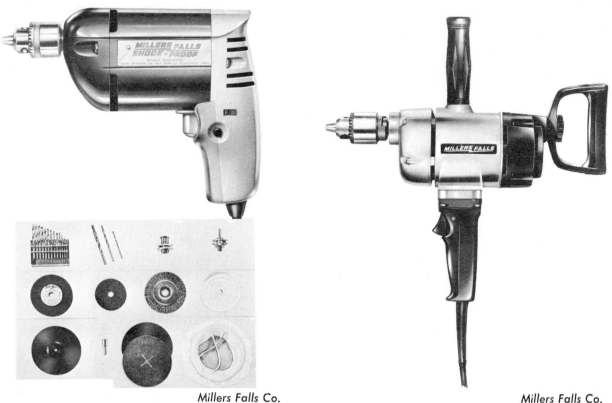

Millers Falls Co.   Millers Falls Co.

Portable Electric Drill

If any portable power tool could be singled out as the one that made the greatest contribution to the ease and convenience of woodworking, the portable electric drill would undoubtedly rate first honors. This handy little time saver started its career as a power convenience for drilling holes. It was then adapted for special bits to make the larger holes traditionally bored with brace and auger bit. But soon it was rigged to perform many other jobs. For the introduction of a wide variety of attachments transformed it into a "do-it-all" about the shop.

While the portable electric drill is now regarded as an almost indispensable power tool, its popularity has caused it to be manufactured in such a multitude of makes and types that much confusion has arisen regarding its real abilities and limitations.

The shiny case (and cut-rate price) of some cheaper 1/4-inch drills may hide mechanical deficiencies which will prevent their functioning for any extended period of time with the various attachments made for them. Of course, this does not hold true of the better drills made by reputable manufacturers. In fact, the reputable man-

ufacturer candidly advertises the limitations of his product.

The shock-proof electric drill shown here, with basic accessories, is rated as one of the best. As well as the double-insulated and indestructible housing which warrants absolute protection against electric shock (with standard 2-prong plug) this drill can be operated at variable speeds and has a reversing switch which adapts it for driving and withdrawing screws. Thus it also functions as a power screwdriver. Accessories include attachments for sanding, circular and saber sawing, grinding, and drill press operations.

Portable electric drills are manufactured in three general classifications; namely, *light*, *standard*, and *heavy duty*. *Light-duty* drills are suitable for light drilling, polishing, and sanding. But they are not too satisfactory for use with attachments, because they overheat under constant or even moderately heavy work loads. *Standard-duty* drills can handle continuous work with average loads. *Heavy-duty* drills are made to take continuous heavy production loads.

Drills are made either with *pistol* grips for accessibility and convenience of handling or with *spade* handles for heavier operations requiring a firmer grip.

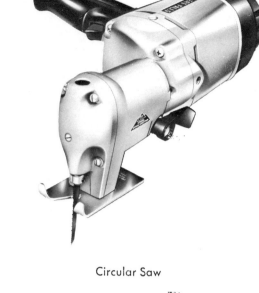

Saber saw

Power Unit with standard attachments
All photographs: Millers Falls Co.

Circular Saw

Orbital Sander

Portable Power Unit

The portable power unit could be called the "big brother" of the versatile electric drill. But, instead of representing itself basically as a hand drill, the power unit introduces an adaptable source of power for the operation of a wide variety of specially designed appliances. With a motor rated at 4.6 amps, turning at a speed of 3200 R.P.M. (which can be reduced 7 to 1 with a speed-reducer attachment), this unit provides greater power for heavier and more continuous work loads. Moreover, it powers a sturdier and more extensive variety of attachments — including a $7\frac{1}{4}''$ tilting-arbor table saw and a 2″ plane. All attachments are driven directly from the motor spindle for smooth, vibration-free operation and maximum power efficiency. With the versatile power unit and its many attachments, you can have a complete power workshop at a fraction of the cost of individually powered tools.

The shockproof model shown offers the advantage of being double-insulated inside by a tough plastic casing enclosing the internal mechanism. Even if normal insulation breaks down, you are protected against dangerous electric shock.

Disk Sander

Bench Grinder

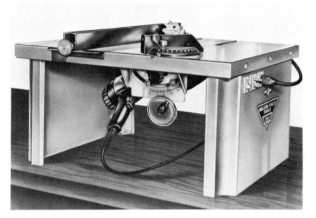

Table Saw

Bench Sander

Drill Press

Bench Buffer

Working Capacity of Electric Drills

The average portable electric drill runs at between 1600 and 2300 revolutions per minute, with horsepower running from about $\frac{1}{14}$ on smaller drills to $\frac{1}{3}$ or more on the heavy-duty variety. Most attachments require a drill rated at an extreme minimum of 1.5 amps, approximately $\frac{1}{8}$ H.P. Saws and reciprocating attachments need at least 2 amps ($\frac{1}{6}$ H.P.) to prevent the motor from overheating and becoming damaged.

The portable power unit, illustrated on the preceding pages, has the extra power needed for heavy-duty operations. The motor is rated at 4 amps and is geared down to 3200 R.P.M., a performance qualifying it to drive the various attachments. This drill offers the advantage of operating attachments *directly from its threaded spindle.* Each attachment is mounted securely to the machined nose of the gear case, putting it in precise alignment with the spindle.

This minimizes vibration, providing better balance and easier handling.

Precautions with Electric Drills

1. *Do not overload the drill.* Dull tools or heavy continuous operations may force the drill to run at slow speeds, thus consuming more current than its rated amperage. This results in overheating and possible burning out of motor. *When a drill becomes hot, turn it off and change to a sharper tool or lighter operation.*

2. Insert drill bits *all the way* so that the chuck grasps the bit *to the full depth of its jaws.* Partially inserted bits damage the chuck.

3. Do not apply *side pressure* unless such pressure is within *1 inch* of the chuck jaws.

4. Do not cover ventilating slots with hands while drill is in operation. This obstructs flow of cooling air, causing motor to overheat.

5. Do not expose drill to moisture. Rust and corrosion can permanently damage motor.

More attachments for the power unit described on the preceding pages. Table attachment, for mounting saber saw, enables scroll sawing in fixed position.

Power plane attachment offers the ease and accuracy of mechanical planing. As pictured at left, this attachment is most useful for squaring edges of boards preparatory to joining. *All photographs: Millers Falls Co.*

Saber Saw

One of the most fascinating portable power tools of relatively recent origin is the so-called *saber saw*. This little "wonder-worker" slices into wood up to 2 inches thick, sawing curves and angles as well as performing straight cross-cutting and ripping. Made by many different manufacturers, in a wide variety of models and designs, it cuts with reciprocating action like a power scroll saw. But it offers the advantage of an "open-end" blade, a condition making it capable of cutting almost anywhere and from almost any position.

Saber saws for this model have a "nose cutting" adjustment that permits sawing up to an adjoining obstruction.

The cutting action of the saber saw is extremely rapid, as high as 3300 strokes per minute. With some makes, as with the Stanley saber saw pictured above, speed can be controlled. Slow speeds can be dialed for starting cuts and you can increase or retard motion of the blade in relation to type of work performed.

Most saws of this type come with a variety of blades which are quickly interchangeable. As well as the standard blades for coarse and fine cutting, special metal-cutting blades are usually included.

One of the most useful attributes of the saber saw is its ability to cut its own starting slot inside the edges of a board or plywood panel. With the saw "nosed over" to a perpendicular position, the tip of the blade simply scratches into the wood until a "through slot" is made. Then the saw is brought down to rest on the surface area, where it continues to cut along the inside outline.

Various makes of saber saws bear their own names and offer their own special features. The two models illustrated are among the most noteworthy.

The Stanley saber saw, shown here, incorporates an *antivibration* mechanism which provides extremely smooth operation. This model also offers a *two-position* base and a special flush-cutting blade. Adjusted to its second position, the Stanley saws from the "nose," thus adapting it for many jobs where it is necessary to work right up to adjoining obstructions.

The self-starting advantage of all saber saws is especially helpful when a series of inside cutouts must be made.

All photographs: Stanley Tools.

Skil "Recipro Saw" has two speed adjustments — high speed (2,000 strokes per minute) for fast cutting of wood, plastic, and compositions, and low speed (1,600 s.p.m.) for steel, aluminum, and brass. The shoe and blade are adjustable to several different positions. *Skil Corp.*

Shopmate "*Blitz*" reciprocal saws offer variable speeds with adjustable shoe and blade for various sawing positions. This model has a built-in light that beams directly on the work. *G. W. Murphy Industries, Inc.*

Reciprocal Saw

Working on the same principle as the saber saw, the reciprocal saw is larger and more powerful. It is designed to be held and operated differently than the saber saw. For cross-cutting and ripping it is held on a slant over the work in much the same position as a manually operated hand saw.

The reciprocal saw is designed for heavy-duty sawing of heavier wood and metal and lacks the flexibility of saber saws for cutting sharp curves. It uses wider and longer blades. However, it is excellent for pocket cuts, roughing-in, ripping and for mild scroll work.

Portable Power Router

The power router works on much the same cutting principle as the shaper. But, being *portable*, it offers greater flexibility of application. Of course, as its name implies, it performs the essential *routing* process, which calls for removal of wood from surface areas *inside* the perimeter of the work. But, like the shaper, the power router can also be used with guides and cutters of various types for shaping edges, rabbeting, grooving, and numerous other edging processes. To these functions of the power router are added other specialties of its own, including dovetailing, mortising, and cutting for inlays and surface ornamentation.

In order to obtain smooth and flexible cutting action, the spindle of the power router revolves at tremendously high speed. In fact, the model illustrated runs at *30,000 R.P.M.!* This enables the cutters to produce an entirely smooth, *machined* wood finish which ordinarily does not require sanding.

While caution must be exercised when operating any power tool with an open cutter revolving at such great speed, the power router is handled with knobs on the top, *with both hands held firmly over, above, and away from the cutting parts at the base.* The cutters, in fact, are fully guarded during operation by the covering body of the router housing.

Some typical power router operations are illustrated and described on the next page. Removed from its router base, the router can also be applied as a power unit for the plane and shaper attachments described on page 112.

Stanley Tools

110

In cutting dados and grooves, an adjustable edge guide is used for accuracy. The cutter can be adjusted to the required depth. "Blind" dados are made by keeping solid margin at each end of the cut.

Edge shaping and rabbeting require an edge guide. This guide has extra-long rods and a screw adjustment for exact cut location.

Edge molding and shaping is performed with special cutters. Because of its high speed, the cutter leaves a smooth, *machined* finish, even on end grain.

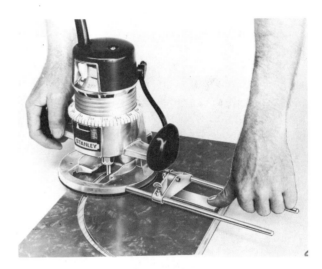

Circular grooves require the use of a trammel point attachment in conjunction with a circular guide. Special decorative effects and grooves for inlay are made this way.

Metal templets are followed by the router for cutting special shapes. Templets are also used for cutting dovetails and mortises and for duplicate operations.

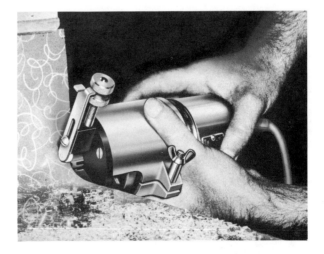

For edge trimming, the power unit is removed from the router base and used free-hand, but guided with adjustable trimmer base. *Stanley Tools.*

Millers Falls Co.

Router-Shaper Attachment

For many jobs it may be desirable to mount the router in a stationary, or *table*, position. This converts it into a *shaper*, which performs the work already described on page 92. However, the shaper attachment illustrated above was specially designed for use with the power router shown on the opposite page. It functions as a simplified "jig" to hold the power unit of this router.

This low-cost attachment, made with a 1″ x 15″ x 24″ plywood table surface, has a built-in motor mount and provision for accurate adjustment. Illustrated below are just a few of the many processes the shaper attachment can perform. Of particular interest is the round-edge shaping made with a circular shaper guide, as shown at the bottom.

Millers Falls Co.

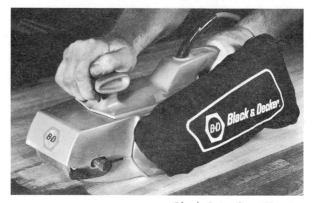

Black & Decker Mfg. Co.

Portable Electric Sanders

For the many different sanding jobs called for in the shop, the portable electric sander provides substantial help. Aside from its basic advantage of always being available to *take to the job*, it is made in a variety of types, each suited for a particular kind of job. Various sanding abrasives, ranging from fine to coarse, may also be selected to fit each type of sander for the kind of work being performed.

Millers Falls Co.

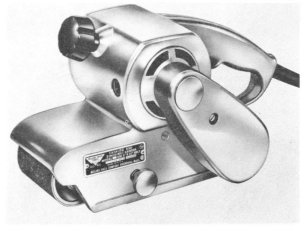

Portable Belt Sander

The portable belt sander has demonstrated itself to be one of the most useful sanding tools yet devised. Because of its *endless belt* action, it surfaces wood in a minimum of time. Thus, sanding with a coarse belt, followed by one of finer abrasive, such a sander can smooth even the roughest stock. Most portable belt sanders are also adaptable for stationary work. This is done by mounting them on their own stand or simply fastening them to a bench.

Portable Disk Sander

The portable disk sander has been described and illustrated previously with the drills and power-unit attachments. But its action is worth special note. Revolving rapidly on a rubber pad, at either *direct-* or *right-angle* drive, the action of the portable disk sander is so fast and effective that it can be used for *shaping* wood as well as sanding. For this reason it must be handled with skill and care in order to avoid damage to the work. One of the best safeguards against such damage is a protective sanding guide, such as the one illustrated. This attachment provides positive control for freehand disk sanding. It is adjustable to any angle to govern *depth and uniformity* of sanding, thus eliminating any erratic streaks or scratches which may occur during unguarded operations.

Orbital Sander

Whenever an exceptionally fine finish is desired on wood, the orbital sander can produce it, and at a rate *approximately twelve times faster than by hand sanding!* Working in *orbital* motion, models like the one illustrated make 4500 *orbits* per minute. The sanding shoe has a sponge-rubber face and can be used with either wet or dry abrasives.

As well as regular sanding, the orbital sander is excellent for sanding between coats of fine finishes. This useful tool is light and easily handled. It is particularly applicable for sanding in tight corners where other types of portable sanders will not fit.

Disk-plate and flexible disk sanders are used for flat or convex curved sanding.

Belt and drum sanders are used for concave curved sanding. Belt sander is also used for flat surfacing. *All photographs: Millers Falls Co.*

Dremel Mfg. Co.

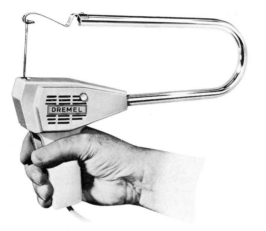

Dremel Mfg. Co.

Electric Utility Tool

The Dremel *Moto-Tool* is designed for light-capacity *drilling, grinding, polishing, shaping, sanding, routing, etching, carving,* and innumerable other fine craft operations. Weighing only 6 ounces, it handles almost as easily as a pencil, thus permitting it to do fine detail work with pin-point accuracy. The Moto-Tool comes with a wide assortment of cutters, grinders, drills, and shapers. A "wrenchless" collet chuck provides a quick means of changing tools.

Electric Coping Saw

This handy tool eliminates the labor and much of the inaccuracy from manual coping saw operations. Weighing only 17 ounces, the *Moto-Saw* can cut to the center of a 19-inch panel. While it works most effectively when cutting thin wood, it can also saw stock up to ¾-inch thick. Its smooth sawing action protects wood edges, thus making it especially good for plywood.

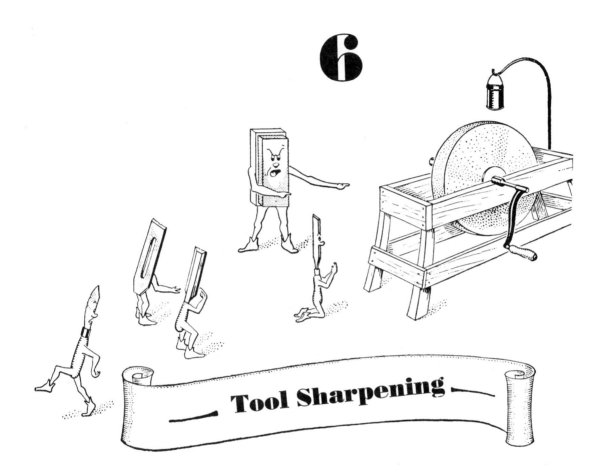

Tool Sharpening

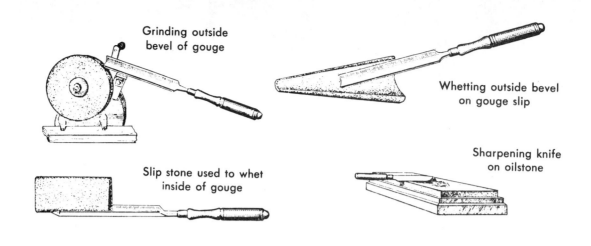

Grinding outside
bevel of gouge

Whetting outside bevel
on gouge slip

Sharpening knife
on oilstone

Slip stone used to whet
inside of gouge

How to Sharpen Hand Tools

One of the first essentials in a well-equipped shop is a hand or power grindstone. As tools are used they are bound to become worn, nicked, and damaged. In order to recondition them, the edges must be ground.

Together with the grindstone, you should have one or more oilstones. These may be purchased in convenient boxes which serve as holders during the sharpening process. They are made with two surfaces: the coarser surface for sharpening and the finer for honing.

Nor does the sharpening equipment stop at this point. The skilled craftsman will insist that his cutting tools be every bit as sharp as a razor. To bring them to this degree of sharpness, he not only hones the cutting edge, but also strops it in razor fashion on a leather strop.

Common shop tools such as chisels, plane blades and spokeshave blades are all sharpened in just about the same manner. These tools have a single, beveled cutting edge and the actual sharpening is performed mostly on this edge alone. Remember always to keep the same degree of bevel along the cutting edge when the tool is being sharpened.

Unless the beveled edge of a blade is badly nicked, rounded, or damaged from too frequent rubbing on the oilstone, it may be resharpened without using a grindstone. This sharpening is performed by spreading a few drops of thin oil on the surface of the stone and then holding the chisel so that it rests evenly on its cutting bevel. Then it is rubbed backward and forward, or with a circular motion on the surface of the stone. However, it must be remembered that the blade should at all times be rubbed on the slant of its cutting bevel. During the sharpening process, the position of the blade is alternated on the stone, the opposite straight side being held flat on the sharpening surface. After the cutting edge has been carefully sharpened, it is ready to be honed and stropped to final razor sharpness.

However, if the cutting edge happens to be worn or damaged, it will be necessary to regrind it. This is done by holding the blade against the grindstone, on the correct beveled slant, and sliding it back and forth evenly on the revolving wheel. For this operation certain power grindstones have an automatic oiling device, to keep the wheels oiled while they revolve.

To prevent burning the blade, certain types of hand-operated stone should likewise be oiled. After the grinding has been performed and the cutting edge of the blade properly reshaped, it should be carefully sharpened, honed, and stropped in the manner outlined in the preceding paragraphs.

Before leaving the power grindstone it should be mentioned that the business of grinding a beveled edge accurately is greatly simplified when a special tool holder is attached to the grinder. The blade is then simply clamped in the holder so that it may be pushed back and forth across the wheel at the exact slant of the cutting bevel.

Gouge chisels and wood-turning tools require a special sharpening technique. Some gouges are beveled on the outside or *convex* edge, while others are beveled on the inside or *concave* edge. Those that are ground from the outside must be held at the required beveled slant against the grindstone and turned in such a manner that the proper bevel is uniformly maintained along the curved edge.

The final sharpening of the inside and outside gouge is performed with a special round edge, wedge-shaped oilstone (gouge slip). The straight edge of the blade is honed perfectly flat. Many of the turning tools, as well as the carving tools, belong to the gouge family and are sharpened, therefore, in the manner suggested.

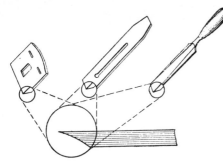

Blade of spokeshave, plane, and chisel,
showing beveled cutting edges

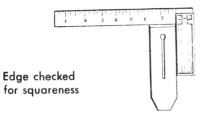

Tool rest of grinder adjusted to proper bevel

Edge checked
for squareness

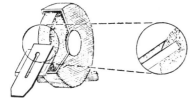

Circular motion used to whet bevel on oilstone
(blade is held on exact slant of bevel)

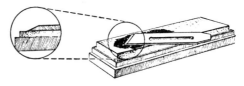

Straight edge of blade kept flat on oilstone

Leather strop used for final sharpening

The grinder-honer is bench-mounted for tool sharpening. This convenient combination of grindstone and revolving hone (top), with adjustable tool rests, is ideal for keeping tools in keen cutting shape. *Black & Decker Mfg. Co.*

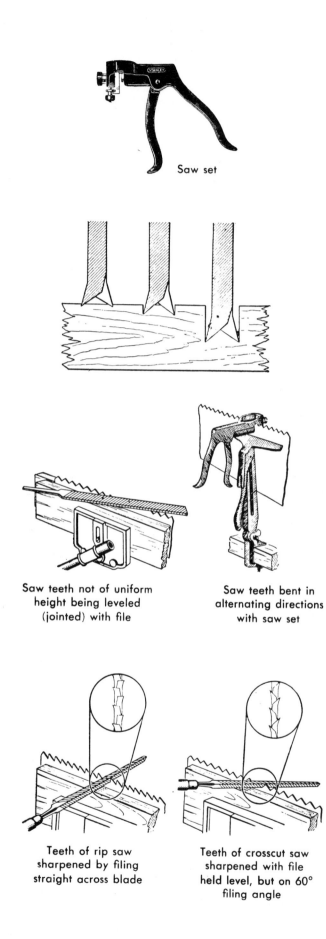

Saw set

Saw teeth not of uniform
height being leveled
(jointed) with file

Saw teeth bent in
alternating directions
with saw set

Teeth of rip saw
sharpened by filing
straight across blade

Teeth of crosscut saw
sharpened with file
held level, but on 60°
filing angle

How to Sharpen a Saw

The sharpening of saws is a rather special job. Unless the worker happens to be interested in the experience, it might be advisable to send any dull saws to a professional saw sharpener who will do the job expertly for a nominal fee.

A saw that has been used over an extended period of time, and as a result has become dull and worn, should first be *jointed*. This term means that the tips of the teeth must be leveled off so as to provide an absolutely straight cutting edge.

In the jointing process, the saw is held in place either with a special clamping device or between two strips of wood in the regular vise, at the work bench. A file or flat emery stone is then rubbed across the points of the teeth, along the entire length of the blade. During this process the teeth are checked with a straightedge until they are found to be perfectly straight and level. It should be noted that if an emery stone is used, extreme care must be observed to avoid spoiling the stone by creasing it in a single groove.

When the blade has been properly jointed, each tooth is filed to a uniform shape. This filing is usually done with a triangular seven-inch file. In the case of the crosscut saw, each tooth is shaped to a perfect triangular point, the filing being performed on the inside edges of the teeth. The file is held at a 60-degree angle thus making a bevel on the front edge of one tooth and at the same time making a similar bevel on the back edge of an adjoining tooth.

It will be noted, however, that the teeth of ripsaws are sharpened to an even chisel edge at the point. The front edge of each tooth forms a perfect right angle to the blade.

Before the saw teeth have been properly filed, it is necessary to set each tooth so that it staggers, or bends in an opposite direction to its neighbor. This set is attained by using a tool which resembles a pair of pliers, called a *saw set*. All teeth should be bent to a uniform *set;* those which spread out too far being brought in while others are spread out to the desired amount of set. The proper amount of bend, or set, is frequently marked on the saw blade, and the saw set may be adjusted to this amount.

The teeth of a saw are set to clear the blade and prevent it from binding. It is interesting to note that soft and wet woods require more set to cut them properly than hard and dry woods.

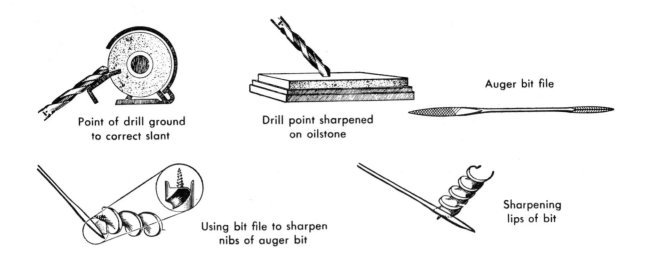

Point of drill ground
to correct slant

Drill point sharpened
on oilstone

Auger bit file

Using bit file to sharpen
nibs of auger bit

Sharpening
lips of bit

How to Sharpen Drill Bits

Bits that are used with the various types of drills are sharpened at the cutting point. The push drill bit, which must move in reverse directions while it actually drills only on the drive stroke, is fluted on both sides. At the slightly pointed tip, each flute forms the edge of a cutter. On the other hand, the drill bit used with the hand automatic and machine drill revolves in a single direction. Its two spiraled cutting flanges form individual cutters at the slightly sloping point.

When sharpening these bits, it should be kept in mind that each type is shaped at the point with two cutters, and that each cutter is slightly slanted to provide a sharp cutting edge. Both types may be sharpened on a grinding wheel. A sharpening stone, or oilstone, may be used to improve their condition.

How to Sharpen Auger Bits

The sharpening of an auger bit is really not a very difficult job. In fact, it only requires the careful use of a small bit file in reshaping the cutting parts.

The cutting, or boring, parts of an auger bit are the *nibs* and the *lips*. The lips consist of the two cutting knives which terminate the spiral above the pointed tip, or tang, of the bit. Each lip should be filed to an even slanted cutting edge on the upper sides. The nibs which project on both sides, on the rim of the spiral, serve to cut the outside circumference of the hole. In sharpening, they should be filed from the inside. If a burr appears outside of the nibs, it should be filed off flush to the circumference of the bit.

How to Sharpen a Scraper

The edge of a cabinet scraper is first bevel-ground in the same manner as a plane blade, and may be sharpened and honed in somewhat similar fashion. After this treatment, however, the sharp edge must be bent over so as to form a shallow lip. Ordinarily it is necessary for this lip to project only about $\frac{1}{32}$ of an inch over the edge. The delicate job of bending the

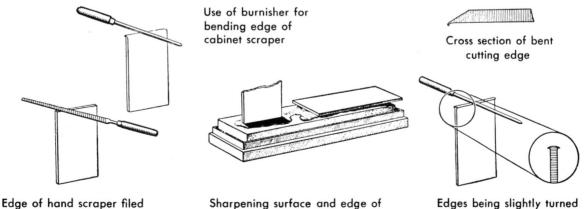

Use of burnisher for
bending edge of
cabinet scraper

Cross section of bent
cutting edge

Edge of hand scraper filed
straight and square

Sharpening surface and edge of
hand scraper on oilstone

Edges being slightly turned
with burnisher

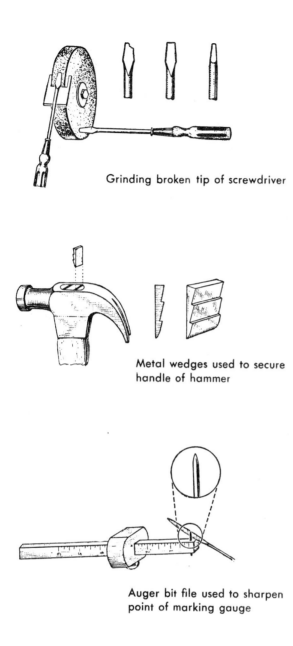

Grinding broken tip of screwdriver

Metal wedges used to secure handle of hammer

Auger bit file used to sharpen point of marking gauge

sharpened lips is most easily performed with an oval-shaped burnishing tool. The burnisher is pressed gently back and forth against the beveled edge. By slow degrees this edge is then bent over to provide the necessary lip. A suitable burnishing tool can be made by grinding the teeth off an old half-round or rat-tail file.

The straightedge hand scraper is not as difficult to sharpen. It is only necessary to file the edges until they become perfectly straight and square. Each edge is then rubbed on the surface of an oilstone, the blade being held at a perfect right angle to the surface. The blade is then placed flat on the surface of the stone and rubbed in this position to remove the burr which has collected along the edge. It will be noted that in the case of the hand scraper, a perfectly sharp and square cutting edge is required.

Keeping Tools in Good Condition

Despite the very best of care, tools and shop equipment are bound to become damaged occasionally. The ends of screwdrivers may become chipped or misshapen, chisels broken, a saw may fall off the bench causing a cracked handle, and working parts of vises and machines may bind and balk. It is usually possible to regrind chipped points of screwdrivers and broken ends of chisels to their original shape. Loose hammer and mallet heads should be tightened promptly. Tools that have become rusted may be brightened by rubbing them with steel wool, followed by a thorough rubbing with anti-rust oil.

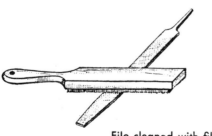

File cleaned with file card

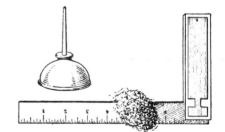

Fine steel wool and oil to keep tools bright

7

— Wood Finishing —

Wood finishing is a broad subject in itself and one which requires special treatment. In general, there are many ways of finishing wood. Those interested in the subject have their own special methods and, with the exception of a few basic steps, on which all agree, there is little in common in the way different people go about the job.

Excellent and highly effective finishes are often obtained through methods which might strike the professional as being quite unusual. Different finishing agents are used in various parts of the world. Some favor methods at which others scoff.

Yet all are agreed that the good finish, regardless of the methods or finishing agents employed, should by all means enhance the final appearance of the article on which it is used. Moreover, if it is a transparent finish, it should bring out to the fullest extent the beauty of the grain and the surface characteristics of the wood.

For this reason it is generally agreed that before any type of finish is applied to an article, the article itself should be carefully prepared for the finishing agents. Indeed, the final appearance of the work is largely dependent on the thoroughness with which the basic steps have been followed.

Preparing the Work for Finishing

Before any of the finishing steps are undertaken, the work should be carefully examined for scratches, mars, grain irregularities, dents, glue spots, and kindred imperfections.

Glue which has adhered at places of joining will not absorb stain and must, therefore, be carefully removed before any further steps are taken. Ordinarily, it can be scraped or peeled off with a sharp knife, chisel, or cabinet scraper.

Dents and depressions may often be lifted by placing a wet piece of blotting paper directly over the spot and pressing it with a hot flatiron. Cracks, unless they are large ones, can ordinarily be filled with wood filler, and toned to the same color as the desired final finish. Stick shellac may be bought in colors which blend exactly with most standard tones of finished wood. This shellac may be used to fill larger cracks or openings. All other imperfections will generally be overcome by the final and thorough use of sandpaper.

Limbering a piece of sandpaper

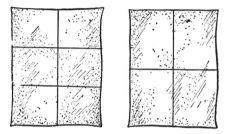

Dividing the sandpaper

Saw being used for cutting
(blade lies on smooth side)

Sandpaper often held on small blocks
or special holder

Too much emphasis cannot be placed on the importance of thorough sanding. Much of the basic sanding should be taken care of even before the work has been put together. The parts are easier to get at in this way. Two grades of sandpaper should be used; first a medium grade and then, for final sanding, a fine grade.

All sanding should be performed with the grain of the wood. To insure an even and thorough job a sandpaper block should be used wherever possible. End-grain portions must be especially well sanded so that the natural grain appears hard and clean. The end grain is especially porous and unless the sanding is very thorough, these portions will absorb the stain and turn a darker color than the rest of the work.

Choice of Stain

Choosing the right stain provides the first point of discussion in the art of wood finishing. There are many different types of stain and each type has its own particular group of followers. In fact, many insist that the richer woods are better off without any stain. However, most people do have occasion to use wood stains at one time or another and it will be well, therefore, to discuss a few of the more common types.

Water Stain is extremely popular because it is easily mixed and does not fade very readily. Pure aniline colors are mixed in hot water and are applied directly and permitted to penetrate and dry on the wood. The water stain is not rubbed. The only objection to stains of this character is that they are apt to raise the grain of the wood, after application. This fault, however, can be overcome by sponging the wood with water and permitting it to dry. The grain, which has been raised during this initial sponging, is then carefully sanded with fine sandpaper, thus providing a protected surface for the water stain.

Spirit Stains, like water stains, are mixed with pure aniline colors. However, the liquid agent is alcohol. Spirit stains must be applied carefully because they dry very quickly. When they are applied with a brush, a degree of skill is necessary in order to avoid streaks where brush strokes overlap. In large furniture factories, stains of this kind are generally applied with an air brush.

Sanding with the grain

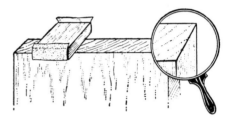

Sanding end grain (fine sandpaper produces interesting graining)

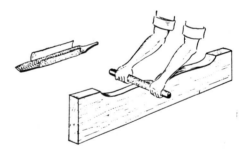

Spindle or file wrapped in sandpaper used for curved work

Sandpaper held loosely for dulling edges

123

Oil Stains are favored by many people because they are very easy to apply, and because they enable the worker to develop many interesting effects of tone and color, which would be difficult to attain with stains of other types. The oil stain is mixed from aniline colors compounded in oil and turpentine. Sometimes a small amount of linseed oil is added to give additional body to the stain. Stains of this type which are sold already mixed may contain benzol, benzine, or naphtha as their mixing ingredient.

The oil stain is a common favorite because it does not dry quickly and may be worked over with a rubbing rag after it has been applied. Moreover, it can be worked for tones and contrasts which cannot be obtained with any of the other varieties.

Common Methods of Staining and Coloring Wood

Distinctive colors are often obtained on wood through the use of various types of acids and other preparations which bring about a chemical reaction in the wood itself. This reaction produces the distinctive color. The variety of these chemical solutions is almost limitless, so it will be advisable to discuss only two or three of the most popular kinds.

Attractive colors and tones may be obtained on oak through the use of ammonia, potash, and bichromate of potassium. When ammonia is used, the work is exposed to the fumes and as a result takes on a dark tone.

Mahogany may be given a rich color through the use of quicklime. This material is applied and later rubbed off with linseed oil. If the quicklime is permitted to stay on, it discolors the work. However, when it is quickly removed with linseed oil, the result is exceedingly rich.

The Use of Wood Filler

In order to obtain an effective finish on wood, it is not only necessary to color it, but, in the case of open-grained woods, it is necessary as well to *fill* those portions which are to be finished. Close-grained woods, on the other hand, do not require a filler because the texture of the wood is not porous or open, and for this reason the ordinary finishing agents, such as shellac, varnish, or lacquer, will provide whatever filling may be necessary.

Wood filler can be purchased in paste form. It consists of silica, a white powder, mixed in linseed oil, turpentine, and japan. The so-called transparent finish is cream-colored and may be tinted to any desired tone or shade through the introduction of oil colors.

Filler should be thoroughly mixed and diluted with turpentine until it is of the consistency of heavy cream. Generally speaking, it is good practice to stain the work before applying the filler. The latter is applied to the work with a stiff brush. It dries and hardens in a relatively short time and for this reason, on large projects it should be brushed on portions at a time, in separate applications. After each portion has been treated and allowed to dry for a few minutes, it is rubbed vigorously across the grain with a coarse rag or piece of burlap. The idea is to work the paste well into the open and porous grain. After the initial cross-grain rubbing has been performed, the filled portions are again rubbed with the grain, this time with a finer piece of cloth.

If the filler adheres and hardens in places on the surface of the work, it should be carefully removed with a rag moistened with turpentine. Excess filler should be removed at intersections and places of joining, with a sharpened stick or knife blade covered with a rag.

While it is not always necessary to do so, sometimes the idea of re-staining the article after the filler has been applied is a worth-while practice. Frequently this operation improves the appearance of the finished product. Naturally, it is rather difficult to color the wood filler to the exact desired shade, and thus when the work is re-stained, the color may be adjusted and brought to the shade desired.

Wood filler should be given at least twenty-four hours to dry and harden before continuing with further steps of finishing.

How to Apply Stain

The application of water or spirit stains is relatively simple, as both of these types of stain are merely brushed on the well-sanded wood and permitted to penetrate into the surface. Sometimes, however, it is necessary to remove carefully with a rag any excess stain from portions of the wood, especially on the end grain. The main idea is to let the stain penetrate and dye the wood.

Likewise, in the application of chemicals and acids which are used to change the color of the

Stain applied evenly from center area

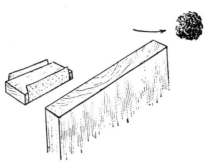

Fine sandpaper or steel wool used to
brighten end grain

Soft cloth used to rub stain, with the grain

Center areas and edges thoroughly
rubbed to produce high lights

wood, it is only necessary to apply them in the regular manner, and remove the excess with a rag.

However, in the application of oil stains, especially where a special effect is desired, the technique is somewhat different. For example, let us say that a small table is being stained. The stain is first brushed freely and quickly on the four legs and the underneath structure. While it remains wet on these portions, it is rubbed carefully with a rag until the grain and surface characteristics of the wood show through. Moreover, in the rubbing process, it is possible to *tone out* certain portions of the wood to obtain either uniform or contrasting effects. Light rubbing with very fine steel wool will help in this process.

With certain types of close-grained woods, notably pine and maple, there is a definite advantage in mixing the oil stain to a fairly heavy consistency. Maple is not very absorbent, while pine is porous and generally absorbs the stain in patches. Unfortunately, these patches cannot be detected until after the stain has been applied. The heavy oil stain, because it permits an opportunity for extra rubbing with cloth or fine

steel wool, is excellent for obtaining tone effects. Its use allows the worker a greater margin of control in obtaining the desired tones and uniformity of color.

High Lighting

Oil stains, especially when they are mixed heavy, lend themselves well to the process of high lighting, or toning an article for contrasting tonal effects. In the finishing of furniture made of pine, maple, oak, chestnut, and certain other woods, it is often desirable to produce varying tones in the finished color. Table tops assume a richer and more vital appearance when the mid-portions and corners are a few shades lighter in tone than other portions. The central area of legs, rails, and aprons should be in contrast, remaining somewhat lighter in tone than the darker sections at the points of joinery. These effects may be obtained by rubbing off the oil stain with additional vigor where the lighter shades are desired. Fine steel wool also helps to remove excessive stain. Indeed, the final appearance of the work will warrant the additional effort involved.

The Shellac Finish

Shellac, as it is prepared commercially, is usually composed of four pounds of shellac gum mixed in one gallon of alcohol. This mixture is referred to as a "4-lb. cut." However, it is not wise to apply the shellac directly to the work in this consistency. It should be diluted.

Before proceeding with any of the steps of shellacking, the worker should be sure that the article to be covered is thoroughly dry and clean, that no dust or dirt is adhering to the surfaces, and that it is altogether ready for the final finishing steps.

For the first coat, the regular commercial shellac should be cut with alcohol in any amount varying from one-third to one-half. It should be almost *water thin*. As shellac dries quickly when it is being applied, the worker should proceed briskly and evenly, working with the grain of the wood to avoid over brushing. The first thin coat is absorbed into the wood and provides a base for further coats.

After each coat of shellac, the work should be carefully rubbed with fine steel wool. Ordinarily, three or four coats of shellac will provide an excellent finish. The final coat may be sprinkled with fine pumice stone and rubbed with an oil-soaked felt pad to obtain perfect smoothness. Afterward the work should be thoroughly waxed, both to protect the finish and to bring it to a beautiful luster.

It is generally agreed that the shellac finish should not be applied over a stain that has been mixed in alcohol; or for that matter, over any other type of spirit stain. The alcohol in the shellac is apt to cut and fade stains of this type.

The Varnish Finish

Varnish has many advantages over other types of finishing agents in that it may be applied more easily and provides an excellent luster. However, it is by no means impervious to damage and, unless a specially fine quality of varnish is used, it will, in time, crack and check, and require refinishing.

One of the first requisites in varnishing is to find a dust-free work room. The very fact that varnish dries slowly, makes it vulnerable to any dust or dirt which may come in contact with it during the drying period.

However, after the varnish has been suitably cut with turpentine, the worker will delight in the fine free fashion in which it flows from the brush. Indeed, as the work is being brushed, ample time can be taken to smooth out the brush strokes, pick up drips, and examine and re-touch all parts of the article.

Although there are a number of quick-drying varnishes on the market, and while most of these are excellent, still the worker should allow ample time for each coat of varnish to become thoroughly dry. When this time arrives, each coat in turn is carefully rubbed and smoothed with fine garnet paper, before the next coat is applied. This provides an even binding surface for the succeeding coat.

Three good coats of varnish generally suffice. The final coat, which should be rubbed to a smooth luster, is polished thoroughly with a mixture of fine pumice stone and rottenstone, or with rottenstone alone. The rubbing is performed with an oil-soaked felt pad. After all parts have been carefully polished, the finished article may be waxed, both for extra luster and to protect the finish.

The Lacquer Finish

Lacquer is a comparatively new commercial finishing product. However, a product bearing this name has been used in the Orient since the beginning of civilization. Because of its many excellent qualities it has been greeted with much enthusiasm by manufacturers. It is used to a great extent by the furniture industry.

Lacquer provides an exceptionally durable finish. It does not crack or mar very readily and it resists the action of liquids, as well as changing climatic conditions. Moreover, it dries quickly and with the proper equipment is not difficult to apply.

Although lacquer may be obtained in various shades and colors, we are concerned at present with its use in clear form, that is, like shellac and varnish. The ingredients of lacquer (it contains a high percentage of lead acetate, or "banana oil") make it injurious to many stained surfaces. For this reason, it is wise to first cover the stain with one or more sealing coats of shellac, before any lacquer is applied.

Because it is extremely quick in drying, the most satisfactory way of applying lacquer is with an air brush. When skillfully sprayed on the work it dries uniformly and evenly. However, if it is properly diluted with its exclusive thinner (lacquer thinner) it may be brushed on, providing, of course, that the worker proceeds with due caution and takes care not to repeat brush strokes.

There are two schools of thought regarding the treatment of lacquer after it has been applied. Some assert that each coat should be sanded or steel-wooled in the manner of varnish and shellac, while others maintain that the dull even luster of the untouched lacquer should provide the final finish. However, if the final coat is carefully rubbed with either fine steel wool or pumice, no harm will result and, indeed, the beauty of the surface may be enhanced by this additional attention.

Natural Finishes—Oil Finish

For bringing out the inherent characteristics of wood, for the beautification of fine graining, and for the development of a lovely natural luster, no type of finish can excel that which is obtained with boiled linseed oil. The luxurious, rich tones which oil produces in natural walnut, gumwood, teak, mahogany, and similar hardwoods, causes this type of finish to be especially desirable. Moreover, the surface which is treated with oil is amply protected against ordinary damage, and it may be freshened up at any time with new applications of oil.

To produce this finish, it is first necessary to thin the boiled linseed oil with an equal quantity of turpentine. It is applied with a brush, excess oil being removed with an absorbent rag. Successive coats of oil are applied, up to three or four, allowing each coat to dry before applying the next. The final coat is carefully rubbed with a clean cloth until a warm luster has been produced. The oil penetrates the wood, and once it has hardened, there is little likelihood of it coming off and soiling covers or clothing.

Orange Shellac Finish

To obtain a beautiful natural finish on light colored woods, pine especially, the work should be left unstained and finished with a mixture of orange and white shellac. The two colors of shellac are mixed to a light orange tone and diluted from one-third to one-half, with alcohol.

Ordinarily three coats of shellac will suffice; each coat, after it has dried, being carefully rubbed with fine steel wool. After the final rubbing, the work is thoroughly waxed.

This natural finish is especially recommended for pine, maple, birch, and cherry, as it permits the wood to age and darken to its own excellent tone.

Wax Finish

It has already been noted that waxing plays an important part in the proper finishing of wood. Indeed, some very effective finishes have been accomplished with stain and wax alone. If the worker so chooses, he may proceed to wax his work immediately after the stain has become thoroughly dry. Let him be reminded, however, that the plain wax finish is absolutely dependent upon perfectly smooth initial sanding. It is not well to attempt such a finish on any woods other than those of the close-grained varieties. Coarse-grained woods must be finished by other methods.

The principal idea in waxing is to obtain and to keep the finished beauty and luster of the wood. As furniture becomes older, it may, from time to time, be waxed again. This process protects its original freshness of finish and also enhances the more mature tones which age produces in wood.

There are several types of wax which may be used in this work. Many wood finishers employ a wax which is obtained by mixing beeswax and turpentine. It is prepared by dissolving beeswax in turpentine for at least two days. To this heavy wax solution is added a small amount of burnt umber for coloring purposes.

The better varieties of commercial paste wax also serve excellently for this work. Burnt umber or a blending of colors in oil should be added to any wax so as to tint it to match the finish. This treatment prevents the possibility of conspicuous smudges where wax is likely to dry. Wax, of natural color, may otherwise adhere in places of joining, leaving such places noticeably off color.

It is well to apply the wax evenly with a small, soft, cloth pad. While usually it is proper to let the wax remain on all parts for an extended period of time before rubbing, it is only advisable to do so when the temperature of the room in which the work is being performed, is sufficiently high to prevent hard setting. The object in letting wax stand is to help the worker in obtaining a proper luster, but in a cold room the wax may become so hard that it will be difficult to remove it successfully. Under such conditions, the wax should be rubbed with a

Small dents and depressions lifted with wet
blotting paper and hot iron

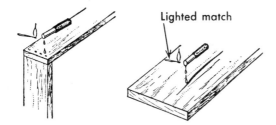

Lighted match

Stick shellac used to fill nail depressions and cracks

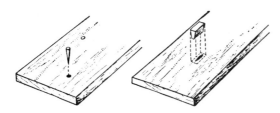

Pegs and wedges used to repair small holes
and damaged areas

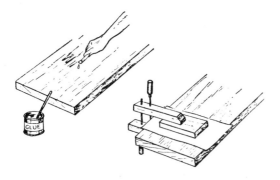

Grain splinters carefully glued and clamped

soft lintless cloth shortly after it has been applied. Subsequent waxing will further develop the luster.

A commercial product (*Minwax*) has appeared on the market which combines stain and wax. It may be applied directly to the work, which is later rubbed to a dull luster.

How to Paint

The same basic rules carry through in painting that apply in preparing work for a natural finish. Naturally, however, painting is not quite as precise an operation as shellacking or varnishing. In most cases, paint will serve to conceal many of the blemishes which might mar or damage the appearance of work which is finished naturally. But it is a good idea to prepare carefully the surface on which paint is to be applied.

Surfaces should be well sanded and free of grease spots, dirt, cracks, or nail holes. Nail holes and cracks can be filled with putty or with a similar filling substance, after the priming coat of paint has dried, and sanded flush to the surface of adjoining parts. Porous, open-grained woods should be carefully filled.

It is always wise to give the work a priming coat of paint before proceeding with additional coats. The priming coat is absorbed by the wood and provides a base for the coats which follow. Where several successive coats are to be applied, each coat, in turn, should be carefully sanded to perfect smoothness. The final coat is then evenly applied and permitted to remain unsanded.

One or more priming coats should always be applied as a base for enamel. One coat of enamel will suffice. Of late, there has appeared on the market a new type of enamel which covers the work thoroughly with a single coat. On new work, however, even with enamel of this character, at least one priming coat of paint should be used.

Lacquer is popularly used where bright color effects are desired. It is especially effective for indoor and outdoor furniture. As previously explained, lacquer is exceedingly fast in drying and as a result it must be applied quickly. Best results are obtained by spraying it on the work. However, if it is properly thinned with lacquer thinner it may be applied by brush. The worker must proceed alertly and *must not repeat brush strokes*. Two or three coats of colored lacquer are usually sufficient.

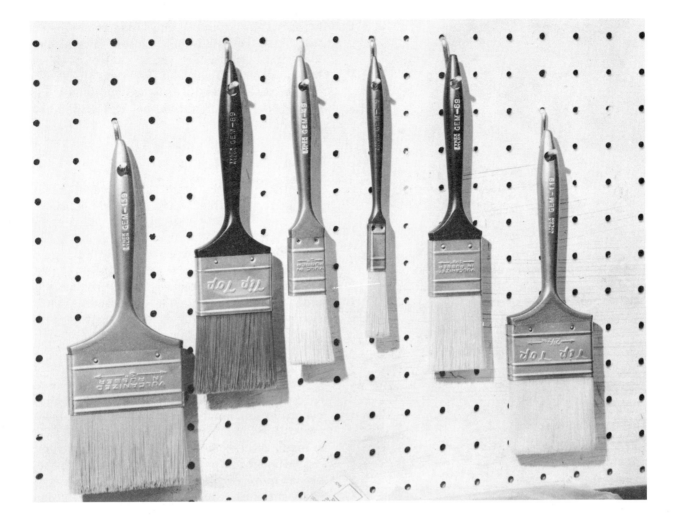

Care of Brushes and Finishing Equipment

It almost goes without saying that paints, shellacs, varnishes, stains, and so forth, should always be kept in air-tight containers when they are not in actual use. White shellac is subject to a degree of damage if it is kept in the light. For this reason it should be kept in an earthenware light-proof container. It will corrode the ordinary metal can and leak away, if kept over an extended period.

A sealed metal container should be kept handy for storing steel wool, rags, pumice stone, and associated materials.

It is a good idea to wash brushes out in a brush-cleaning solution, various brands of which may be purchased in hardware stores, after they have been used. In this way the bristles are kept clean and soft. They may be left in water to which a small amount of the cleaning powder has been added, but they should never be permitted to rest on their bristles. This causes the

New *Snap-a-Brush* has disposable cartridge of polyurethane foam; it can be inexpensively replaced to eliminate brush cleaning. *U.S. Plywood-Champion Papers, Inc.*

129

Spray finishes, in cans, are handy for small projects or for touching up finished parts. *Pittsburgh Plate Glass* Co.

Spraying equipment can be used to advantage for finishing most projects. Skillful spraying produces professional results. *Burgess Vibrocrafters, Inc.*

Paint rollers save time when finishing large areas. They can be used to advantage for painting full-size panels. *Pittsburgh Plate Glass Co.*

bristles to bend and in time renders the brush worthless. To avoid this damage, it is a good idea to hammer a tack in the mid part of the brush handle and suspend the brush on the rim of the can so that its bristles, while they are immersed in the liquid, do not rest on the bottom of the can.

Sprayers and Rollers

In the industrial paint shop, production finishing is performed with elaborate spraying equipment. Usually the article to be finished moves along a conveyor belt and is rapidly spray-finished by an expert operator. The entire process of finishing a piece of furniture requires but a few minutes. Because of the scientific techniques employed and the professional proficiency of the operator in handling the spray gun, the resulting finish is excellent.

While it would not be practical for the home craftsman to invest in elaborate spraying equipment, modified models of compressor-sprayers are available for home use. If a large volume of finishing work is contemplated sprayers of this type should be investigated.

Small, electric sprayers of the type illustrated can be bought at nominal cost — and while they do not quite produce the results of the heavy-duty spraying equipment, they do save time when quantities of work require finishing. Also, various types of paints, stains, and clear finishes may now be purchased in aerosol cans for pressure spraying. These are especially useful for finishing small projects — or, for touch-up of present finishes.

Regardless of what type of spraying equipment is used, the beginner will discover that there's a definite trick to spraying. The idea is to work fast and systematically. Sprayed areas should not be *oversprayed*. Finishing agents tend to build up and produce ugly drips and "curtains" if sprayed too heavily. The best idea is to try some practice spraying on scraps of wood before progressing to actual projects.

Another important time saver is the paint roller. When large surfaces are to be finished, the roller can outperform the paint brush in a fraction of its time — and usually produces much smoother results. Rollers are now designed for practically every painting and finishing purpose. They come in various sizes, shapes, and types. Investigate their variety and many applications if a large volume of work is anticipated.

Stain and Plastic Coating

1 Chair with finishing materials, ready for staining and finishing.

2 All parts are thoroughly sanded with fine sandpaper.

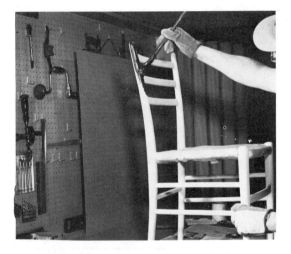

3 Stain is started at the top and brushed along one part at a time.

4 Excess stain is removed with rag from each part.

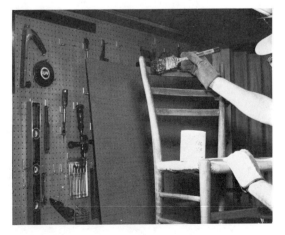

5 After stain becomes thoroughly dry, plastic coating is brushed on.

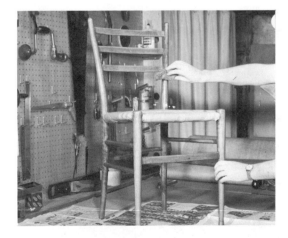

6 Between coats, after drying period, fine steel wool is used to polish all parts.

Color Matching

One of the greatest boons for the do-it-yourself painter and wood finisher is the color matching system recently introduced by prominent paint manufacturers. With this system you can take a sample of practically any color to your paint dealer and after making a spectrum analysis of the tones involved, he can mix paints and enamels to match the exact colors you want.

When the colors have been matched, the dealer affixes code numbers to the container specifying the precise ingredients. Thus if you need to reorder and duplicate the color it is only necessary to give your dealer the code numbers.

This is especially helpful when you happen to spot an exact shade of color — or, compatible combinations of colors — which please your taste for interior decor. All you need are samples of the colors themselves. You can even duplicate them from color pages of magazines and homemakers' literature.

Also, as illustrated below, you can now match wood stains to tones of related furniture. A stain matching system, called Weldwood Color Tones, makes it possible to mix over one hundred separate wood tones to match any desired shade. The stain is made of colorants which come in plastic pods to be mixed with two bases — light and dark. To obtain the exact stain tone, it is merely necessary to refer to dealers' color chip samples which show the various tones and specify the required mixture of colorant and base to produce each shade.

This new stain system differs from other pigmented wiping stains because penetration is controlled by a formula which ensures uniform effects on both soft and hard woods.

Color tone stains are mixed to match over 100 selected tones. *Photos courtesy U.S. Plywood-Champion Papers, Inc.*

Matched stains are brushed evenly on the wood and allowed a few moments to penetrate.

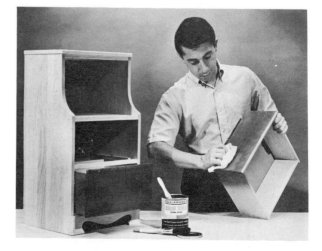

Especially effective for finishing traditional furniture, Minwax antique stain finishes, available in tones, are easy to apply and produce professional results.

Paste wax, made by Minwax, produces a soft luster on antique finishes. It complements the stain finish at left. *Photographs above: Minwax Co.*

Foam-N-Tone is a quick-drying foam stain recently introduced by U.S. Plywood-Champion Papers, Inc. It comes in aerosol pressure cans in a variety of natural wood tones. It is easy to apply and washes off hands with soap and water.

Weldwood "Award" is a liquid emulsion of lemon oil that cleans, polishes, and protects finished surfaces, *Photographs below: U.S. Plywood-Champion Papers, Inc.*

Danish Oil Finish

An excellent product, called *Watco Danish Oil Finish*, performs wonders in the natural finishing of rich grained woods. It is particularly effective for such woods as teak and walnut where it penetrates to enrich the tone and surface graining. Because of its special ingredients, successive coats act as a sealant to fill the slight porosity of these woods and thus produce a soft, lustrous surface.

As shown in the accompanying photo-sequence, Watco Danish Oil is extremely simple to apply. The finishing job only requires brushing on the oil, letting it penetrate into the wood, and then rubbing off the excess with a soft rag. It dries and does not leave an oily surface. The beauty of this finish is that it can always be refreshed with another application.

1 For final smoothing use fine sandpaper with hand block, working with the grain.

2 Oil is first applied to center areas, brushing toward edges and ends.

3 As brushing of oil progresses toward ends, watch out for "dry-out" of absorbent areas and retouch.

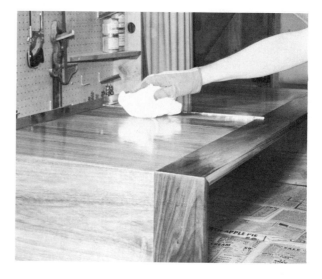

4 Within half an hour, rub off excess oil. Polish is obtained after second coat.

8

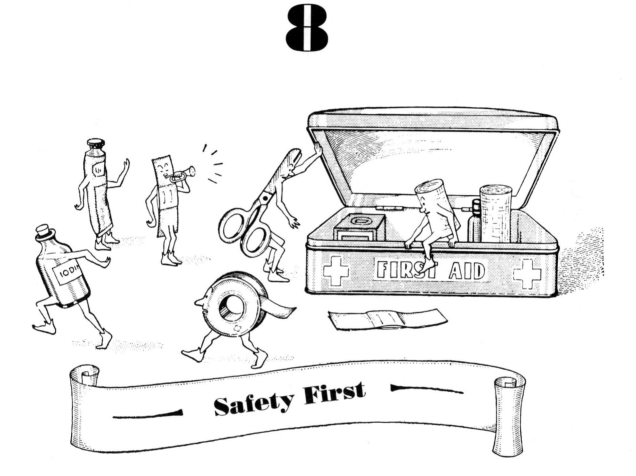

Safety First

Safety First in the Shop

We have all heard the slogans: "Watch your Step! — Look Before You Leap! — Take It Easy!" and dozens of others meaning the same thing. We have also heard that very important slogan "Safety First!"

Safety First is a practice that should be followed at all times. It is not restricted to any single type of activity but carries over to all activities and works its way into our general method of living.

Each year thousands of accidents occur which might have been avoided. Carelessness is the cause of most accidents. The classic example of "The Man who didn't know the gun was loaded" demonstrates the exact manner in which many of these accidents occur. Also remember that the shop is a place where accidents *can* and *do* occur. So is the bathtub. But this circumstance does not prevent us from taking a bath.

When working in the shop, however, we should become acquainted with the things that *may* cause trouble. If we know about them we can avoid them. So, let us review some of these shop hazards and see what can be done to prevent accidents.

Undoubtedly there are more *safe ways* of doing a job than there are *unsafe ways*. Being in a hurry or trying to take short-cuts to gain speed, frequently ends up in a serious accident. You may be able to get away with a few occasional short-cuts, but according to the law of averages you will get hurt sooner or later.

Don't take chances! We hear lots of talk these days about different types of machines being "fool-proof." Unfortunately there is generally a fool who will come along to revoke this claim. Most of our woodworking machinery, properly equipped with guards and safety devices, may be considered practically fool-proof. Still, if it is not used the right way, accidents may occur that could have been prevented.

There are a number of safety suggestions that we should consider. First of all it is not a good thing to let the shop floor become strewed with scraps and debris. Under such conditions the worker may slip and fall, the chances of serious accidents being magnified with the presence of sharp-edged tools and machinery. If nails are

Nails left in board . . .   accidentally stepped on . . .   cause injured foot.

not removed from boards the unwary person may step on them. Don't leave boards lying around that have nail points sticking out beyond the surface.

Sharp edges and rough edges of boards are the cause of many cuts and sliver wounds. Handle rough lumber carefully. You won't be considered effeminate if you wear gloves!

Rough boards . . .   carelessly handled . . .   cause painful splinters.

Certainly the shop is not a place for horseplay or fooling around. Many tragic accidents have resulted from practical jokes and silly activity. In most cases the trouble was started by levity on the part of an individual.

We all know that the live current in the electric light socket, or floor outlet, is just waiting for a contact in order to produce active electricity. When this contact is made by a misguided person who inserts a nail, or metal object, into the socket, a severe shock will follow. We can

Live sockets and wires . . .   touched with metal objects . . .   cause severe shock.

imagine the dreadful result if this experiment is made on a high voltage power line! It is a good idea to snap off the main switch before making repairs on electrical equipment. In his repair work the electrician uses rubber gloves and tools that have insulated handles.

Never put brads, tacks, or screws in your mouth. Should you cough or stumble while they

Nails, tacks, and screws . . .   held in mouth . . .   may lead to operating table.

are in your mouth, you may swallow a few. Screws and nails are also germ carriers. There are many cases reported where acute infection has resulted from this practice.

Overheated condition . . .   when in draft of open window . . .   may cause colds and serious illness.

You may get yourself overheated while you are working and be tempted to open wide a window, in order to cool off. With your pores open and perspiration flowing freely, this is a fine way to get pneumonia. Don't do it.

Avoid the practice of throwing tools and articles to another person. This game may work out all right in a grocery store or on a skyscraper construction job, where riveters are practiced in

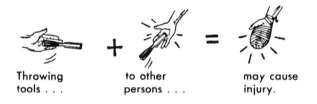

Throwing tools . . .   to other persons . . .   may cause injury.

the job of throwing hot rivets. In the shop, however, there is a possibility of your catching the sharpened edge of the tool and thus getting an ugly cut.

Get Acquainted With Your First-Aid Kit

It goes without saying that every shop should be equipped with a complete first-aid kit. Handy kits are available containing the various items that are necessary for first aid. They should be kept within easy reach.

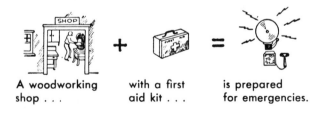

A woodworking shop . . .   with a first aid kit . . .   is prepared for emergencies.

Regardless of how trivial you may consider a cut, be on the safe side and have it looked after. In so doing you may avoid serious infection.

Small cuts and scratches may be cleansed with antiseptic soap and warm water. They should be treated with an antiseptic solution. A sterilized bandage or covering placed directly over the wound prevents exposure to dust and dirt. Various types of small prepared bandages are now on the market. They are very easily applied.

Antiseptic and bandage . . .   immediately applied to cut . . .   provides safety first.

If the cut is large and bleeding freely it is wise to see a doctor or nurse immediately. Cuts which enter veins or arteries must be given first aid with tourniquet treatment. This means that the flow of blood must be stemmed at a point above the cut. For such treatment improvise a loose sling, inserting a stick to twist and tighten. Pressure may be applied directly by pressing the fingers against the blood vessel leading to the wound, thereby stopping the flow of blood. Then take the patient to the hospital.

The layman is not qualified, except in extreme emergencies, and where a doctor is not available, to treat cuts and injuries that are of a serious nature. Nor should the layman "play doctor" in amateur fashion.

Bruises and burns require special treatment. A bruise is a type of injury in which the skin itself has not been broken, but the tissues beneath have been torn, thereby allowing blood to

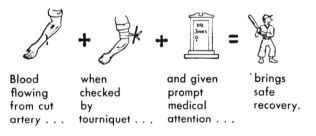

Blood flowing from cut artery . . .   when checked by tourniquet . . .   and given prompt medical attention . . .   brings safe recovery.

ooze into this area without coming to the surface. You may be tempted to open the bruise and release the "bad blood," *but don't do it.* This blunder may result in further irritation and even cause infection. When severe bruises must be opened, this is a job for a doctor.

Safety First and Power Machinery

Power machinery does, of course, present the greatest amount of risk. Circular saws, band saws, jointers, lathes, shapers — all of them — with their sharp cutting parts exposed and turning at very high speed, must at all times be watched. The error of a single second may result in a serious accident.

Fortunately, most of these machines are being manufactured with adequate guards so that their danger of operation is reduced to a minimum. Even so, they are not entirely fool-proof, and if they are not operated correctly accidents may result.

Get into the habit of paying strict attention to your work while operating a machine. The

Revolving blades and cutters . . . properly guarded . . . are safer for hands.

old trolley cars displayed a large sign which read "Don't Talk to the Motorman." This precaution should likewise be observed when a person is operating a machine.

The student or amateur should, of course, be thoroughly instructed before attempting to use a machine. There are certain definite *do's* and *don't's* which should be followed, many of which may be demonstrated. This writer recalls the instance of an instructor who was so conscientious in his demonstration of the *do's* and *don't's* that he cut off his own index finger while demonstrating a *don't*!

We all like to be helpful and it is a common thing to see amateur woodworkers trying to help each other in the operation of a machine. This should be avoided, excepting when long planks are being cut which virtually require two people for handling. Even then one person should take care of the operation of the machine while the other person walks along slowly to guide and support the extremity of the plank.

In most instances the operating of woodworking machinery is strictly a one-man job. After all, no two persons can safely operate a car at the same time. In carrying this idea over to woodworking, the would-be helpful "back-seat driver" is generally the one who causes the accidents.

Frequently we see one person snap the switch, to start a machine for another person. This practice, of course, is extremely dangerous. Suppose the worker has his hand, or a part of his

Person turning on switch . . . while another stands **unaware** at machine . . . may result in trip to hospital.

body, in the vicinity of the moving parts of the machine when the switch is snapped on!

Get into the habit of staying at your post, at the machine, even after the switch has been turned off. Modern machinery operates so quietly that it is often difficult to tell whether or not the machine is running. If you leave the machine while it is still running under full power, or while it is coasting to a stop, another person may accidentally come in contact with the moving parts and be seriously injured.

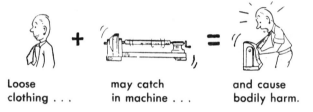

Loose clothing . . . may catch in machine . . . and cause bodily harm.

Even your clothing may provide a cause of accidents. Loose neckties and cuffs may get caught in the moving parts of the machine. It is a good idea to roll up your sleeves and tuck in your necktie before starting to work. In this way you are ready for action and thus you minimize the risk of accident.

Most of our modern machinery is equipped with guards which cover the belts, gears, pulleys, and shafts. If your machinery is not safely equipped you can probably obtain guard attachments. They are a very good investment.

Slippery floors . . . and resulting falls . . . may cause serious injuries.

A basic precaution in safeguarding the operation of a power machine is to be sure that at all times the floor in the immediate vicinity of the machine is free of any obstructions. Moreover, the area where the operator stands should afford firm and solid footing, and should be kept free of anything which might cause it to become smooth or slippery. Wide mats of corrugated rubber are often attached to the floor around the machines, which seems to be a very sensible precaution. Also, wet paint is sometimes sprinkled with fine sand, providing a non-skid footing as soon as the paint has thoroughly dried.

Then too, the person operating the circular saw must always be careful to keep his hands a good distance from the blade. If small pieces of wood are to be cut, special sticks and feeders should be introduced to safeguard the hands.

Generally speaking, it is unwise to attempt to cross-cut pieces to a required length by feeding with the material against the ripping fence. The pieces are apt to bind momentarily between the revolving blade and the ripping fence and then

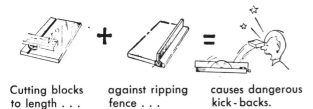

Cutting blocks to length . . .   against ripping fence . . .   causes dangerous kick-backs.

"kick back" in the direction of the operator at terrific speed. It is risky too, to attempt to rip very small pieces of wood. Here again lurks the danger of a kick back.

Operating grinder . . .   without eye protectors . . .   may result in eye injuries.

The power grinder is usually equipped with a wide lens through which you look when a tool is being sharpened. This lens is put there so that you will not get fragments of steel or abrasive in your eyes. If the grinder is not equipped in this way, a pair of goggles should be used.

Using a jointer . . .   for smoothing small blocks . . .   is extremely hazardous.

The jointer is considered by many to be one of the most dangerous machines in the shop. Indeed, there is good reason for its evil reputation, for as the cutting blades revolve at a tremendous speed there is very little hope for anything which might get in the way. Ordinarily the operator is able to keep his hands a good distance from the revolving blade as the work is being fed into the machine. It is both wise and sensible to avoid using the jointer for surfacing small pieces of wood.

Even the ordinary wood-turning lathe has several risks attached to its operation. Primarily, of course, the operator must be careful to secure all loose clothing. Then too, the various working tools must be correctly held so that they do not catch in the work and cause an accident. The lathe can be a really vicious and dangerous machine when not used in a sensible manner, and so above all — *safety first*! First and foremost, be sure the stock is securely fastened so that there is no danger of it flying out and injuring some one. This rule holds true for work mounted upon the face plate as well as for stock which is being spun between the two centers. It is always well to test the final adjust-

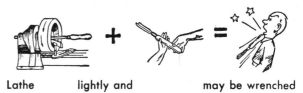

Lathe tools . . .   lightly and improperly held . . .   may be wrenched from hands.

ments by "spinning" the lathe by hand before turning on the mechanical power. And by all mean always practice on small pieces of *softwood*.

Be sure the stock is well balanced so as to avoid excessive vibration which, in itself, creates a tendency to tear the stock out of the lathe. Also, the extent of vibration increases with the increased speed; so run the lathe at slow or medium speeds until the stock is perfectly round. Be sure the tool rest is securely fastened so that it does not slip, which might cause either the cutting tool or the tool rest itself to get caught by the edges of the rough stock.

A necktie or any other flowing bits of one's clothing can easily get caught in the lathe. More than one person with long hair has had a great deal of it painfully torn from his scalp when stooping before a spinning lathe, as it became wrapped upon the fast moving cylinder. The answer to this lurking danger is: *Avoid wearing anything which may be grabbed by the spinning parts.*

Another sane caution is to refrain from touching the stock while it is in motion. A piece of wood with splinters, or edge breaks, may look perfectly smooth when spinning at high speeds. The eye, as you know, is much too slow to be able to detect these dangerous spots on rapidly turning stock and thus many a hand has been injured.

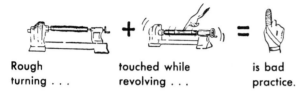

Rough turning . . . touched while revolving . . . is bad practice.

Safety First With Hand Tools

Nor are these risks limited to the operation of power machinery. Indeed, hand tools may cause severe injury if they are not used with the right amount of care. Chisels especially, are dangerous if not properly handled. The worker should always take care to use the chisel in such a way that the cutting is performed in the direction *away* from the parts of his body. Clamping the stock firmly in place and using *two hands* to operate a chisel, obviously eliminates the danger of cutting the one hand which might otherwise be used as the holding agent.

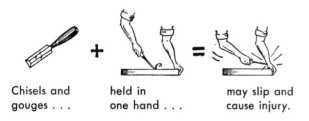

Chisels and gouges . . . held in one hand . . . may slip and cause injury.

Automatic screwdrivers should be carried about and used in such a way as to avoid the chance of the screwdriver point snapping out to full extension and injuring oneself or neighbor. Knives, and even saws, must be watched. Fortunately, in the case of hand tools, when the tool is correctly used the possible risk remains at a minimum. It is usually the careless individual who injures himself.

More accidents are caused by dull cutting tools than by those which have keen cutting edges. The sharp tool does a fine job with very little effort. On the other hand, when using a dull cutting tool such as a knife, hatchet, chisel, or saw, the work may slip or the dull tool may glance off, causing injury. After the worker has exerted and fatigued himself trying to cut with a dull tool he is apt to become careless and at this point the tool may slip and a serious cut result. Keep your tools sharp!

When handing an edged tool to another person, extend the handle first. This is both courtesy and sound practice toward accident prevention.

Even when you are carrying tools, there is a safe way of going about it. Hold the sharp edges down so that they will not come in contact with any one who is standing or walking nearby.

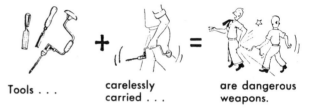

Tools . . . carelessly carried . . . are dangerous weapons.

Accidents are avoided when tools are used in the proper way. Even the plain, old-fashioned hammer, may in its blunt, unintentional way, cause trouble. Think of the number of times that people have missed the nail and bruised their thumb!

Be sure that your tools are in good condition. There is always danger that the heads of hammers, mallets, and hatchets, if not properly attached, will fly out and seriously injure some one. Loose handles on saws, chisels, and other tools may cause similar trouble.

Hammers, mallets, and hatchets . . . not properly secured . . . are extremely dangerous.

Other Causes of Shop Accidents

There are certain things that happen again and again in the woodworking shop that might just as easily be avoided. Often when driving screws people will run their finger over the head of the screw after the job has been completed. This may result in the person getting a sharp metal splinter from the screw head in the tip of his finger. While the screw is being turned a small "barb" of sharp metal may become loosened from the edge of the slot. This razor-sharp chip of metal is ready to imbed itself into the finger tip.

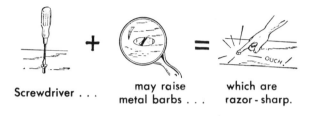

Screwdriver . . .   may raise metal barbs . . .   which are razor-sharp.

Common wood clamps are sometimes a source of trouble. Work that has been clamped together is extremely bulky and unwieldy while the clamps are fastened on it. Accidents have occurred where people have stumbled into the ends of these protruding clamps, resulting in bodily or facial injury. It is well to put the clamped work away so that people cannot stumble over it.

Beware of all things overhead! How frequently people bang their heads on protruding shelves or parts of construction that extend outward at head level. Plan your shop in such a way as to minimize this danger. Tools and lumber stacked in this manner are sources of danger to every one in the shop.

Fire Prevention as Part of Safety First

Unless it is carefully guarded the shop may become a virtual fire trap. Wood shavings and dry wood provide perfect fuel for a fire. Moreover, the materials used in wood finishing add considerably to the risk.

Kerosene, gasoline, turpentine, and other inflammable finishing solutions, should be kept tightly sealed either in bottles or metal containers. Rags and waste which has been soaked in turpentine, linseed oil, or kerosene may cause spontaneous combustion. They should either be burned after use or stored in covered metal cans. Lighted matches, pipes, or cigarettes, must of course be carefully guarded. As a general thing smoking should be prohibited in the woodworking shop.

If the shop is kept clean and tidy the fire risk will be greatly reduced.

A Healthy Shop is a Safe Shop

The shop should be a pleasant place, where you will enjoy your work. Large manufacturers have learned that shop accidents are greatly reduced when the shop itself is well lighted and well ventilated. The introduction of ventilating and blower systems which free the air of dust

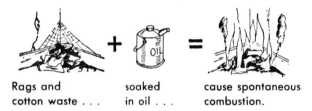

Rags and cotton waste . . .   soaked in oil . . .   cause spontaneous combustion.

and particles of dirt, have gone a long way toward reducing accidents. Good lighting, both natural and artificial, likewise safeguards the worker. Together with the other things that have been mentioned, these features are tremendously important. The healthy shop is the safe shop. After all, the protection of health is the first rule of "Safety First in the Shop."

A woodworking shop . . .   hygienically planned . . .   is a healthy place to work.

9

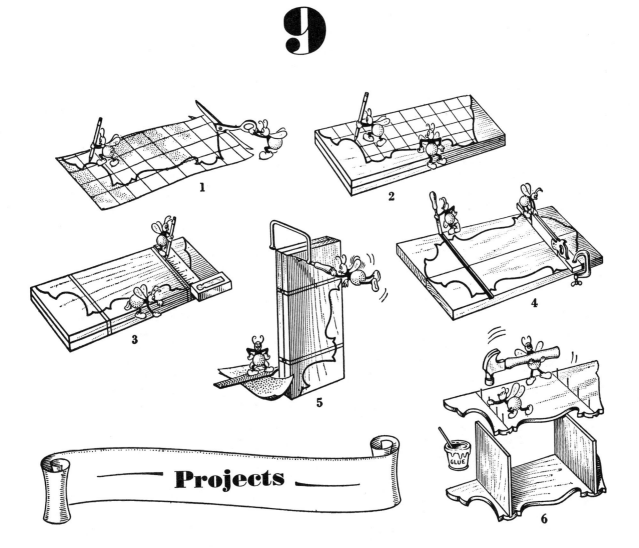

1

2

3

4

5

Projects

6

Woodworking Projects

The following fifty pages of project designs and plans are intended to offer diversified ideas which will challenge the skills of both amateur and advanced woodworkers. Obviously, no attempt has been made to restrict this offering to projects of homogeneous style or purpose. To the contrary, styles and types of projects are deliberately mixed in the hope that the assortment may guarantee something of interest to all.

But an intense effort has been made to offer projects of positive value — designs that are in good taste and that when carefully constructed will reward the maker with something useful and attractive to compliment his craftsmanship. Considering the wide range of woodworking skills — *from beginners to master craftsmen —* it was deemed desirable to provide project designs for all grades of abilities. Thus, starting with the most elementary shelves and projects of prefabricated, put-together parts, they then progress to advanced joinery, wood turning and the more sophisticated woodworking techniques detailed in text of preceding chapters.

Workbench, Tool Board, and Supply Cabinet

The sturdy workbench, illustrated below, brings together a variety of desirable features. It is made of stock materials — 2″ x 4″ legs, 1″ x 4″ rails and aprons, with plywood reinforcement panels bracing the ends and back. Since all parts are sawed square to be butted, bolted, and nailed together, there are no constructional complications.

Following this plan, you can build your workbench to any desired length. The top is made of heavy planking or a double thickness of ¾″ plywood.

Make the tool board backing with a panel of pegboard of standard 8′ length or sawed to desired length. Framing boards and shelves are squared to size of ¾″ x 6″ lumber. Since the pegboard back panel also braces the frame, nails can be used for fastening. However, before driving nails near the ends of framing boards, drill pilot holes to prevent end splitting.

A supply cabinet, such as the one on page 146, provides compartmented shelf space for a number of powered tools as well as additional room for materials and supplies. It complements

Designs by author for Millers Falls Co.

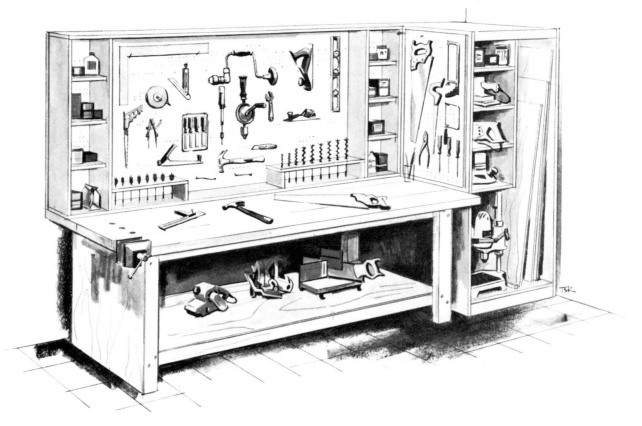

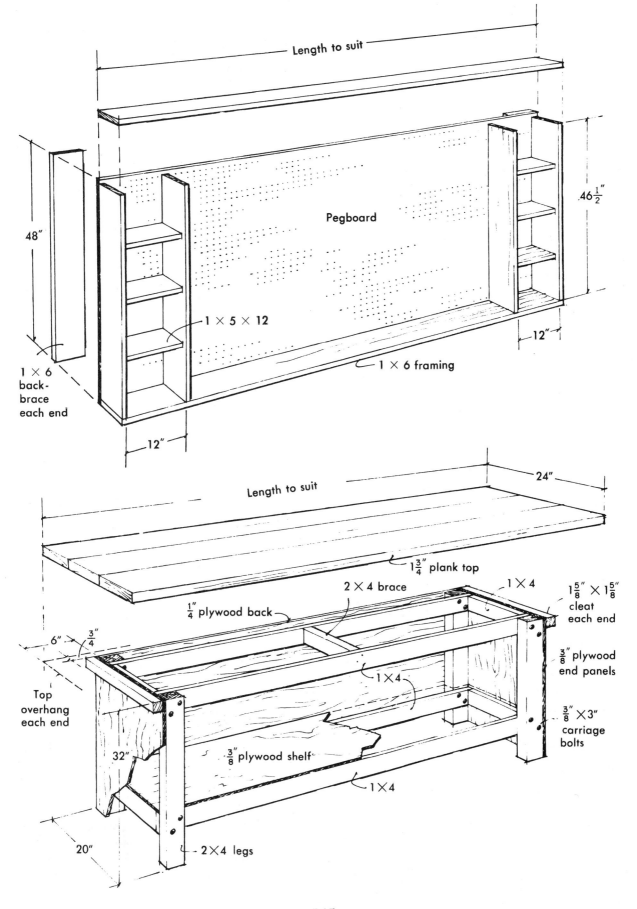

Length to suit

48"

.46 1/2"

Pegboard

1 × 5 × 12

1 × 6 framing

1 × 6
back-
brace
each end

12"

12"

Length to suit

24"

1 3/4" plank top

1 × 4

1 5/8" × 1 5/8"
cleat
each end

2 × 4 brace

1/4" plywood back

6"   3/4"

3/8" plywood
end panels

1 × 4

3/8" × 3"
carriage
bolts

Top
overhang
each end

32"

3/8" plywood shelf

1 × 4

20"

2 × 4 legs

145

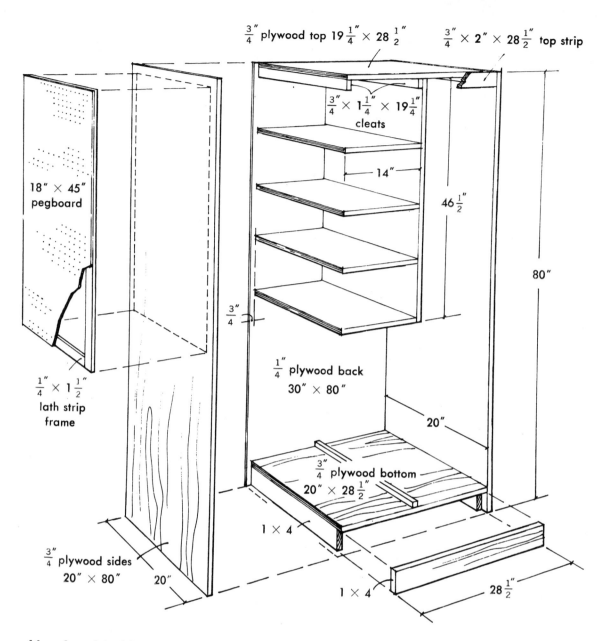

$\frac{3}{4}''$ plywood top $19\frac{1}{4}'' \times 28\frac{1}{2}''$

$\frac{3}{4}'' \times 2'' \times 28\frac{1}{2}''$ top strip

$\frac{3}{4}'' \times 1\frac{1}{4}'' \times 19\frac{1}{4}''$ cleats

14"

$46\frac{1}{2}$

80"

18" × 45" pegboard

$\frac{3}{4}$

$\frac{1}{4}''$ plywood back 30" × 80"

20"

$\frac{1}{4}'' \times 1\frac{1}{2}''$ lath strip frame

$\frac{3}{4}''$ plywood bottom 20" × $28\frac{1}{2}''$

1 × 4

$\frac{3}{4}''$ plywood sides 20" × 80"

20"

1 × 4

$28\frac{1}{2}''$

the workbench and tool board designs and completes the organization of a practical workshop. While the supply cabinet is usually made of ¾" plywood it can also be built of lumber. Like the preceding workshop designs, all parts are simply and strongly butted together and fastened with nails and screws.

Beginning Projects

Start something simple. But be sure it's practical and attractive. Few homes, for instance, have enough shelves or places to put books. Yet the work involved in producing wall shelves and bookcases requires only a few tools and little woodworking skill.

Illustrated at the right, and on the following

nine pages, with construction details, are some elementary ideas of this sort which can be undertaken by the beginner.

Shelf-type projects, shown on the next two pages, are made of standard boards squared to desired lengths. Other easy projects are better built of plywood.

Starting with these simple but useful ideas the beginning craftsman may progress to the more advanced projects which follow. While the first few projects require only beginners' instructions of Chapter 3, constant reference should be made to instructional chapters of the book for specific information on related aspects of project construction. Whatever instruction the job requires is explained in one or more of the preceding chapters.

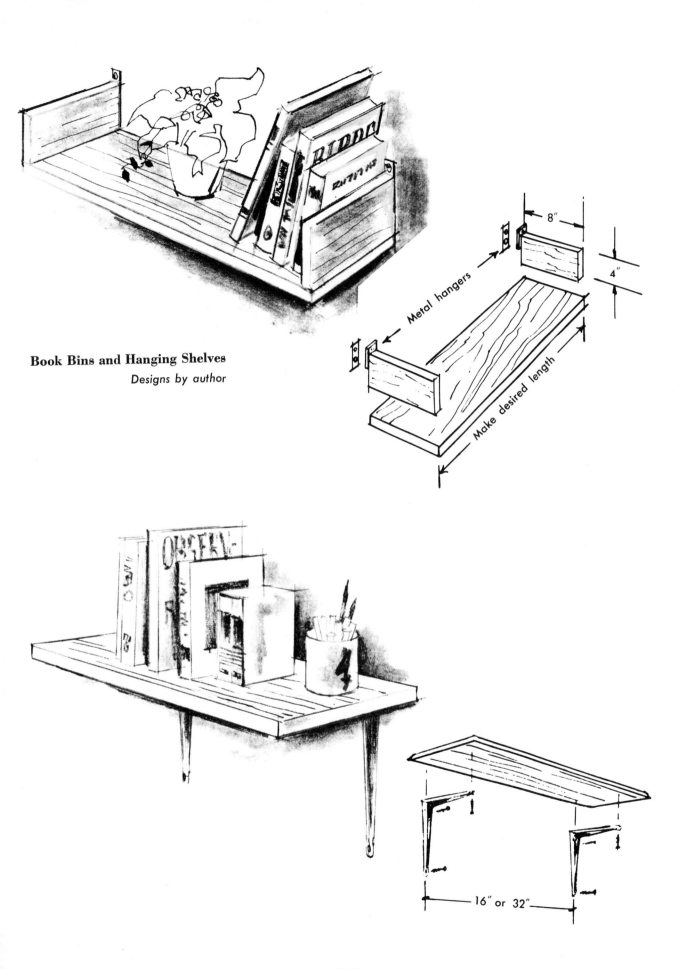

Book Bins and Hanging Shelves
Designs by author

8"

4"

Metal hangers

Make desired length

16" or 32"

147

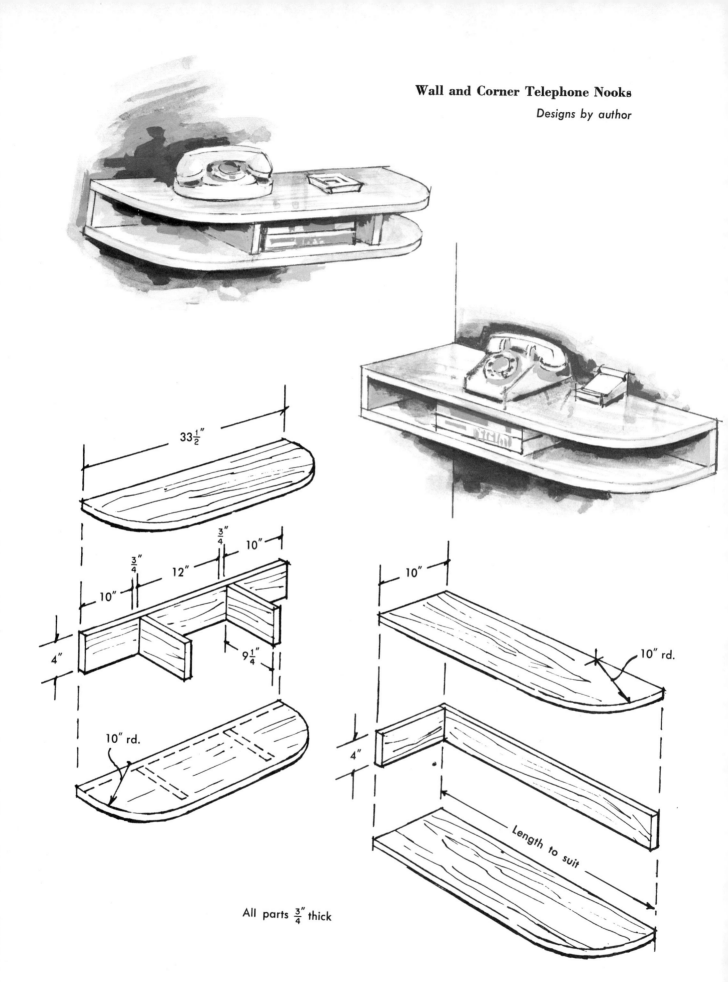

33$\frac{1}{2}$"

$\frac{3}{4}$"

$\frac{3}{4}$"

10"

12"

10"

10"

4"

9$\frac{1}{4}$

10" rd.

10" rd.

4"

Length to suit

All parts $\frac{3}{4}$" thick

148

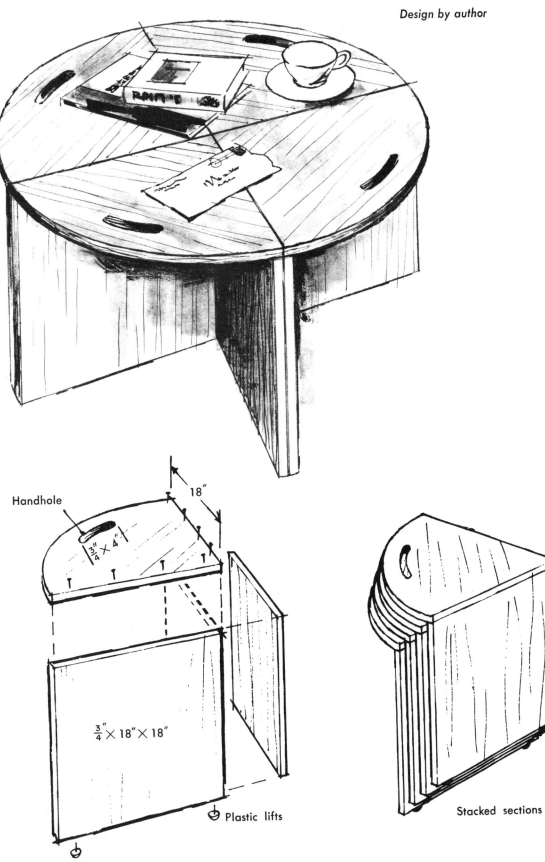

Handhole

18"

$\frac{3}{4}" \times 4"$

$\frac{3}{4}" \times 18" \times 18"$

Plastic lifts

Stacked sections

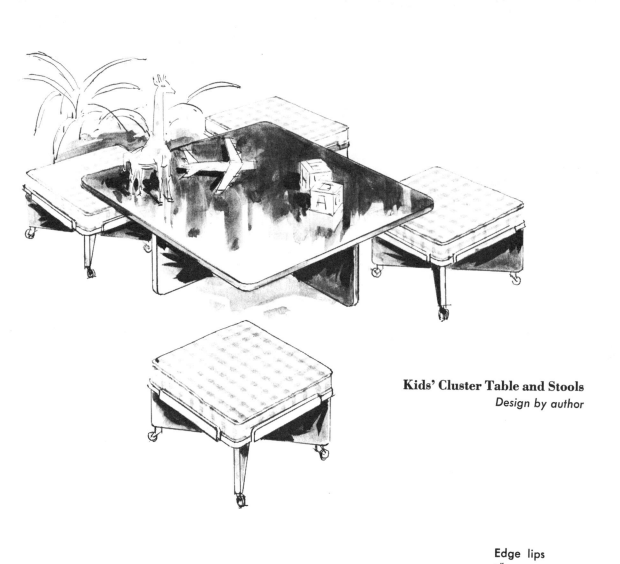

Kids' Cluster Table and Stools
Design by author

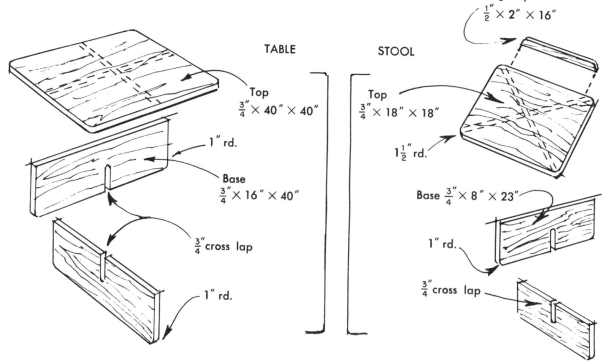

TABLE

Top
$\frac{3}{4}" \times 40" \times 40"$

1" rd.

Base
$\frac{3}{4}" \times 16" \times 40"$

$\frac{3}{4}"$ cross lap

1" rd.

STOOL

Edge lips
$\frac{1}{2}" \times 2" \times 16"$

Top
$\frac{3}{4}" \times 18" \times 18"$

$1\frac{1}{2}"$ rd.

Base $\frac{3}{4}" \times 8" \times 23"$

1" rd.

$\frac{3}{4}"$ cross lap

150

Cross-Lap Companions

Bases for a variety of attractive tables and stools are made by the simple process of sawing half-way, center slots for reciprocal, cross-lap fitting. (See the discussion of lap joints on pages 70 and 71.) The joint is then secured with glue. These designs are made of plywood which is sanded and painted in accordance with instructions of Chapter 7.

Design by author

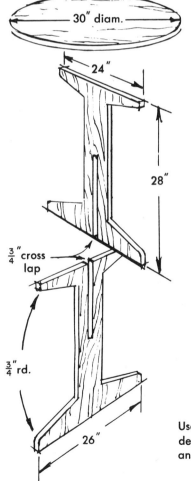

30" diam.

24"

28"

$\frac{3}{4}$" cross lap

$\frac{3}{4}$" rd.

26"

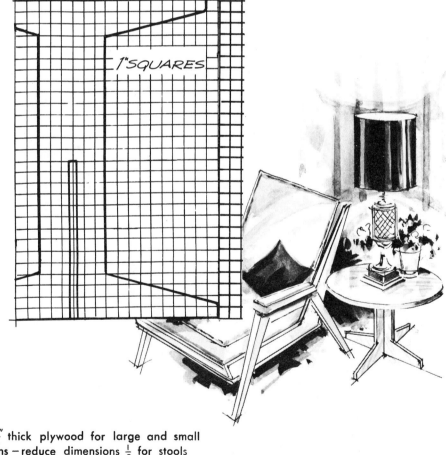

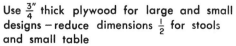

1"SQUARES

Use $\frac{3}{4}$" thick plywood for large and small designs — reduce dimensions $\frac{1}{2}$ for stools and small table

Book Bins
Design by author

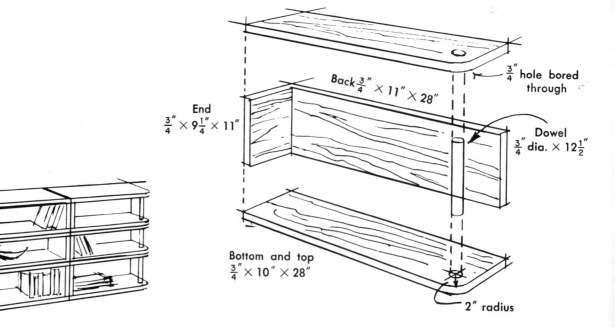

Back $\frac{3}{4}'' \times 11'' \times 28''$

End
$\frac{3}{4}'' \times 9\frac{1}{4}'' \times 11''$

$\frac{3}{4}''$ hole bored
through

Dowel
$\frac{3}{4}''$ dia. $\times 12\frac{1}{2}''$

Bottom and top
$\frac{3}{4}'' \times 10'' \times 28''$

2" radius

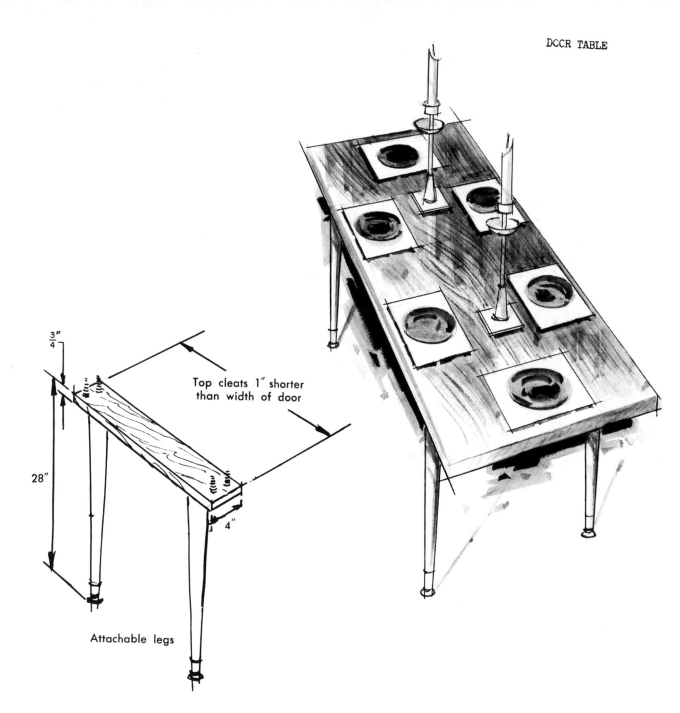

$\frac{3}{4}''$

Top cleats 1" shorter than width of door

28"

4"

Attachable legs

Instant Tables

Flush-panel doors — the hollow-core type that can be bought inexpensively at lumber yards and building supply stores — provide the clue to quick construction of various types of tables. When mounted on attachable legs they make practical furniture which belies the simplicity of its origin.

Most commonly manufactured in lengths of 80" and in widths, graduating by 2", from 18" to 36", the doors are laminated of thin plywood with Philippine mahogany, birch and maple most commonly used as surface veneers. Wood staves, bonded diagonally, are spaced to rein-force the hollow core. For this reason, durable fastenings for leg connections cannot be made within the hollow area. Thus, as shown in accompanying detail, flat cleats are glued to the under surface with end screws catching the solid edges.

The 80" lengths of most flush doors may exceed room requirements. However, they can be sawed off to manageable lengths by following the step-by-step procedures pictured on page 56. The surface veneers of most doors have good natural graining which may be enhanced with stains and/or clear finishes. But they can also be covered with *MACtac* self-adhesive vinyls or rich wood veneers as described in Chapter 3 .

Work Table

If you need a handy work table which can be taken apart for closet storage and is light enough to lift from room to room, nothing is easier to make than the design pictured at the left. As shown in working detail, construction consists merely of fastening attachable legs to a plywood top. While the resulting table may be painted, its appearance is improved when the top is covered with *MACtac* self-adhesive vinyl veneer with legs stained to match.

It should be noted that many types of large and small tables may be easily assembled on the same principle. Dimensions of the top may be altered to individual needs — and the attachable legs come in various lengths for high or low elevations.

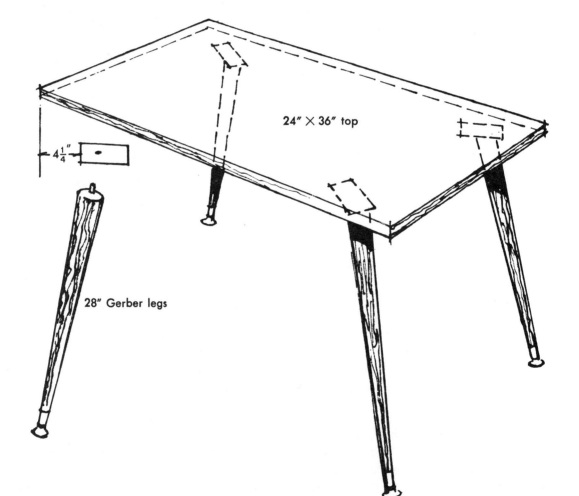

4¼″

24″ × 36″ top

28″ Gerber legs

Pedestal Console

With the help of pre-assembled pedestal bases, low tables to sit beside chairs or sofas may be quickly assembled simply by adding a plywood top. Pedestals are also available in 28″ heights for full-size tables. The tops, of course, can be of any desired shape — square or round.

While the work of producing pedestal furniture may be further simplified by merely sanding and painting the top, richer effects are obtained when the plywood is veneered. This can be done in Formica, vinyl, self-adhesive covering or with natural wood veneers as illustrated with the model pictured. The various veneering processes are described in Chapter 3.

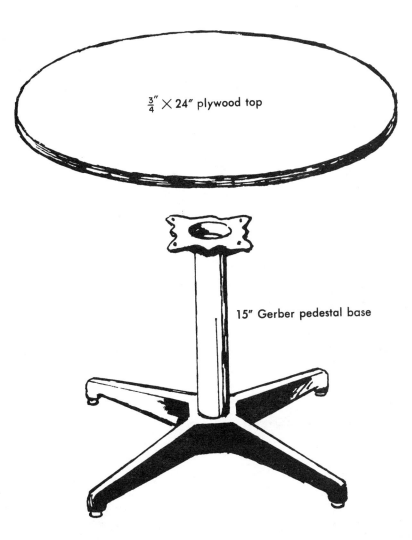

$\frac{3''}{4} \times 24''$ plywood top

15″ Gerber pedestal base

Magazine Rack

Don't let the idea of making special iron legs stop you from building this useful accessory. You can make a plywood base instead, if you choose, simply by butting two pieces of plywood together to the dimensions shown on plan.

Cut spacers and ½″ fir plywood partitions to size, sand edges and round top corners slightly. Fasten both spacers to edge of center partition with glue and 8d nails driven through from each side. Then cover nails by attaching front and back partition to spacers with glue and 6d finish nails. Set heads slightly, fill, sand, and finish as recommended to contrast with color of legs. (Design courtesy American Plywood Association.)

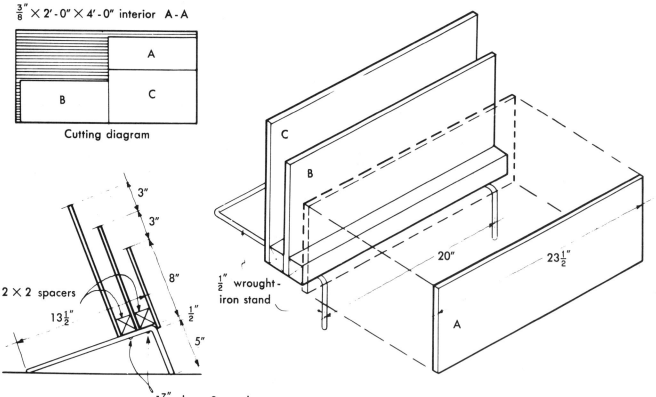

$\frac{3}{8}″ \times 2′\text{-}0″ \times 4′\text{-}0″$ interior A-A

A

B   C

Cutting diagram

3″

3″

8″

½″

5″

2 × 2 spacers

13½″

½″ wrought-iron stand

20″

23½″

C

B

A

$1\frac{7}{8}″$ r.h. no.8 wood screws

Ladder Bench

Casual ladder benches are fine for furnishing most rooms. They can be used beside room dividers, or can be stretched along walls with colorful throw cushions for auxiliary seating. Construction requires only the patience of boring a series of ¾″ dowel holes and simple fitting of cross rails and attachable legs. When boring the dowel holes, the two side rails should be clamped together and bored simultaneously to assure accuracy of alignment. Following the same construction, you can also shorten the bench to make a luggage stand to fit at the foot of a bed. (Photo courtesy American Plywood Association.)

Rail—end detail

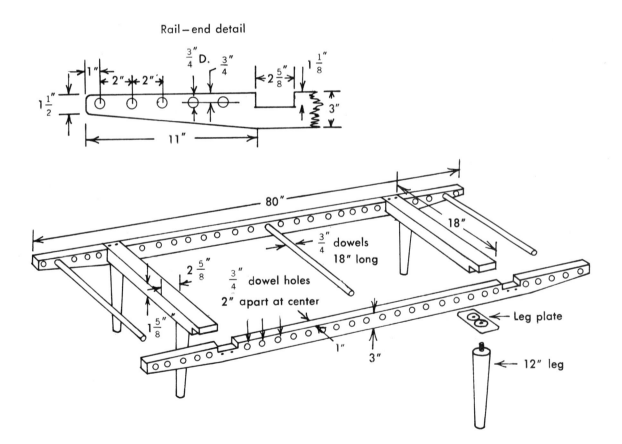

Laminated Cutting Boards

Because of the many services they perform around the house, laminated cutting boards have become extremely popular. As well as providing a base for slicing bread and chopping vegetables, the more substantial boards illustrated here can carry the roast for table carving or be used as a serving board for cheese and crackers or between-meal snacks.

These are heavy boards, laminated of walnut and maple. The strips are bonded together with waterproof glue — so, there should be no fear of their coming apart when washed in warm water. Occasional scrubbing with metal-wool followed by fresh applications of vegetable oil will keep your cutting boards bright and serviceable.

Design by author

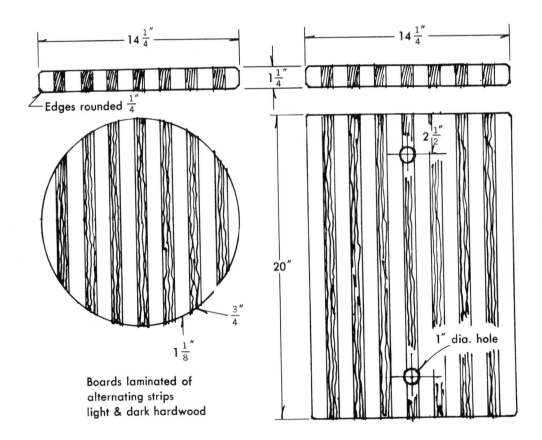

$14\frac{1}{4}''$

Edges rounded $\frac{1}{4}''$

$14\frac{1}{4}''$

$1\frac{1}{4}''$

$2\frac{1}{2}''$

$20''$

$\frac{3}{4}''$

$1''$ dia. hole

$1\frac{1}{8}''$

Boards laminated of
alternating strips
light & dark hardwood

Carving Caddy

Acting as a sturdy housing for the rectangular cutting board pictured on the opposite page, the carving caddy will find plenty of uses in your kitchen — and it can also be brought in alongside the dining table for carving and serving the roast. For this purpose, ball casters should be attached as suggested in the plan.

Construction of the caddy introduces a new and simplified method of plywood joinery. This involves only butt fastening — nailing and gluing together — of four, integral, side and leg sections. This eliminates the necessity of making separate joints to connect the legs and top aprons. And since the plywood maintains strength in both directions, the resulting table frame is practically as strong as it would be if made of one piece.

Design by author

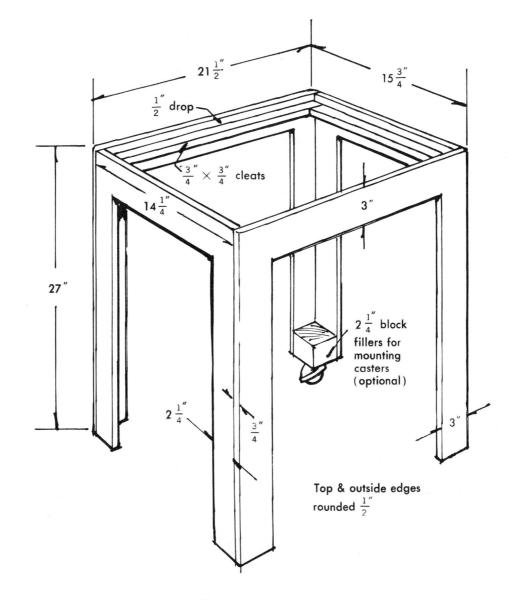

$21\frac{1}{2}''$

$15\frac{3}{4}''$

$\frac{1}{2}''$ drop

$\frac{3}{4}'' \times \frac{3}{4}''$ cleats

$14\frac{1}{4}''$

$3''$

$27''$

$2\frac{1}{4}''$ block fillers for mounting casters (optional)

$2\frac{1}{4}''$

$\frac{3}{4}''$

$3''$

Top & outside edges rounded $\frac{1}{2}''$

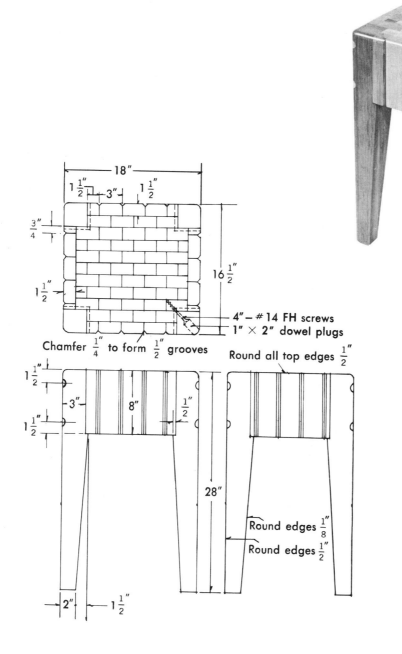

18"

1½" 3" 1½"

¾"

1½"

16½"

4" – #14 FH screws
1" × 2" dowel plugs

Chamfer ¼" to form ½" grooves

Round all top edges ½"

1½"

3" 8" ½"

1½"

28"

Round edges ⅛"
Round edges ½"

2" 1½"

Design by author

Butcher Block

The current craze for butcher blocks as an auxiliary to kitchen furnishing — and their considerable cost when purchased at department stores — suggested the special design and construction of this baby elephant! While the size has been modified to space limitations of average kitchens, this should not be regarded as a diminutive affair. Indeed, it consists of 70 chunks of hardwood laminated together with waterproof glue — and it weighs approximately 70 pounds.

Obviously, the butcher block is not a project for the beginning woodworker. Its construction requires precise joinery of layers of wooden blocks which are glued and clamped together in two separate operations: First the blocks are edge joined to form slabs which are then dressed flush and surface glued together to produce the brick-like end-grain pattern. This is machine sanded and treated with repeated applications of vegetable oil.

Serving Car

Indoor or outdoors — in living room or patio — the serving car brings snacks and beverages to your delighted guests and saves you many steps going back and forth to the kitchen. The jumbo trays are removable for independent service — and the entire affair can be folded flat for closet storage.

Made of plywood and soft, do-it-yourself aluminum tubing (which may be purchased with fittings at hardware stores) the serving car is much easier to build than the illustration may suggest. The aluminum tubing may be cut to required lengths with woodworking saws. Special fittings which go with the tubing simplify assembly of parts. Plywood trays should be veneered with Formica or vinyl sheeting.

Design by author for Reynolds Metals Co.

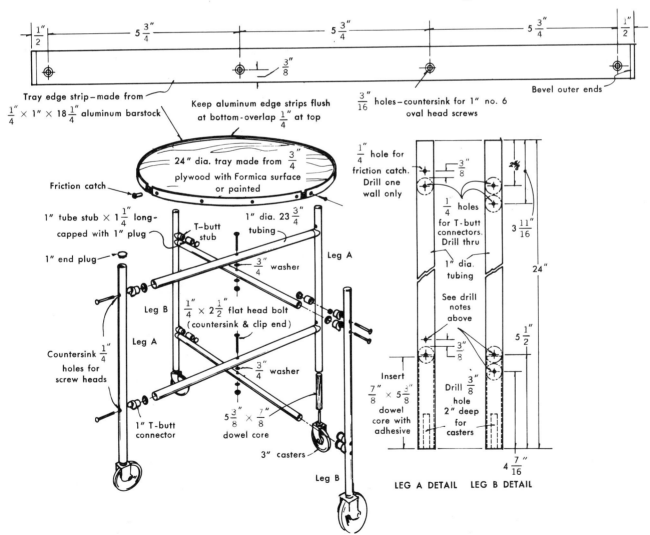

Tray edge strip — made from $\frac{1}{4}$" × 1" × 18 $\frac{1}{4}$" aluminum barstock

Keep aluminum edge strips flush at bottom — overlap $\frac{1}{4}$" at top

$\frac{3}{16}$" holes — countersink for 1" no. 6 oval head screws

Bevel outer ends

24" dia. tray made from $\frac{3}{4}$" plywood with Formica surface or painted

Friction catch

$\frac{1}{4}$" hole for friction catch. Drill one wall only

1" tube stub × 1 $\frac{1}{4}$" long — capped with 1" plug

T-butt stub

1" dia. 23 $\frac{3}{4}$" tubing

Leg A

1" end plug

$\frac{3}{4}$" washer

Leg B

$\frac{1}{4}$" × 2 $\frac{1}{2}$" flat head bolt (countersink & clip end)

Leg A

Countersink $\frac{1}{4}$" holes for screw heads

$\frac{3}{4}$" washer

1" T-butt connector

5 $\frac{3}{8}$" × $\frac{7}{8}$" dowel core

3" casters

Leg B

$\frac{1}{4}$" holes for T-butt connectors. Drill thru

1" dia. tubing

See drill notes above

Insert $\frac{7}{8}$" × 5 $\frac{3}{8}$" dowel core with adhesive

Drill $\frac{3}{8}$" hole 2" deep for casters

$\frac{3}{8}$"

2 $\frac{7}{8}$"

3 $\frac{11}{16}$"

24"

5 $\frac{1}{2}$"

4 $\frac{7}{16}$"

LEG A DETAIL   LEG B DETAIL

$\frac{1}{2}$"   5 $\frac{3}{4}$"   5 $\frac{3}{4}$"   5 $\frac{3}{4}$" $\frac{1}{2}$"

$\frac{3}{8}$"

Bench

Back in the colonial days benches were used more frequently than chairs. In fact, during the first period of settlement, chairs were reserved only for the head of the household.

Here is a copy of an early Colonial Bench. You will notice that the construction is extremely simple, and yet the bench is very sturdy. That is the way furniture was made in the old days.

Through mortise-and-tenon joints hold the rail and uprights. The tenons are then keyed in the typical old-time manner. *Counter boring, rounding of edges,* and the *cutting of templates* are among the processes involved in the building of this bench. All of these processes are explained in your text.

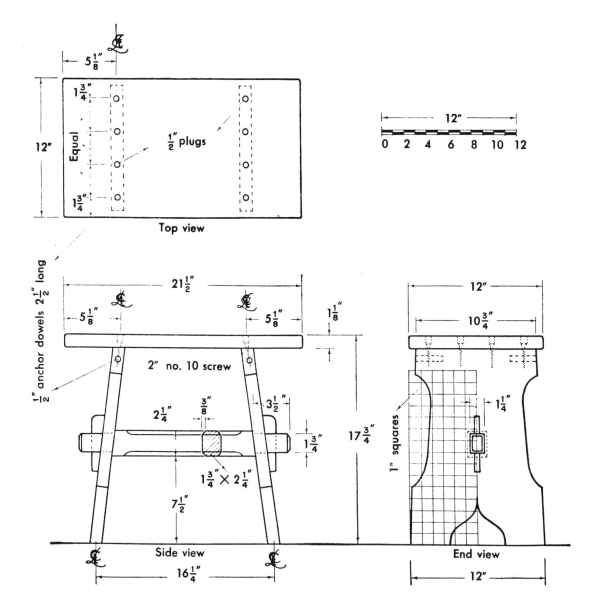

Top view

Side view

End view

Sconce

These little single shelves lend a quaint touch to the Colonial room. Originally they were used to hold tallow candles. The design illustrated is quite typical of those made in New England during the latter part of the seventeenth century.

As indicated in the illustration, the little wall shelf is well adapted for holding potted plants or trailing ivy. It may likewise be used for decorative objects or hobby collections. Obviously, this design is extremely easy to follow, even for the beginning woodworker.

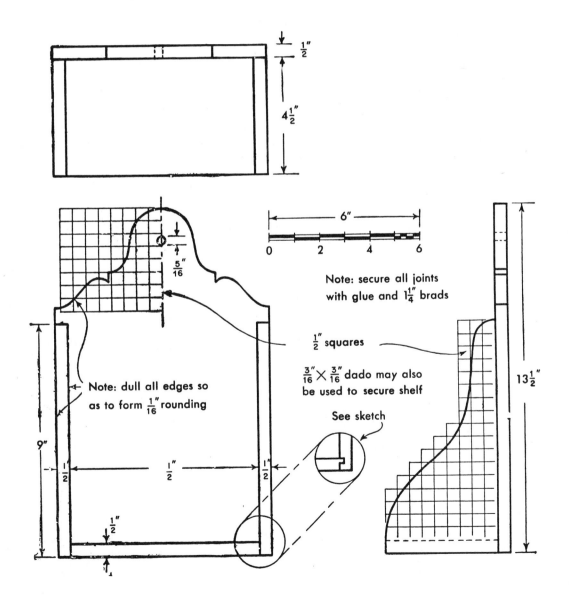

Note: secure all joints with glue and $1\frac{1}{4}''$ brads

$\frac{1}{2}''$ squares

$\frac{3}{16}'' \times \frac{3}{16}''$ dado may also be used to secure shelf

See sketch

Note: dull all edges so as to form $\frac{1}{16}''$ rounding

Fireside Stool

This peg-legged stool was inspired directly by the early fireside stools used so commonly in the early American homes. Nowadays it finds a variety of practical uses both for seating purposes or as a demure end table when placed beside your favorite chair.

This stool introduces the interesting process of peg-legged construction which is explained in Chapter 4. This article is extremely easy to make and can be constructed by the careful beginner.

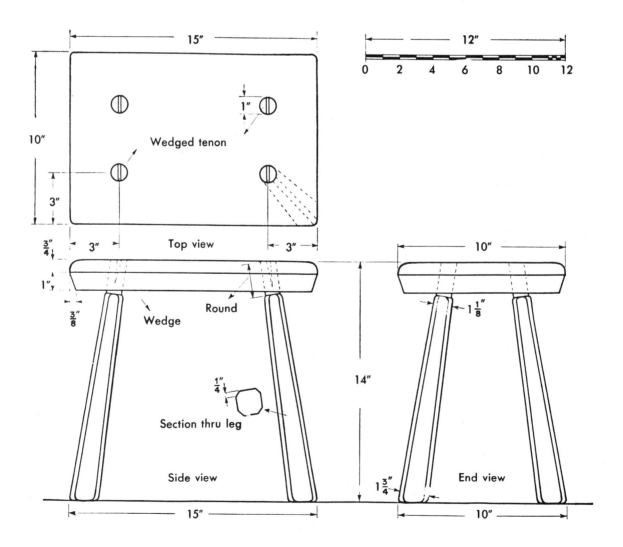

164

Magazine Holder

The village smith used a box similar to this to hold nails and tools when he was shoeing the old gray mare. It is another one of those reminiscent designs which are always attractive when put to modern use. As indicated in the illustration the blacksmith box not only contains magazines, but can be used as well for holding ash trays and other articles.

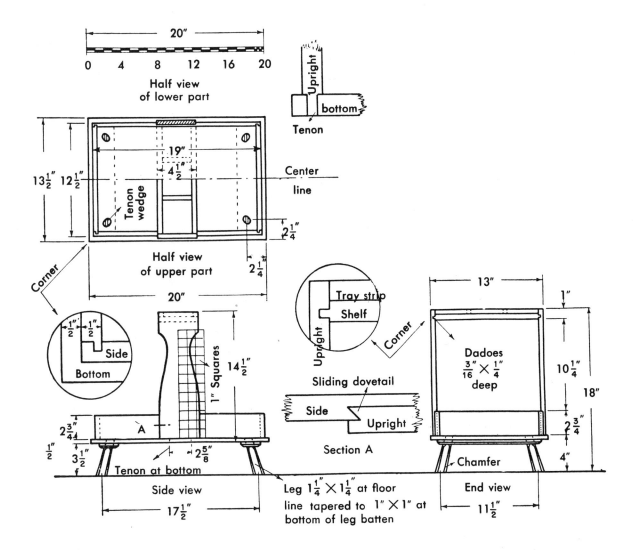

Sea Chest

Every boy should have a sea chest for the safe keeping of his valuables. Here is the ideal strongbox for baseballs, gloves, tops, bits of fishing tackle, and those many other interesting things which form your prize collection. These items are bound to get lost unless you keep them in a definite place, under lock and key.

The Sea Chest introduces us to the interesting process of dovetailing. The base molding is mitered at the corners. Refer to your text for the edge· shaping, and other interesting procedures which the job requires.

Design by author

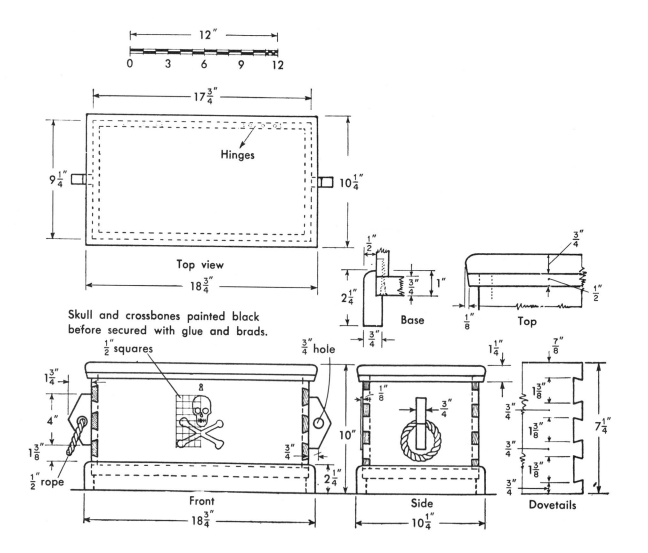

Ship's Ladder Wall Shelves

These hanging wall shelves are built like a ship's ladder; the side supports for the lower shelves are hung sailor-fashion with knotted rope. The nautical effect goes well in a boy's room, a hobby or recreation room, or a summer cottage. White pine or Philippine mahogany $\frac{5}{8}$" thick is used in construction.

Construction involves nothing more difficult than good aim with your coping saw, the art of boring a few holes, and a little careful practice at hammering nails. Use white boat rope, knotted at both ends to link the shelves.

Design by author

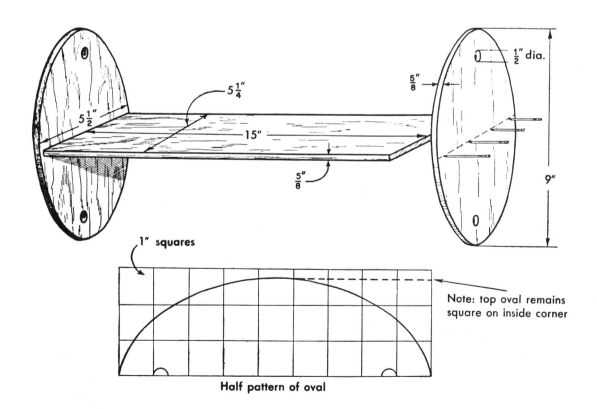

Note: top oval remains square on inside corner

Half pattern of oval

167

TV Hassock

To solve that "extra" seating problem created by television, TV hassocks may be just the answer, especially for those young people who would rather *perch* than *sit*. Even the not so young may stretch out at ease by using this hassock as a leg-rest extension to their favorite chair. As well as furnishing foam-rubber comfort, the TV hassock also provides ample storage space for books and magazines.

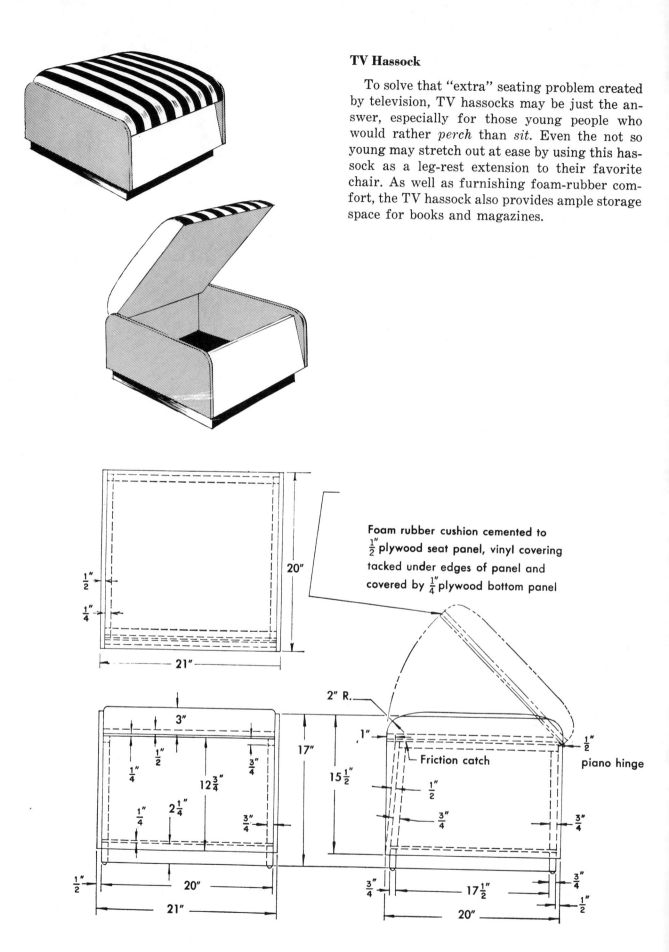

Foam rubber cushion cemented to $\frac{1}{2}$" plywood seat panel, vinyl covering tacked under edges of panel and covered by $\frac{1}{4}$" plywood bottom panel

20"

$\frac{1}{2}$"

$\frac{1}{4}$"

21"

3"

$\frac{1}{2}$"

$\frac{3}{4}$"

$\frac{1}{4}$"

$12\frac{3}{4}$"

$\frac{1}{4}$"

$2\frac{1}{4}$"

$\frac{3}{4}$"

$\frac{1}{2}$"

20"

21"

17"

$15\frac{1}{2}$"

2" R.

1"

Friction catch

$\frac{1}{2}$"

piano hinge

$\frac{1}{2}$"

$\frac{3}{4}$"

$\frac{3}{4}$"

$\frac{1}{2}$"

$\frac{3}{4}$"

$17\frac{1}{2}$"

20"

Table Desk

The student's room and the family room are places where this table may provide just the proper paper-work area. It has a clean, neat design and requires a minimum of space. It is easy to keep tidy and does not complicate house-cleaning operations.

Design by author

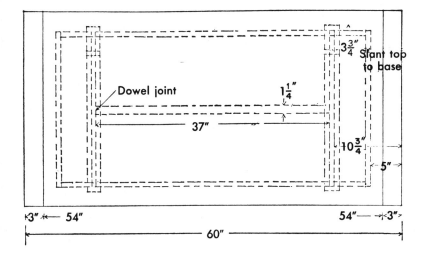

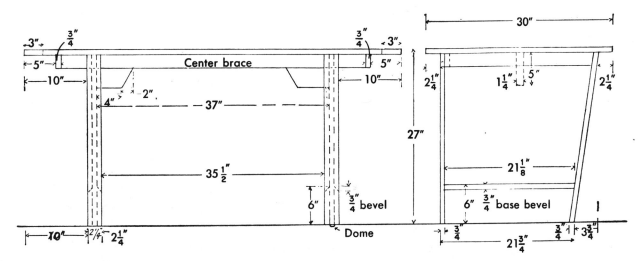

Colonial Shelves

Colonial craftsmen were experts in the design of scrolled wall shelves. The design pictured at left was taken from an antique original displayed at Longfellow's Wayside Inn at Sudbury, Massachusetts. The flowing side scrolls, which typify the best of early colonial design, are augmented with other features of authentic construction. The shelves are joined with exposed dado and dovetail joints — a type of construction used by our forefathers years before glue became a common commodity.

The shelves should be built of pine or cherry with optional choice of walnut if you prefer darker and richer tones of natural wood. All processes involved, including dadoing and dovetailing are described in Chapters 3 and 4.

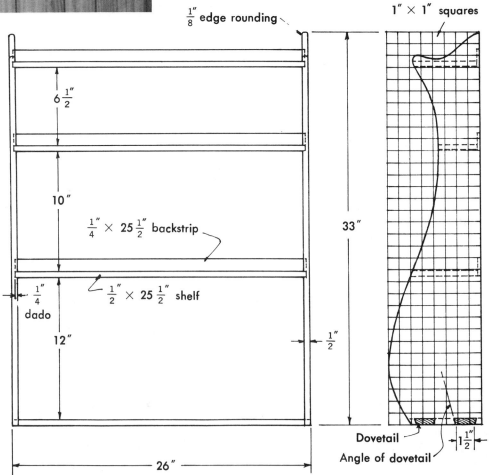

Wall Table

Here is something different in table design. It is called a table rather than a shelf because the top is deeper than a conventional shelf and it is mounted on the wall at table height above the floor. This design is especially attractive when used as a console in the hallway or as part of a dressing table group with a mirror above and a bench below. The woodworker will delight in making this project. It calls for good craftsmanship and should encourage the effort of any one who wants to do a good job on a good design. If desired, a simple dado may be substituted for the sliding dovetail.

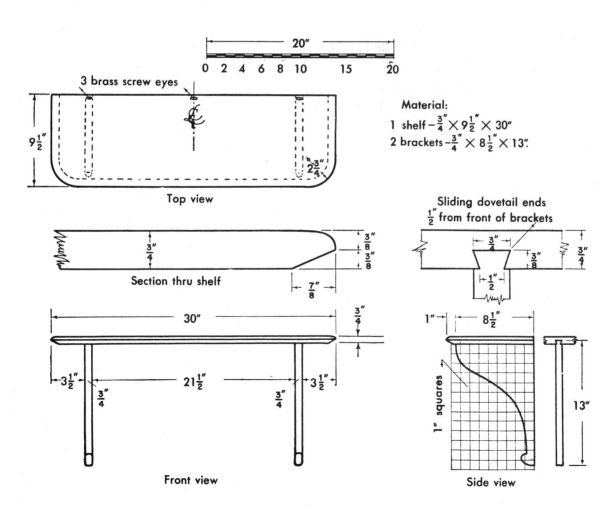

3 brass screw eyes

$9\frac{1}{2}''$

$2\frac{3}{4}''$

Top view

Material:
1 shelf — $\frac{3}{4}'' \times 9\frac{1}{2}'' \times 30''$
2 brackets — $\frac{3}{4}'' \times 8\frac{1}{2}'' \times 13''$.

$\frac{3}{4}$

$\frac{3}{8}$
$\frac{3}{8}$

Section thru shelf

$\frac{7}{8}''$

Sliding dovetail ends $\frac{1}{2}''$ from front of brackets

$\frac{3}{4}$

$\frac{3}{8}$

$\frac{3}{4}$

$\frac{1}{2}$

30''

$\frac{3}{4}''$

$3\frac{1}{2}''$ $21\frac{1}{2}''$ $3\frac{1}{2}''$

$\frac{3}{4}''$ $\frac{3}{4}''$

Front view

1'' $8\frac{1}{2}''$

1'' squares

13''

Side view

Scrolled Valances

As far as can be determined, our colonial forefathers didn't go in for window valances. But since they serve the purpose of tying together the solid wood elements of the contemporary colonial interior, we are inclined to favor them. The designs shown employ typical colonial scalloping and scrollwork. As you will see from the construction sketches, they are of simple two-sided box construction and are easy to make. They can be constructed of white pine and finished in natural tones to match other furniture components.

Design by author

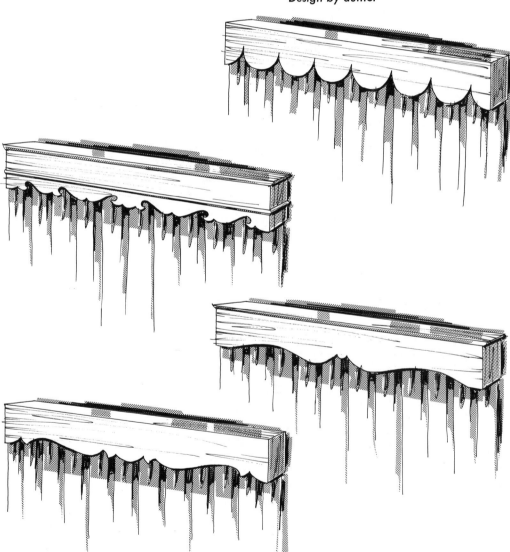

172

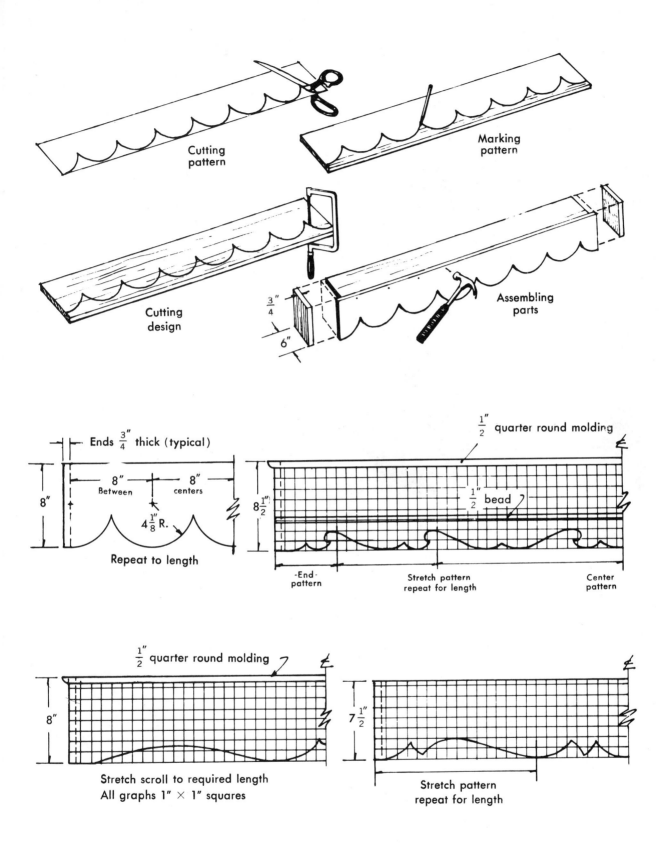

Cutting
pattern

Marking
pattern

Cutting
design

$\frac{3}{4}''$

$6''$

Assembling
parts

Ends $\frac{3}{4}''$ thick (typical)

$8''$
Between

$8''$
centers

$8''$

$4\frac{1}{8}''$ R.

Repeat to length

$\frac{1}{2}''$ quarter round molding

$\frac{1}{2}''$ bead

$8\frac{1}{2}''$

-End-
pattern

Stretch pattern
repeat for length

Center
pattern

$\frac{1}{2}''$ quarter round molding

$8''$

Stretch scroll to required length
All graphs 1″ × 1″ squares

$7\frac{1}{2}''$

Stretch pattern
repeat for length

The Thingamajig

The "Thingamajig" is a change-about affair which, as the photos indicate, may be turned on end, side or bottom to serve as table-stand-rack-storage bin or whatever. Because of its versatility, you are bound to find many uses for it about the home. As the plan indicates, it is made of ½" plywood put together with aluminum angle braces for easy take-apart. Since both the inside and outside are exposed in its various positions, all surfaces should be finished. The model pictured at the left was laminated of two layers of prefinished, plywood wall paneling. This was glued together on the unfinished surface with the prefinished surfaces exposed.

Design by author

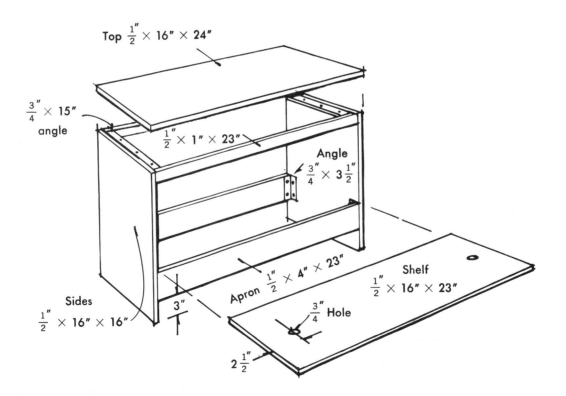

Vada Table

Here is a contemporary table style now enjoying wide popularity. Comparing the illustration with the plan there may appear to be some difference between the basic box construction and the *apparent* detail of separate legs which appear in photograph at right. Explanation is that the four-sided, box plywood construction was veneered for the photograph, giving the appearance of separate legs and aprons.

Actually, despite its sophisticated appearance, this is one of the easiest and most attractive tables you can make. As the plan shows, it is simply glued and nailed together of four plywood sections with the top inserted flush to the leg framework. For further simplification the final assembly can be painted. However, the design is considerably enriched when the plywood is veneered.

It should be observed that the same box construction can be applied to all sizes of tables. You may wish to enlarge this design and revise the proportions for full-size dining tables, or make smaller tables of the same construction for special purposes.

Design by author

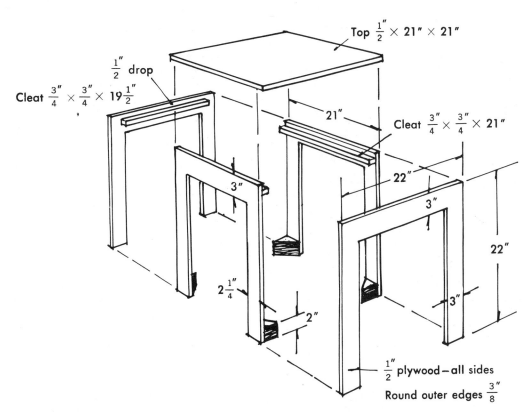

Top $\frac{1}{2}'' \times 21'' \times 21''$

$\frac{1}{2}''$ drop

Cleat $\frac{3''}{4} \times \frac{3''}{4} \times 19\frac{1}{2}''$

Cleat $\frac{3''}{4} \times \frac{3''}{4} \times 21''$

21"

3"

22"

22"

3"

3"

2$\frac{1}{4}$

2"

$\frac{1}{2}''$ plywood—all sides
Round outer edges $\frac{3''}{8}$

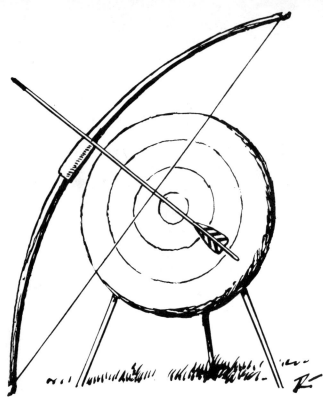

Bow and Arrow

Did you know that the strongest bows are shaped from staves of wood that have been *split* from the timber? If you saw the staves you are bound to cut *across the grain* somewhere along the length of the piece. Naturally, this weakens your bow and causes it to snap, or to bend unevenly.

The best bows are made from lemonwood, yew, osage orange, lancewood, and hickory. Those woods may be purchased at lumber supply dealers or from dealers in archery supplies.

Why not form an archery club and make your own bows and arrows? Incidentally, every young archer should be cautioned never to draw his bow beyond the length of the arrow. Many good bows have been needlessly broken because this precaution was overlooked.

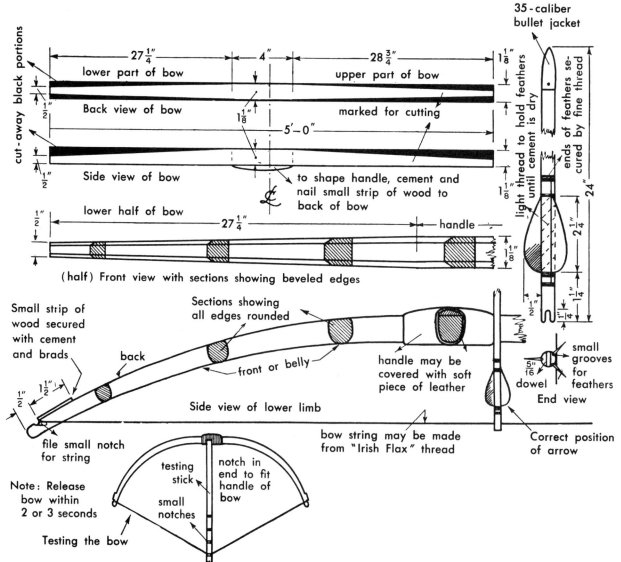

Water Skis

Your success at making water skis depends entirely on how well you can bend wood. But if you select a good quality of straight lumber and carefully follow instructions for wood bending, as explained in Chapter 3, you should finish up with a practical pair of skis. Since these are rather expensive to buy, you may thus apply your woodworking skill to save money *and* have fun.

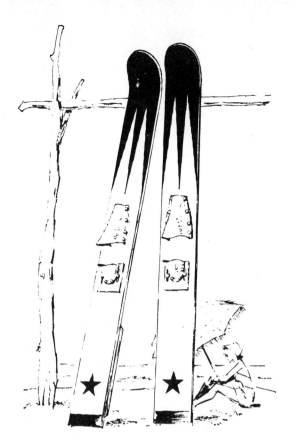

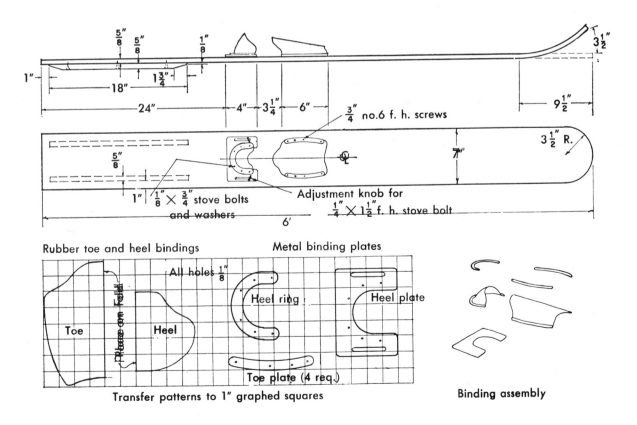

Rubber toe and heel bindings

Metal binding plates

All holes $\frac{1}{8}$"

Toe   Heel   Heel ring   Heel plate

Toe plate (4 req.)

Transfer patterns to 1" graphed squares

Binding assembly

Bookcase

In the average home it would seem there are never enough bookcases. This goes especially for bedrooms and other places where people want to retreat for relaxed reading. In answer to this need the bookcase illustrated is designed to contain a good stock of books and, at the same time, contribute to the decor of the room in which it is used. The style, of course, is colonial — which remains the favorite of many people.

You can build the bookcase of pine and finish it in honey tones of colonial furniture. Plywood can also be used if you prefer to paint your workmanship. It will be noted the construction is simple and follows the process and joinery procedures explained in Chapters 3 and 4.

Design by author

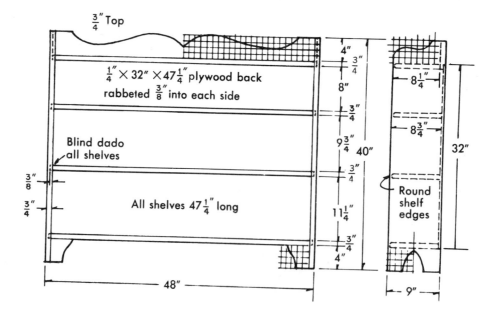

$\frac{3''}{4}$ Top

$\frac{1}{4}'' \times 32'' \times 47\frac{1}{4}''$ plywood back rabbeted $\frac{3}{8}''$ into each side

Blind dado all shelves

$\frac{3}{8}''$

$\frac{3}{4}''$

All shelves $47\frac{1}{4}''$ long

48"

4"

$\frac{3}{4}''$

8"

$\frac{3}{4}''$

$9\frac{3}{4}''$ 40"

$\frac{3}{4}''$

$11\frac{1}{4}''$

$\frac{3}{4}''$

4"

$8\frac{1}{4}''$

$8\frac{3}{4}''$

32"

Round shelf edges

9"

Rod, Reel, 'n' Tackle Rack

The "compleat angler" would be at a loss without one (at least) of these handy racks. There are notches here for a half dozen of your favorite rods, while the pegboard back houses an infinite variety of lures. In the drawer, below, go your extra reels, hooks, and fish line.

Design by author

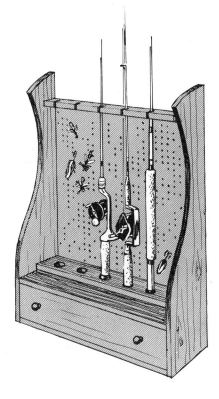

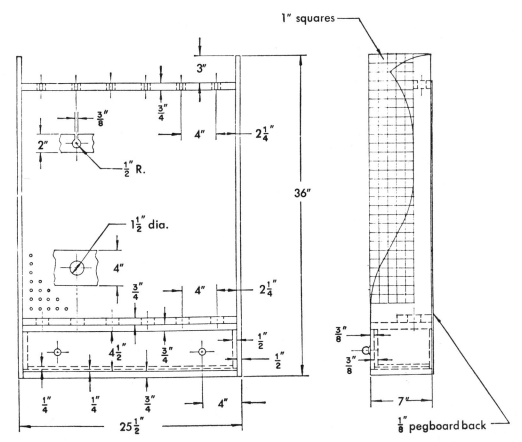

179

Stacking Hassocks

Score a big hit with your family by building a set of these handy hassocks. They are easily put together with plywood and aluminum fittings which may be purchased at most hardware stores. If your wife happens to share your home-crafting enthusiasm, enlist her help in selecting fabrics and sewing covers for the foam cushions. (Covered foam cushions may also be bought in standard sizes.) Paint the hassocks in contrasting colors and stack them for use singly or in pairs as shown in illustration.

Design by author for Reynolds Metals Co.

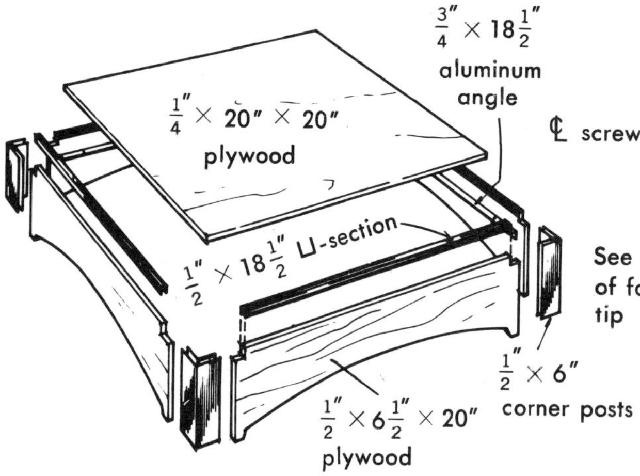

$\frac{3}{4}'' \times 18\frac{1}{2}''$ aluminum angle

$\frac{1}{4}'' \times 20'' \times 20''$ plywood

$\frac{1}{2}'' \times 18\frac{1}{2}''$ U-section

$\frac{1}{2}'' \times 6''$ corner posts

$\frac{1}{2}'' \times 6\frac{1}{2}'' \times 20''$ plywood

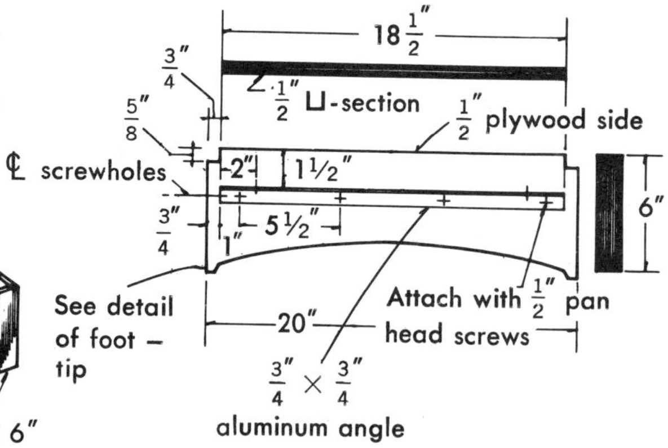

$18\frac{1}{2}''$

$\frac{3}{4}$

$\frac{5}{8}$

$\frac{1}{2}''$ U-section

$\frac{1}{2}''$ plywood side

$\mathcal{C}$ screwholes

$2''$ $1\frac{1}{2}''$

$\frac{3}{4}''$

$1''$ $5\frac{1}{2}''$

$6''$

Attach with $\frac{1}{2}''$ pan head screws

See detail of foot — tip

$20''$

$\frac{3}{4}'' \times \frac{3}{4}''$ aluminum angle

SIDE DETAIL

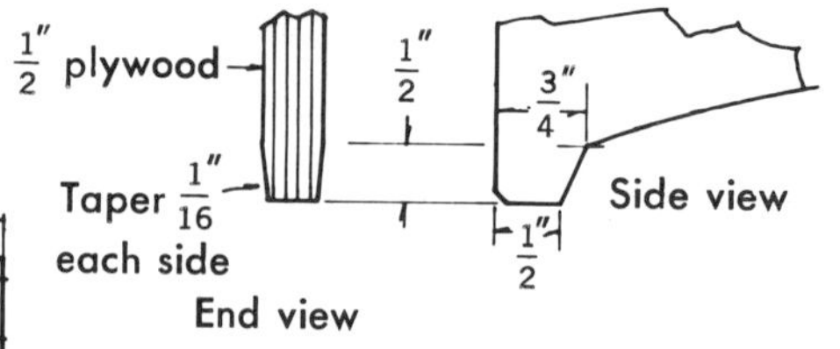

$\frac{1}{2}''$ plywood

Taper $\frac{1}{16}''$ each side

End view

$\frac{1}{2}''$

$\frac{3}{4}''$

$\frac{1}{2}''$

Side view

FOOT TIP DETAIL

$\mathcal{C}$

$1''$ squares

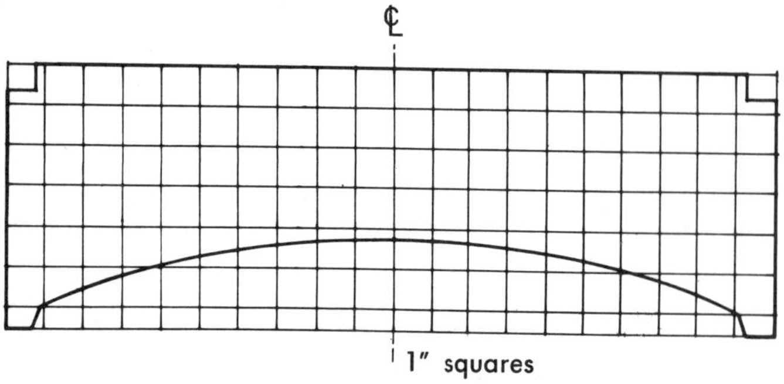

SIDE CUTTING PATTERN

Wall Desk

This smart looking little drop-lid desk is altogether unobtrusive when folded flat against the wall. But it provides a spacious, 16″-wide writing surface when the lid is extended. Inside, there's room for stationery, books, and scads of elusive pencils. Use it in the kitchen or bedroom as well as other living areas. Construction is quite simple; about the only word of caution is to attach it securely to the wall studding. As noted on plan, the wall desk is made of plywood and the design (reillustrated here) was originated by the American Plywood Association.

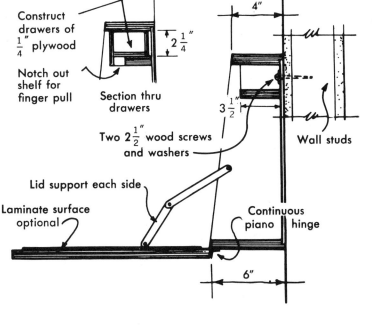

Construct drawers of $\frac{1}{4}$″ plywood

Notch out shelf for finger pull

Section thru drawers

Two $2\frac{1}{2}$″ wood screws and washers

Lid support each side

Laminate surface optional

Continuous piano hinge

Wall studs

$2\frac{1}{4}$″

4″

$3\frac{1}{2}$″

6″

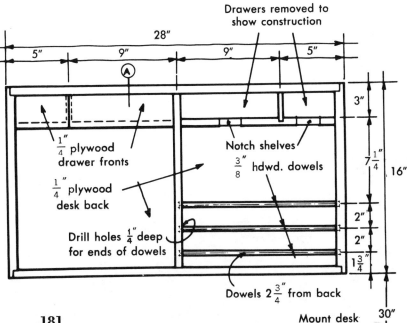

Drawers removed to show construction

28″

5″   9″   9″   5″

Ⓐ

$\frac{1}{4}$″ plywood drawer fronts

$\frac{1}{4}$″ plywood desk back

Drill holes $\frac{1}{4}$″ deep for ends of dowels

Notch shelves

$\frac{3}{8}$″ hdwd. dowels

Dowels $2\frac{3}{4}$″ from back

3″

$7\frac{1}{4}$″   16″

2″

2″

$1\frac{3}{4}$″

Mount desk above floor   30″

181

Plank Table

If you want the ultimate in spacious coffee table — the giant-jumbo size that spreads out before your sofa allowing room for all manner of magazines and incidentals — this one is for you. It was made with a standard, 28″ wide, hollow-core door sawed off to 54″ length. (Make it longer if you like — and be sure to check the step-by-step instructions on sawing doors in Chapter 3 .) This is mounted on 3″ square legs which are braced with cross-lapped boards and strip cleats.

The table shown was veneered entirely with walnut "Flexwood." Hand-rubbed oil finish produces the handsomely grained, planked effect.

Design by author

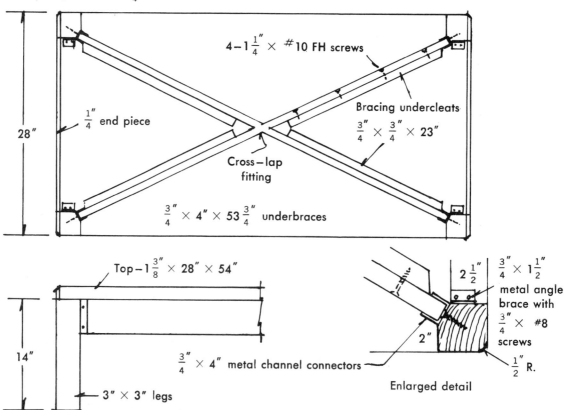

All top edges rounded $\frac{1}{4}''$

$4 - 1\frac{1}{4}'' \times$ #10 FH screws

$\frac{1}{4}''$ end piece

Bracing undercleats
$\frac{3}{4}'' \times \frac{3}{4}'' \times 23''$

28″

Cross-lap fitting

$\frac{3}{4}'' \times 4'' \times 53\frac{3}{4}''$ underbraces

Top — $1\frac{3}{8}'' \times 28'' \times 54''$

$2\frac{1}{2}''$

$\frac{3}{4}'' \times 1\frac{1}{2}''$
metal angle brace with
$\frac{3}{4}'' \times$ #8 screws

14″

$\frac{3}{4}'' \times 4''$ metal channel connectors

2″

$\frac{1}{2}''$ R.

3″ × 3″ legs

Enlarged detail

Butler's Coffee Table

If you are looking for a gift to make for a gracious lady (your mother, wife, or best girl), we suggest this tray-table. Made of light but strong half-inch plywood, it is as easy to lift and carry as the ordinary serving tray. Note the four convenient cut-out handholds.

Design by author

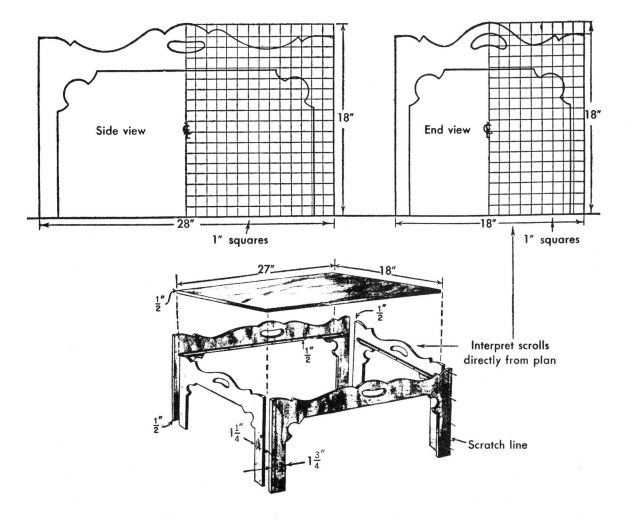

183

"I"-Trestle Table

Aren't you pleased with the idea of having a small coffee table that's a miniature edition of your big trestle dining table? One day it occurred to the designer that you could build a big table or a little one from the same set of plans.

All you have to do is to scale the dimensions of the full-size design down to half, with just one exception — the thickness of the table top. The full-size tables measure six feet long by thirty-four inches wide; the small ones are therefore three feet long by seventeen inches wide.

Take your choice of two designs — the crossed-leg one shown on the next page or the one with straight supports shown on this page. Build your table of a good quality of soft white pine, thoroughly seasoned — no cracks, twists or warps. Your dealer will help you select boards which will have interesting matched grain.

Note: For Coffee Table reduce all dimensions *one half* — excepting top which should be ¾″ thick.

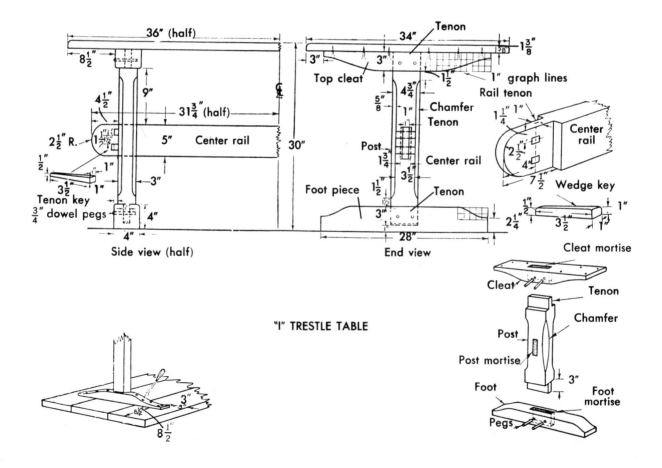

"I" TRESTLE TABLE

184

"X"-Trestle Table

Like the tables shown on the preceding page, the X-Trestle design is also of pure early American origin and can be made either full size or as a half-dimension coffee table. You will be pleased with either example. The good, old-fashioned craft elements that go into this construction should recommend the job to many.

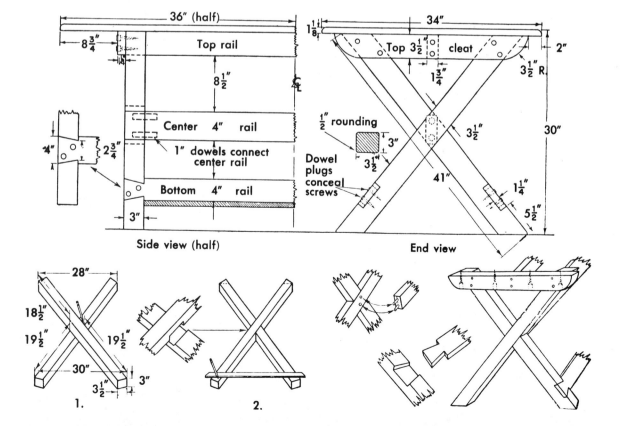

Turned Table

Any craftsman who is seeking a perfect exercise in wood turning can stop right here. For the vase and ball turning of this piece is shaped to near perfection and all other elements go nicely together to make this an excellent project on which to demonstrate your craftsmanship. Make the table of pine, cherry, walnut or maple. Instructions on wood turning can be found in Chapter 5.

In colonial days the little turned tables were used as candle stands. Obviously, their applications today are more widespread — and because of the beauty of their design they are bound to brighten any spot where they are used.

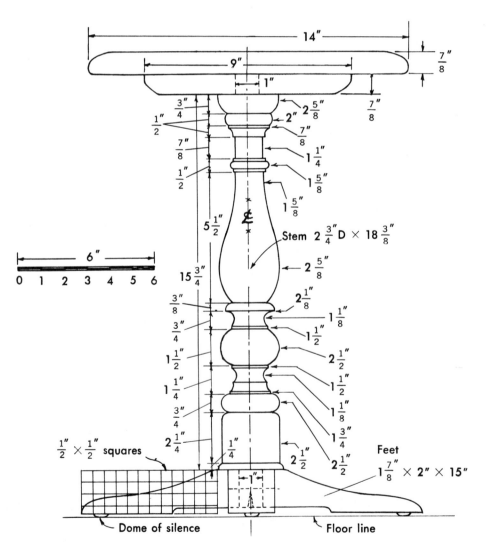

Butterfly Table

This little charmer has done more to influence our admiration for the craftsmanship of our forefathers than any other single article of early colonial furniture. The wing supports and top were originally made of pine while the turned members were usually of maple or birch. This is another excellent project for craftsmen interested in the art of wood turning as described in Chapter 5.

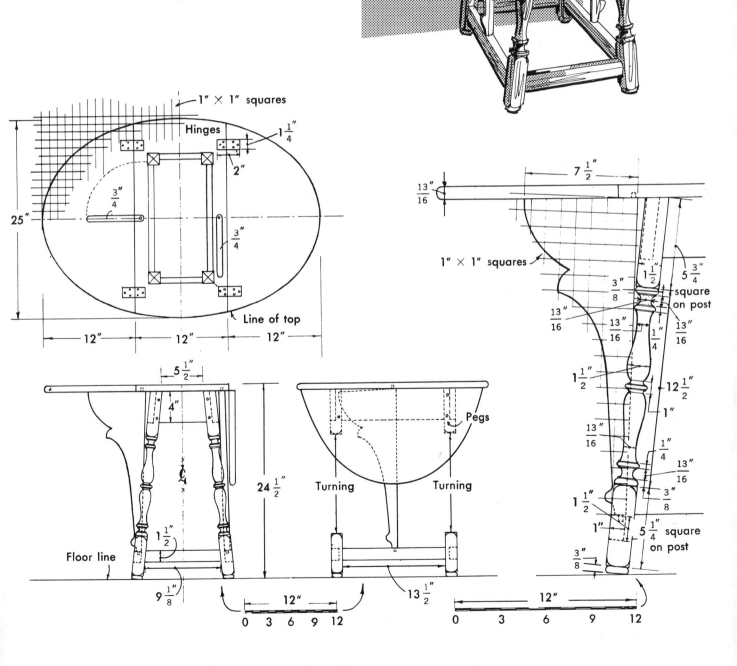

1" × 1" squares

Hinges

1 1/4"

2"

3/4"

3/4"

25"

Line of top

12"   12"   12"

5 1/2"

4"

24 1/2"

Floor line

1 1/2"

9 1/8"

12"

0 3 6 9 12

Pegs

Turning   Turning

13 1/2"

12"

0   3   6   9   12

7 1/2"

13/16

1" × 1" squares

13/16

3/8

13/16

13/16

1 1/2"

13/16

1 1/2"

1"

1 1/2"

1 1/2"

5 3/4"
square
on post

13/16

1 1/4"

12 1/2"

1"

1/4"

13/16

1/4"

3/8"

5 1/4" square
on post

3/8"

Gate Leg Tables

Tables of gate leg design originated in England during the seventeenth century. Like all other furniture made in that country during the period, they were built rather heavy and it is reasonable to believe that stout gate legs were required to support their broad massive leaves. The gate leg idea was also employed at an early date by our own colonial craftsmen. In fact, the grace and beauty of Colonial tables of this type seemed at times to exceed that of their English contemporaries.

In America the design of turning differed from that used on the other side. Likewise, there appeared other features, such as tongue and groove, leaf joints, and peculiarities of construction, which distinguished American gate leg tables from those made elsewhere.

It is believed that the Gate Leg Trestle Table, differing structurally as it does from the conventional gate leg table, is an early American innovation.

Here is an excellent design for the skilled craftsman. Obviously, there is a quantity of turning involved, but the craftsman who undertakes the job has the satisfaction of knowing that he is making something of definite and lasting value.

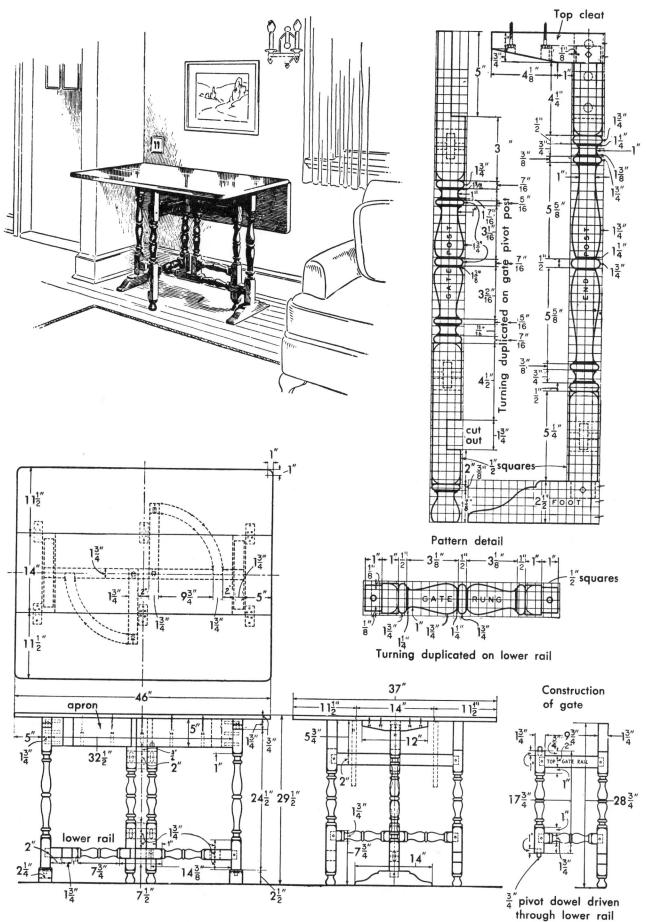

Top cleat

Turning duplicated on gate pivot post

GATE POST

POST END

cut out

2" ½" squares

FOOT

Pattern detail

GATE RUNG

½" squares

Turning duplicated on lower rail

Construction of gate

apron

lower rail

TOP GATE RAIL

¾" pivot dowel driven through lower rail

189

Design by author

Pole Systems, Wall Shelving, and Room Dividers

Probably there's nothing more practical — nor more highly decorative in many individualized installations — than the various pole systems of contemporary furnishing. With the simple device of spring-loaded tension poles, which fit snugly between floor and ceiling, you can create the attractive shelving effects shown here. But this only offers a hint of greater possibilities — because you can amplify this arrangement with storage cabinets and various combinations of modular furniture.

Indeed, you become your own designer when you install sectional pole systems. For they can be arranged any way you please; to stretch across entire walls, to bend around corners or to jut out from mid-areas to form room dividers. Moreover, they can be put up, taken down, and rearranged at any time to refresh your decor.

You need not be an expert to build your own pole systems, and save money in the process. As detailed in the working drawing on the facing page, the systems illustrated require only stock materials. The poles are made of standard "two-by-threes" which cost less than one dollar apiece. Shelving is of plywood or seasoned lumber. You can even avoid the labor of boring the pole ends for the homemade dowel and spring details, if your hardware dealer stocks the spring-loaded tops which are now on the market. These spring-loaded caps fit over standard two-by-threes. With them it is only necessary to saw the standards to required lengths.

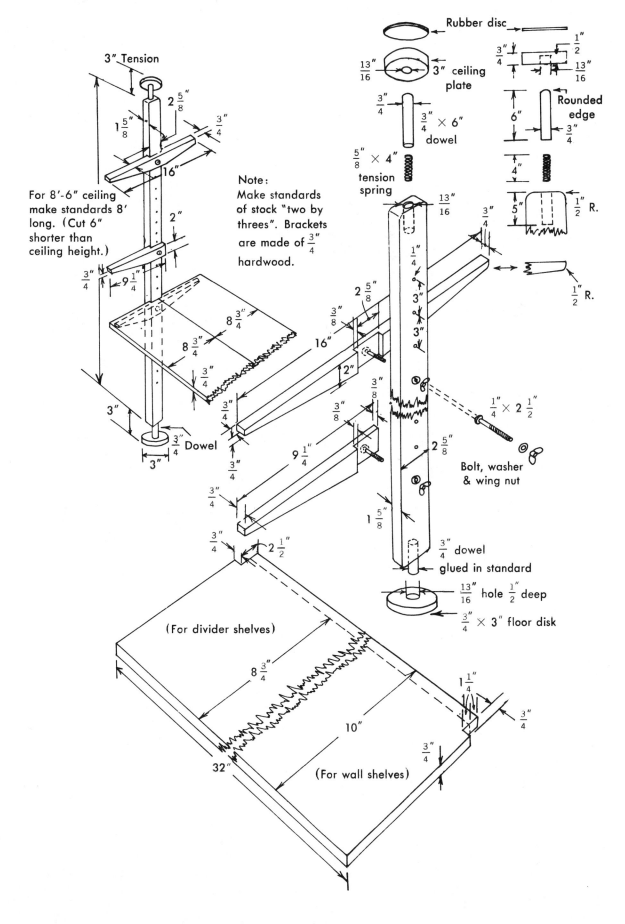

3" Tension

2 $\frac{5}{8}$"

1 $\frac{5}{8}$"

$\frac{3}{4}$"

16"

For 8'-6" ceiling make standards 8' long. (Cut 6" shorter than ceiling height.)

2"

$\frac{3}{4}$"

9 $\frac{1}{4}$"

Note:
Make standards of stock "two by threes". Brackets are made of $\frac{3}{4}$" hardwood.

8 $\frac{3}{4}$"

8 $\frac{3}{4}$"

$\frac{3}{4}$"

3"

$\frac{3}{4}$" Dowel

3"

$\frac{3}{4}$"

$\frac{3}{4}$"

$\frac{3}{8}$"

2 $\frac{5}{8}$"

16"

2"

$\frac{3}{8}$"

$\frac{3}{4}$"

9 $\frac{1}{4}$"

$\frac{3}{4}$"

$\frac{3}{4}$"

$\frac{3}{4}$"

2 $\frac{1}{2}$"

(For divider shelves)

8 $\frac{3}{4}$"

10"

32"

(For wall shelves)

1 $\frac{1}{4}$"

$\frac{3}{4}$"

$\frac{3}{4}$"

Rubber disc

$\frac{13}{16}$

3" ceiling plate

$\frac{3}{4}$

$\frac{1}{2}$"

$\frac{13}{16}$

$\frac{3}{4}$

$\frac{3}{4}$" × 6" dowel

6"

Rounded edge

$\frac{3}{4}$

$\frac{5}{8}$" × 4" tension spring

4"

5"

$\frac{1}{2}$" R.

$\frac{13}{16}$"

$\frac{3}{4}$"

$\frac{1}{4}$"

3"

3"

$\frac{1}{2}$" R.

$\frac{1}{4}$" × 2 $\frac{1}{2}$"

Bolt, washer & wing nut

2 $\frac{5}{8}$"

1 $\frac{5}{8}$"

$\frac{3}{4}$" dowel glued in standard

$\frac{13}{16}$" hole $\frac{1}{2}$" deep

$\frac{3}{4}$" × 3" floor disk

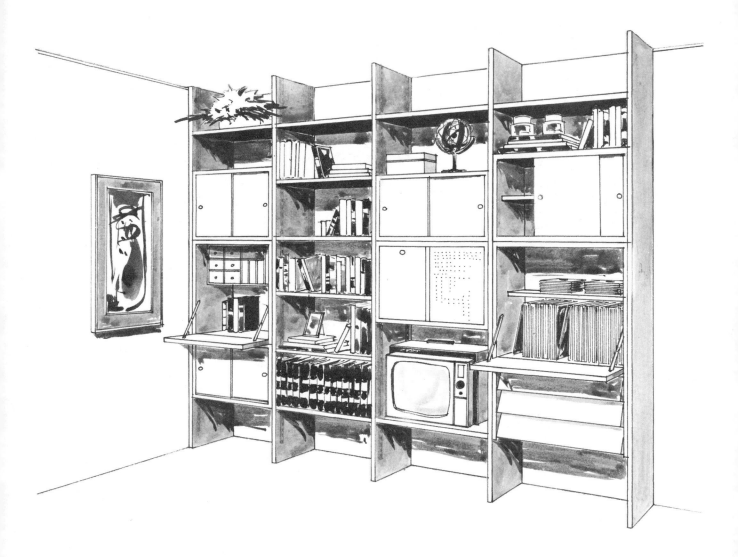

Flexible Wall Storage

As the detailed plans of the next two pages indicate, construction of all built-in units of flexible wall storage, illustrated above, would call for ambition and patience above and beyond that of the average homecraftsman. Anybody could make a season's project of building all the cabinets, desks, record holders, shelves, and drawers encompassed in the complete assembly. But the beauty of this undertaking is that the building can be done piece-by-piece in sections of modular components. Thus, you can start with basic construction of the shelved sections

and add the cabinet units as you find time to make them. They simply slip in between the uprights and are screw fastened as shown on plan.

The overall design, which was originated by the American Plywood Association, combines vertical dividers which run from floor to ceiling. Between these go the shelves and box-shaped units which hold drawers, folding desk, and sections with sliding doors. Other arrangements can be made with these units and the entire assembly can be constructed to fit your wall space by adding, subtracting or altering sections to your individual requirements.

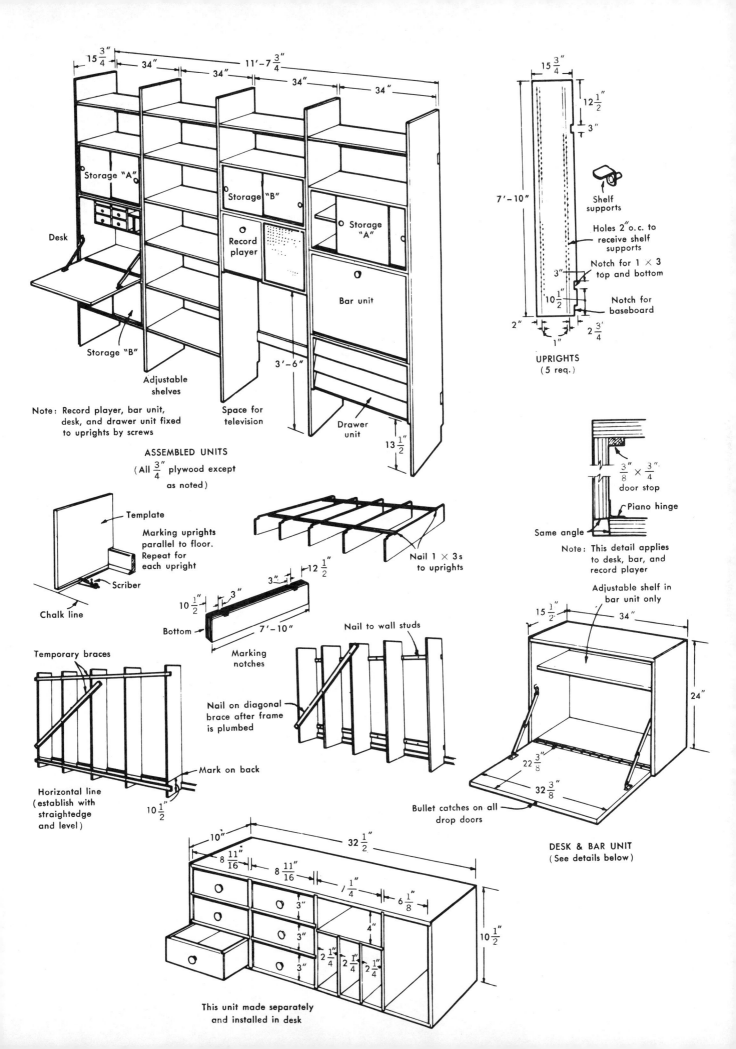

$15\frac{3}{4}''$ $34''$ $11'-7\frac{3}{4}''$ $34''$ $34''$ $34''$

Storage "A"

Storage "B"

Desk

Record player

Storage "A"

Bar unit

Storage "B"

Adjustable shelves

$3'-6''$

Note: Record player, bar unit, desk, and drawer unit fixed to uprights by screws

Space for television

Drawer unit

$13\frac{1}{2}''$

ASSEMBLED UNITS
(All $\frac{3}{4}''$ plywood except as noted)

$15\frac{3}{4}''$

$12\frac{1}{2}''$

$3''$

$7'-10''$

Shelf supports

Holes $2''$ o.c. to receive shelf supports

Notch for 1×3 top and bottom

$3''$

$10\frac{1}{2}''$

Notch for baseboard

$2''$ $1''$ $2\frac{3}{4}'$

UPRIGHTS
(5 req.)

Template

Marking uprights parallel to floor. Repeat for each upright

Scriber

Chalk line

Nail 1×3s to uprights

$12\frac{1}{2}''$

$3''$

$10\frac{1}{2}''$ $3''$

Bottom

$7'-10''$

Marking notches

Nail to wall studs

Temporary braces

Nail on diagonal brace after frame is plumbed

Mark on back

Horizontal line (establish with straightedge and level)

$10\frac{1}{2}''$

$\frac{3}{8}'' \times \frac{3}{4}''$ door stop

Piano hinge

Same angle

Note: This detail applies to desk, bar, and record player

Adjustable shelf in bar unit only

$15\frac{1}{2}''$ $34''$

$24''$

$22\frac{3}{8}''$

$32\frac{3}{8}''$

Bullet catches on all drop doors

DESK & BAR UNIT
(See details below)

$10''$

$8\frac{11}{16}''$

$32\frac{1}{2}''$

$8\frac{11}{16}''$

$1\frac{1}{4}''$

$6\frac{1}{8}''$

$3''$

$3''$

$3''$

$4''$

$2\frac{1}{4}''$ $2\frac{1}{4}''$ $2\frac{1}{4}''$

$10\frac{1}{2}''$

This unit made separately and installed in desk

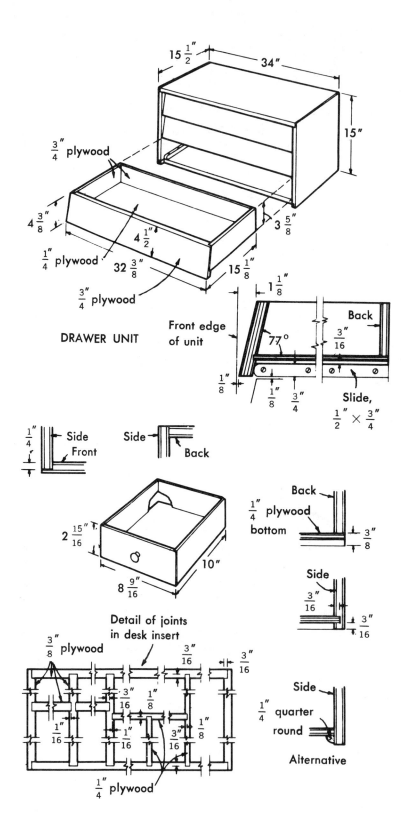

$15\frac{1}{2}''$

$34''$

$15''$

$\frac{3}{4}''$ plywood

$4\frac{3}{8}''$

$4\frac{1}{2}''$

$3\frac{5}{8}''$

$\frac{1}{4}''$ plywood

$32\frac{3}{8}''$

$15\frac{1}{8}''$

$\frac{3}{4}''$ plywood

DRAWER UNIT

Front edge of unit

$1\frac{1}{8}''$

Back

$77°$

$\frac{3}{16}''$

$\frac{1}{8}''$

$\frac{1}{8}''$

$\frac{3}{4}''$

Slide,
$\frac{1}{2}'' \times \frac{3}{4}''$

$\frac{1}{4}''$

Side

Front

Side

Back

$2\frac{15}{16}''$

$10''$

$8\frac{9}{16}''$

Back

$\frac{1}{4}''$ plywood bottom

$\frac{3}{8}''$

Side

$\frac{3}{16}''$

$\frac{3}{16}''$

Detail of joints in desk insert

$\frac{3}{8}''$ plywood

$\frac{3}{16}''$

$\frac{3}{16}''$

$\frac{3}{16}''$

$\frac{1}{8}''$

$\frac{1}{16}''$

$\frac{1}{16}''$

$\frac{3}{16}''$

$\frac{1}{8}''$

$1''$

$\frac{1}{4}''$ plywood

Side

$\frac{1}{4}''$ quarter round

Alternative

194

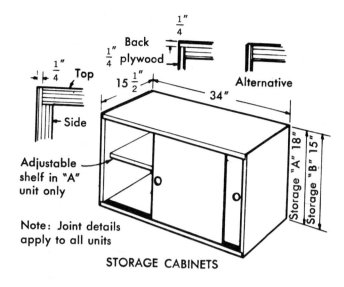

$\frac{1}{4}$ Back plywood

Alternative

$\frac{1}{4}$ Top

Side

15 $\frac{1}{2}$ "

34"

Storage "A" 18"

Storage "B" 15"

Adjustable shelf in "A" unit only

Note: Joint details apply to all units

STORAGE CABINETS

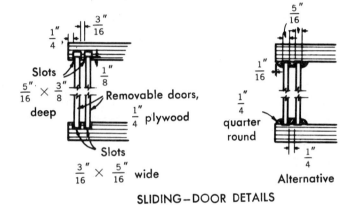

$\frac{1}{4}$ "

$\frac{3}{16}$ "

Slots

$\frac{5}{16}$ " × $\frac{3}{8}$ " deep

$\frac{1}{8}$ "

Removable doors, $\frac{1}{4}$ " plywood

Slots

$\frac{3}{16}$ " × $\frac{5}{16}$ " wide

$\frac{5}{16}$ "

$\frac{1}{16}$ "

$\frac{1}{4}$ quarter round

$\frac{1}{16}$ "

$\frac{1}{4}$ "

Alternative

SLIDING—DOOR DETAILS

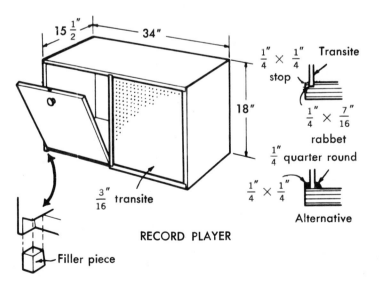

15 $\frac{1}{2}$ "

34"

18"

$\frac{1}{4}$ " × $\frac{1}{4}$ " stop Transite

$\frac{1}{4}$ " × $\frac{7}{16}$ " rabbet

$\frac{1}{4}$ quarter round

$\frac{1}{4}$ " × $\frac{1}{4}$ "

Alternative

$\frac{3}{16}$ " transite

Filler piece

RECORD PLAYER

Note: This detail applies to record player, desk, drawer unit, and bar unit

INDEX